Presented at the IDRC/Nacore Joint Meeting
December 5, 2000
New York, New York

Compliments of the
Virginia Economic Development Partnership
804-371-8100; www.YesVirginia.org

VIRGINIA
Is For Business

"Stephan Haeckel offers a fresh perspective on leadership, accountability, and commitment."

ARVIN F. MUELLER,
VICE PRESIDENT, GENERAL MOTORS

"*Adaptive Enterprise* is a must read for anyone whose firm is under technological attack. Its useful insights will be essential for both corporate executives and entrepreneurs who wish to understand the differences between the sense-and-respond business model of today's digital economy and the traditional make-and-sell approach."

GEORGE H. CONRADES,
CHAIRMAN AND CEO AKAMAI TECHNOLOGIES, INC. AND PARTNER,
POLARIS VENTURE PARTNERS

"Steve Haeckel takes the 'sense and respond' and 'managing by wire' concepts to a new level of precision and practicality."

PIERRE HESSLER,
EXECUTIVE BOARD MEMBER, CAP GEMINI GROUP

"*Adaptive Enterprise* is that rarest of business books that is rooted deeply in intellectual theory and at the same time offers critical advice for the practice of management. Understanding the principles articulated in *Adaptive Enterprise* will be the top priority of any business leader who wishes to survive—let alone prosper—in the emerging information economy."

RASHI GLAZER,
PROFESSOR AND CO-DIRECTOR, CENTER FOR MARKETING AND TECHNOLOGY,
HAAS SCHOOL OF BUSINESS, UNIVERSITY OF CALIFORNIA AT BERKELEY

"At last, a theoretical framework that helps companies understand their business and strategic choices in times when the old rules no longer apply. *Adaptive Enterprise* provides a practical handbook for business leaders who are serious about improving the future profitability of their companies. I wish I had had it years ago to use as part of my armory."

REG MUNRO,
EXECUTIVE GENERAL MANAGER, OLD MUTUAL, SOUTH AFRICA

"If you think you know what your future will be, this book is of little value. If, however, you are *realistic* about the future of your company, *Adaptive Enterprise* is of inestimable value!"

VINCE BARABBA,
GENERAL MANAGER, STRATEGY AND KNOWLEDGE DEVELOPMENT,
GENERAL MOTORS CORPORATION

"Read *Adaptive Enterprise* to learn about the new fundamentals for designing and managing organizations. Stephan Haeckel's conceptual framework for a sense-and-respond organization is concrete, clear, and highly applicable to today's needs."

CHRIS ARGYRIS,
JAMES B. CONANT PROFESSOR, HARVARD UNIVERSITY

"Steve Haeckel has given new meaning to the idea of customer focus. Effective strategies will presume continuously changing customer priorities."

GORDON WYNER,
VICE PRESIDENT, MERCER MANAGEMENT CONSULTING

"*Adaptive Enterprise* is an important and well-written contribution to the management literature. In an age where the only certainty is rapid, unpredictable change, Haeckel offers an intelligent, powerful presentation of the customer-driven, sense-and-respond organization necessary for an enterprise to survive."

FREDERICK E. WEBSTER, JR.,
CHARLES HENRY JONES THIRD CENTURY PROFESSOR OF MANAGEMENT,
THE AMOS TUCK SCHOOL OF BUSINESS ADMINISTRATION

"*Adaptive Enterprise* is an excellent resource for business leaders who need to improve their firm's capabilities to anticipate and respond to rapidly changing external conditions. By providing the framework, examples, and leadership requirements, *Adaptive Enterprise* will help executives develop their sense-and-respond organization."

H. PAUL ROOT,
DIRECTOR, KNIGHT RIDDER CENTER FOR EXCELLENCE IN MANAGEMENT,
FLORIDA INTERNATIONAL UNIVERSITY

ADAPTIVE ENTERPRISE

ADAPTIVE ENTERPRISE

Creating and Leading Sense-and-Respond Organizations

STEPHAN H. HAECKEL

Foreword by
Adrian J. Slywotzky

HARVARD BUSINESS SCHOOL PRESS
Boston, Massachusetts

Printed in the United States of America

03   02   01   00   5   4   3   2

Library of Congress Cataloging-in-Publication Data

Haeckel, Stephan H.
    Adaptive enterprise: creating and leading sense-and-respond
organizations / Stephan H. Haeckel; foreword by Adrian J.
Slywotzky.
        p.   cm.
    Includes index.
    ISBN 0-87584-874-5
    1. Organizational change—Management.   2. New business
enterprises—Management.   3. Management.   4. Corporate
culture.
    I. Title.
    HD58.8.H34   1999
    658.4'063–dc21   98-33201
                                                            CIP

The paper used in this publication meets the requirements of
the American National Standard for Permanence of Paper for
Printed Library Materials Z39.49-1984.

In memory of my father

Lester C. Haeckel

who had nothing

and everything

to do with this book

CONTENTS

FOREWORD

Adrian J. Slywotzky

For some time now, I've been following the development of a strategic model called sense-and-respond, formulated in a variety of articles and whitepapers by Stephan Haeckel. Haeckel's point of departure is the logic of an information economy and the implications of that logic for business strategy, structure, and governance. My own approach to strategy is more empirical: unearthing the business design choices that explain why certain successful companies have been able to sustain their success over decades. Interestingly, both roads lead to a common strategic imperative: What a company does these days must be driven by a deep understanding of how customer needs are changing, customer by customer. I find the ideas and logic of sense-and-respond compelling, and I am delighted that they have now been gathered into a book.

Adaptive Enterprise deserves to be read carefully from beginning to end. It contains a degree of prescription rare in "idea books," including the several very good ones that have appeared in the last few years describing how the business landscape is changing and how the rules determining business success have been fundamentally altered.

Very few of these great diagnostic books provide usable ideas on how to integrate a management concept for dealing with the unpredictable change they describe. *Adaptive Enterprise* falls into a different category. Haeckel provides not only insightful diagnosis but a persuasive prescription for creating new business designs that systematically make sense out of turbulent change and respond adaptively to it.

To be sure, following the prescription is not easy. But then, no significantly new model for creating value is ever easy to internalize. You must change the wiring in your mind from make-and-sell (which has been deeply imprinted into our thinking) to a different mode—sense-and-respond. Implementing this transformation involves a conceptual as well as an operational challenge. Among other things, it requires shifting from a product-centric to a customer-centric way of looking at things.

THE TRANSITION TO A SENSE-AND-RESPOND BUSINESS DESIGN

Haeckel maps stages in the transformation to sense-and-respond against the four strategic choices that define a firm's business model: customer selection, value capture, scope definition, and strategic control point. Stark and revealing differences emerge from stage to stage.

The parameters of a business's scope, for example, differ greatly in a sense-and-respond organization as compared to make-and-sell: They are not the traditional *markets* served and *products* offered. Rather, because increasing unpredictability about what products and services customers will want is a built-in feature of information economies, the sense-and-respond firm defines its scope in terms of first, the repertoire of personalized *customer value attributes* it will address, and second, the repertoire of *capabilities* that can be marshaled by the firm into responses. Even more significantly, the firm has the ability to systematically and dynamically change its scope in response to signals from the environment.

What Haeckel calls customer-back behavior closely resembles the customer-centric approach that characterizes many of today's most successful companies. He describes it this way: "The search for the next profit zone begins with an ability to sense and interpret changes in the customer value zone."

It's true. Examples such as the Plastics Division of General Electric (described in detail in my book, *The Profit Zone*) demonstrate that a firm can provide significant and differentiating value to its customers by exploring the larger economic system of which their specific requests are a part. Often this leads to insight about value of which customers themselves may be unaware—because their businesses are fragmented into independent parts. Customer-back means making investments to find patterns your customers don't see and responding with extended value propositions of which preexisting products and services are only a part. It means making sense out of influences on customers' businesses that they still think of as noise—factors that don't even show up as meaningful blips on their current radar screens. GEers are fond of saying, "We're not smart enough to predict the future, so we have to get better at reacting to it more quickly." You couldn't ask for a better articulation of the sense-and-respond imperative.

This change in mindset will no doubt come more easily for some, such as investment bankers, engineering firms, consultants, and others accustomed to constantly reorganizing themselves around customer requests. It will be very difficult for manufacturers, bankers, utilities, and other firms accustomed to organizing themselves around their own production capabilities. But the absolute necessity of facing up to this shift applies to us all.

Adopting a sense-and-respond orientation produces multiple benefits for an organization. I'd like to point out three benefits over and above those articulated by Haeckel: new business building, solving the medium-term growth crisis, and preempting future competitive opportunities.

New Business Building

One of the major obstacles to effective new business building by large companies is the "Big Opportunity" trap. To varying degrees, we are all caught in it. It works like this: "We're a $20BB company. If the new business proposal is not a $1BB opportunity, we don't have time to pursue it."

The consequence of falling into this trap? Dozens of good, profitable but apparently "small" new business ideas are killed. The silent assumption underlying their execution: We know what the size of the opportunity will be. But, in reality, we are clueless. Another reality: Many of these dozens of discards go unrecognized as bridges to the next opportunities in a constantly unfolding marketplace.

Standing in year one, it's hard—often impossible—to say whether the rejected new business (which seems to have "only" a $100MM potential) is a stand-alone opportunity or a significant bridge to a future profit zone. If the latter, is it a bridge to an island? An archipelago? A whole new continent?

The point is, you don't know. You can't tell. The more rapidly the market changes, the more difficult it is to assess the bridge value of a business. But if you're not building these apparently "small" (and, incidentally, profitable) bridges, you shouldn't complain that somebody else got to the new continent first. The capability to systematically sense important opportunities while they are still small will become a survival trait as change becomes more and more unpredictable.

MEDIUM-TERM GROWTH CRISIS

The second benefit of sense-and-respond behavior relates to the medium-term growth crisis that plagues most of the Fortune 500. The crisis develops this way:

- The best business managers in the company are put in charge of operating units.

- They focus completely on the next four quarters, and they operate in make-and-sell mode because that's the only way they know to make their numbers in the short term.

- Meanwhile, numerous highly talented people and high value new business ideas percolate in R&D. (Most of these ideas have zero potential in year one and enormous potential in years two to five.)

- But the near-term focus of the best management talent leaves these R&D people with no one on the business side to talk to about investing in the commercialization of those new business ideas.

- As the unending sequence of "four quarter horizons" rolls on, the company's "new growth" gap gets bigger. After a few years, it becomes insurmountable.

Companies that learn sense-and-respond behavior will begin redeploying some of their best business talent from make-and-sell activity. Even a 5 percent shift will have dramatic consequences, because sense-and-respond forces companies to look outside themselves to their customers and to look two or three years forward. Having 5 percent of the talent looking "outside" will greatly improve the odds that the company will sense the next major opportunities.

On the response side, R&D will gain managerial dialogue partners with proven abilities to make things happen. The result will be profitable connections between emerging customer priorities and new organizational capabilities. In those cases where the company doesn't have the needed capabilities, it will get them, driven by the attractiveness and immediacy of the opportunity. Sense-and-respond, as it becomes the dominant mindset, will constitute the company's key mechanism for creating the "next act" for growth, even as most of the managerial talent still thinks make-and-sell and the next four quarters.

The experience of a high-tech make-and-sell communications equipment maker illustrates the benefit of making this shift. This company's behavior was driven by what it knew how to do; its mindset was dominated by core competency thinking. Attracted by the emergence of a major potential new market, it experimented with building a next generation business model driven by opportunity rather than core competency. The new market opportunity was very attractive, but required several new skills and competencies.

Abandoning "what got us here" wasn't an easy process. An ongoing debate emerged between managers whose starting point was "what we know how to do," and those whose thinking was driven by "what customers want, and where future profit will be." Ultimately, the latter mindset prevailed. But the debate cycle extracted a cost. The company's new business model was created a full twelve months behind the leader in the new market space.

But the leadership learned, as Haeckel says, "how to play games with customers, rather than games against competitors." Even as it was introducing its new business model, the company was already beginning to sketch out its next business design based on early feedback from its leading customers. At its current rate of progress, the new business design will hit the market months ahead of the competition.

ANTICIPATE AND PREEMPT

The third benefit grows out of the second. Playing sense-and-respond reinforces itself. Once a company gets into a dynamic mindset, it learns; it gets better. Its know-how extends beyond archery, aiming at a static target, to include skeet shooting, taking on a moving target. As the company develops its sense-and-respond skill set, it elevates sense-and-respond from listen and comply to anticipate and preempt.

Sense-and-respond helps us be on time—on market time. Very good sense-and-respond helps us be early. But a superior ability to sense and interpret signals about changing customer needs before they mature into formal requests helps us get there sooner still, soon enough to preempt the next major opportunity and to create an unassailable leadership position. This is the core of customer-back behavior: investing in a relationship that provides privileged and unique access to signals about changing customer patterns so they can be leveraged to enhance customer value.

Anticipate and preempt has tended to be the preserve of fast-moving, close to the customer, risk-taking entrepreneurs. As a result, the majority of value migration winners in the last decade have been newcomers, not incumbents. But no law says that it must be this way. Several notable exceptions show that incumbent stagnation, far from preordained, is something incumbents allow to happen. Operating in rigid make-and-sell mode helps to stack the odds in favor of the newcomer's initiatives. Operating in a sense-and-respond mode shifts the odds back in favor of the incumbent.

Moving a company away from pure make-and-sell to a hybrid operating mode dramatically lowers the incumbent's risk of "economic arteriosclerosis." It initiates a mind shift and skill shift that paves the way for anticipate and preempt. A process of learning and skill development results that enables sustained profit and value growth for the organization.

I cannot emphasize enough that the transformation to sense-and-respond—particularly for large organizations—requires a fundamentally different way of thinking about how companies create value. The story of the past two decades shows that the firms creating the most value change their business designs every five years or so. This book explains why that follows unavoidably from doing business in an information economy—and why the life cycle of business designs will continue to shrink.

Adaptive Enterprise will influence the influencers of business thought. Its contribution lies not simply in describing sense-and-respond as a required behavior but in presenting it as a conceptual model for the post-industrial corporation—a prescription for designing and operating businesses that can continuously, systematically reinvent themselves.

INTRODUCTION

Increasingly unpredictable and rapid change follows un-avoidably from doing business in an Information Age. What could be more strategically important than coming to grips with the im-plications?

The message of *Adaptive Enterprise* is that large, complex organizations must and can adapt systematically—and success-fully—to this kind of change. *Systematic* is a property of the sense-and-respond model described in this book. *Success* will be determined by leadership's competence in making a particular set of choices within the model framework.

The only kind of strategy that makes sense in the face of un-predictable change is a strategy to become adaptive. Speed-to-market, customer intimacy, operational excellence, and organi-zational agility, however important, are not adequate strategic objectives in and of themselves. They are attributes of the real ob-jective: successful and systematic adaptation. Adaptation implies more than agility. It requires *appropriate* organizational response to change. And when change becomes unpredictable, it follows that the appropriate response will be equally so.

In this environment, therefore, *planned* responses do not work. If the underlying reality is an inherent unpredictability in what customers will actually need, having sufficient organizational agility to get to market first with quality offerings based on cus-tomers' predictions of what they will want is a fool's errand.

This is why complexity theory has recently attracted atten-tion as a new way of thinking about strategy. Certain (but not all) systems operating far from equilibrium consistently demonstrate an ability to self organize and display emergent properties that enable them to adapt in unpredictable environments. Why not reconceptualize businesses as complex adaptive systems? Companies will no longer have to develop appropriate strategies—they will simply emerge. Strategy collapses into a universal imperative: Become a complex adaptive system. Next case.

Complexity theory has an enormous amount to contribute, and some of its principles constitute major underpinnings of the sense-and-respond model. But it is insufficient, because it does not address the unique properties of *social* systems—which is precisely what human organizations are. Individuals can and do make decisions *within* the system *about* the system. These decisions include if and how to change their own behaviors inside the system, the structure and rules of the system, and even its purpose. For this reason, the sense-and-respond model adds *intentionality* and *purposefulness* to complexity, adaptiveness, and system as essential organizational properties.

An enterprise's ability to adapt depends on how it processes information. From complexity theorists we learn that all successfully adapting systems have something in common: They transform apparent noise into meaning faster than apparent noise comes at them. Sense-and-respond organizations leverage this insight into a generic way of fostering adaptive sensemaking and action. The particulars of what is sensed and of how it is interpreted are role-specific, and depend on the amount of adaptability required. No role requires more careful design of its adaptive loop than the one accountable for translating apparent noise into meaning about when and how to adapt the *way* the organization adapts. That role, of course, is leadership.

Unpredictability implies that organizational behavior must be driven by current customer requests—tacit as well as articulated—rather than by firm-forward plans to make and sell offerings. Customer-back adaptiveness means dispatching capabilities on demand, as opposed to scheduling them efficiently in advance. This, in turn, implies a modular organizational structure, which cannot be effectively managed with a command and control governance system.

The sense-and-respond model addresses these issues first, by organizing information in a specific way to represent and support systematic adaptiveness by key roles in the firm (the adaptive loop); second, by organizing assets and capabilities as a system of modules that can be dynamically dispatched into one-off value chains (modular organization); and third, by replacing command and control with a commitment-centric governance system that propagates the purpose, bounds, and essential structure of the business throughout the organization. It manages the interactions—rather than the actions—of modular capabilities through a universal and general commitment management protocol (a technology-assisted commitment management system).

A sense-and-respond organization, then, is a collection of capabilities and assets managed as a purposeful adaptive *system*. This presupposes an ability to manage organizations as systems—an idea too rarely preached and almost never practiced in today's large enterprises. The theme threads its way through this entire book, because a deep appreciation of this concept will be vital to the leadership of sense-and-respond organizations.

In this book the term *sense-and-respond* refers both to a type of organizational behavior and to a specific prescription for systematically achieving it. Sense-and-respond *behavior,* that is, the triggering and determination of a firm's operations by the requests of individual customers, characterizes many small and some intermediate-sized organizations, but only a very few large, complex ones. (Some systems integrator firms come to mind.) The sense-and-respond *model* is a new conceptual design for producing this behavior economically and at large scale. Its successful implementation will require the adoption of some new concepts, new tools, and new leadership competencies. As yet, no complete exemplars of the sense-and-respond model exist. But prototype implementors have put its various parts into practice.

The prescription is radical. The first few chapters of *Adaptive Enterprise,* therefore, will establish the conditions under which leadership will find it imperative to undertake the required transformation. A detailed description of sense-and-respond behavior and some of its important underlying concepts follows. Subsequent chapters explore elements of the sense-and-respond model, the responsibilities of leadership, and the early experiences of some sense-and-respond pioneers. Examples help flesh out sense-and-respond theory, bringing it to life in the context of real companies dealing with difficult cultural and business issues as they work through this transformation. These chapters also describe several principles and some early conclusions about good practice.

We will need books that explore the learning curve of shaping and managing successful sense-and-respond organzations. They will be written as good practice emerges from those who commit themselves to the transformation from offering to responding. But these practices will have to be grounded in a model with sound conceptual underpinnings. First things first.

I believe readers need to understand the theoretical building blocks of sense-and-respond so that they can draw their own conclusions about the quality of its foundations and the logic used to synthesize them into a model. But I also recognize that the case for sense-and-respond should be presented as simply and clearly as possible, without diversionary excursions into complexity theory, systems theory, information theory, decision theory, computer science, or linguistics. To resolve the conflict between these two needs, I have used endnotes and appendices to expand on some of the core ideas behind sense-and-respond. Michael Shank's description of modular organizations in appendix A, and the discussion of adaptive decisionmaking by Michael Kusnic and Daniel Owen in appendix B, make particularly important contributions. The references and bibliography will be useful to those who want to delve more deeply into these and other subjects.

As the reader will discover, I believe that the careful use of words is very important for leaders as well as authors—especially when using familiar ones to explain something new. Words such as *leadership, accountability, commitment, collaboration, trust, process, procedure,* and *governance* mean many things to many people, but they have very specific meanings in the sense-and-respond model. For ease of reference, the sense-and-respond definitions of these and other important terms are provided in a glossary.

CHAPTER 1

*I hold that man is in the right who is most closely in
league with the future.*

—I B S E N

THE PREMISE AND PROMISE

OF SENSE-AND-RESPOND

BETWEEN MAY 1994 AND NOVEMBER 1998, MORE THAN
three thousand executives from a variety of industries, government agencies, and educational institutions attended strategy
courses at IBM's Advanced Business Institute. All were asked a
question deeply relevant to the future survival and success of their
organization: What kind of change do you expect your organization to face during the next decade? Fifty-two percent replied that
their future business environment would be one of "continuous
discontinuity." Another 25 percent foresaw "a one-time discontinuity, followed by continuous but incremental change." More than
three-quarters of these senior managers, in other words, expected
to face discontinuity and the challenge of guiding their large, complex organizations through an increasingly unpredictable future.

These executives' conclusions accord with the realities encountered by many firms during the last decade, especially those
in information-intensive businesses. In the late 1980s and early

1990s, leading computer firms, including Wang, Digital, and IBM, experienced drastic, unforeseen changes that threatened not only their industry leadership, but their survival. Of those three, only IBM remains a major independent player. Similarly, financial institutions have faced and continue to face the challenges of deregulation and electronic commerce. As early as 1985, executives at Westpac, Australia's largest bank, after interviewing senior executives of several global banks, were unable to find anyone who felt able to predict reliably what new products and services customers would favor even one year in the future.

These instances of unpredictability are not accidental or unconnected. They stem from a fundamental and lasting economic change affecting more and more businesses. Harvard sociologist Daniel Bell characterized this change as a shift in the basis of wealth creation. Wealth, once based on tangible and scarce resources such as land, labor, energy, and capital, is today increasingly based on intangibles that are not consumed, don't wear out, and don't depreciate—information and knowledge.[1] The software industry, a mere thirty years old, demonstrates the new economic importance of intangibles: The value of software resides in intellectual content captured as symbols in computer code, not in the disks on which those symbols are recorded. Software represents what economist Brian Arthur calls "congealed knowledge," as opposed to the "congealed resources" of traditional manufactured goods.[2]

Increasingly today, global wealth derives from codified knowledge and the ability to manipulate it at electronic speed. Because these intangibles can be transformed and transmitted so quickly, rapid and discontinuous change has become the hallmark of information-intensive industries. Widespread discontinuous change makes unpredictability a given. Uncertainty is not a passing symptom, but a fact of economic life in the information era.

Peter Drucker was one of the first business thinkers to call attention to the growing certainty of uncertainty. He made very clear its implications for planning and strategy when he wrote "uncertainty—in the economy, society, politics—has become so great as to render futile, if not counterproductive, the kind of planning most companies still practice: forecasting based on probabilities."[3]

To survive, organizations must prepare themselves to deal with such a future. As Drucker suggests, however, traditional planning is useless in the face of great uncertainty. The essential question organizations must answer is this: What must we do—in fact, what must we *become*—if we are to successfully navigate the treacherous waters of unpredictability?

When asked to describe their strategies for coping with discontinuity, the executives polled at the Advanced Business Institute named many prescriptions from recent management literature: reengineering, team structures, identifying core competencies, outsourcing, value-based leadership, lean and flexible manufacturing, customer relationship management, and so on. Discussions of these approaches brought out three underlying themes: business focus must shift from products to processes and competencies; individuals close to the firing line must be empowered; and customers' needs must receive increased attention.

It is not difficult to understand the appeal of these prescriptions. The efficiencies promised by reengineering, lean manufacturing, and outsourcing may, in fact, be essential to success; and customer focus and empowerment, as we will see, are necessary ingredients of adaptiveness. But even collectively, they are insufficient, because they are almost always piecemeal attempts to deal with a problem that calls for a systemic, transformational solution. Given the fundamental differences separating the Industrial Age economy from the Information Age economy, only a fundamentally different kind of business organization will suffice. Continuously discontinuous change demands a new business model. The dominant large corporations of the twenty-first century will succeed only by embracing new concepts, not by better executing the old ones.

The sense-and-respond model provides a means for meeting the challenges of discontinuity. A sense-and-respond organization does not attempt to predict future demand for its offerings. Instead, it identifies changing customer needs and new business challenges *as they happen,* responding to them quickly and appropriately, before these new opportunities disappear or metamorphose into something else. Adaptability has come to be increasingly valued in recent years, and the terms *flexibility, agility,* and *responsiveness* crop up frequently in business discussions today. Most people have yet to come to grips, however, with the deeper implications of *adaptiveness:* To be truly adaptive, an organization must have a fundamentally new structure; it must manage information in a particular way; it must be managed as a system; and its leaders and employees must commit themselves to very different behaviors and responsibilities. Traditional organizations cannot just add adaptiveness to their current set of capabilities. They must *become* adaptive organizations.

In other words, no acquired tips, habits, or techniques will transform a traditional organization into an adaptive one. Instead, large organizations must challenge long-established concepts of leadership, strategy, and responsibility. The basic questions to ask are these:

- What do the new economic realities imply for the structure and behavior of large organizations?

- If it is possible for large, complicated organizations to adapt rapidly and systematically to discontinuous change, how should they do so?

- What does strategy mean in an environment of discontinuous and unpredictable change, an environment in which future demand for products and services is intrinsically unknowable?

- What role must leaders play in empowered, decentralized organizations if the organization is to achieve coherent, enterprise-level behavior?

To understand the necessity for a new organizational concept and what would be its essential characteristics, let's begin by contrasting it with the more familiar idea of what a business is and does, the Industrial Age make-and-sell model.

MAKE-AND-SELL VS. SENSE-AND-RESPOND

The simplified representation in Figure 1.1 illustrates two very different ways of thinking about business. Neither is right or wrong. A model is right if it corresponds to the level of pre-

FIGURE 1.1

Two Ways to Think about a Business

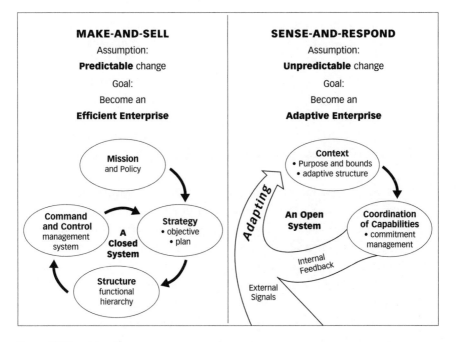

Source: IBM Consulting Group.

dictabilty of the world in which a given firm operates. Where change occurs gradually and incrementally, for example, a sensible management approach would stress efficiency in doing what management already knows should be done: forecasting what the market will want and minimizing the cost and expense of making and selling it. Such a business will articulate its mission and policies and regard them as a constant, as its North Star. These basic declarations will rarely be modified, because doing so would be disruptive, and disruption is the enemy of efficiency. Leadership in a make-and-sell organization operates a closed system, ignoring for as long as possible signals that a change may be required. It articulates strategy as a set of objectives and a broad plan of action to achieve them. Although management will revisit the strategy once or twice a year, the company's course and speed will be kept as steady as possible, with some mid-course corrections. When dramatic changes in strategy are espoused, they will be resisted in the interest of avoiding the substantial cost in time and money required to "turn the ship around."

Structure-follows-strategy organizational design maximizes the efficient execution of the firm's strategy. Changing the strategy is disruptive and inefficient, because it means changing the structure—and reorganizing—with all the attendant breakage and relearning costs. Rather than undertake that, management keeps the ship on as even a keel as possible, issuing directives from the bridge on what to do and seeing that employees learn the repeatable procedures designed to maximize the efficiency of operations.

But in unpredictable markets, in which customers themselves become unreliable predictors of their future needs, adaptiveness must take precedence over efficiency. Premiums now flow to those who sense early and accurately what their customers currently want and who respond in "real time" to those needs—individual customer by individual customer. To enable this behavior, leadership in the sense-and-respond organization must create a context that unambiguously establishes what the firm does and the constraints on how it does it. Leaders must also specify how employees interrelate to achieve the organization's purpose. The elements of the context thus established can be seen as analogous to the traditional concepts of mission, policy, and organization, but with important differences, to be described later. As long as employees stay within the parameters defined by the context, the business empowers them to determine for themselves how best to deliver the results for which they have been made accountable. The organization becomes a pool of modular capabilities that can be dynamically combined and recombined to respond to the current requests of individual customers. Because it has more information about individual customers, the business can differentiate its value proposition from customer to customer. Its strategy is expressed in the form of an adaptive organizational design for dispatching modular capabilities in response to current customer requests; "reorganization" is continuous. Commitments, tracked using a commitment management governance system, define the dynamic interactions between capabilities. *Context and coordination* replaces *command and control*. As individuals in the organization adapt to differing customer requests, always staying within the current organizational context, leadership actively seeks out environmental and internal signals that will help it improve the organizational context itself.

The successful large corporations of the twentieth-century Industrial Age have been make-and-sell organizations. Automobile manufacturers, appliance manufacturers, and even the computer makers of past decades were superbly organized to produce large quantities of products efficiently and then sell them to customers whose needs they could assume, predict, or even, to some degree, control. Henry Ford created the archetype of make-and-sell corporations: the assembly-line manufacturer turning out large numbers of identical items with machine-like efficiency. Human workers in Ford's world functioned as parts of the machine, each carrying out a specified, unvarying sequence of tasks. In fact, the appropriate metaphor for make-and-sell companies is efficient, offer-making machines. Like most machines, such firms are designed to consistently carry out particular purposes in predefined ways. They are characterized by replaceable parts, economies of scale, and replaceable people executing repeatable procedures in accordance with prescribed business plans. Many large industrial corporations, including General Motors, General Electric, Johnson & Johnson, and IBM, became great because they could anticipate demand, efficiently making and selling products in tempo with predicted changes in customer needs—and often enough shaping those needs themselves through marketing.

When customer needs change rapidly and unpredictably, however, this make-and-sell model begins to break down—as many large firms have discovered in recent years. It does not matter how good you are at making widgets if the market for widgets disappears or if your competitors offer dramatically new and improved widgets faster than you can. Even if make-and-sell firms could find ways to better track their customers' rapidly shifting preferences, they could not retool or rebuild their complicated production machines quickly or efficiently enough to keep up. Offer-making machines may be efficient, but they are not very flexible.

Many business thinkers and executives realize that the stable world that enabled make-and-sell organizations to thrive is disappearing. Don Hackworth, Group Executive of the General Motors North American Car Group, the largest of all twentieth-century make-and-sell firms, recognized the importance and magnitude of the change and described it in 1997 at the end of a GM Manufacturing Strategy Immersion Day:

> This world of make-and-sell is basically over. We're in the transition to something else. The world that we know is one in which you make a lot of something and then give it to the customer at a certain price, whether they want it or not. That world is over. It's the world of high volume, a lot of output per brand, some very specific techniques to produce it, and a certain way that you market it. That world is over.
>
> We are now moving to a world that I call the world of sense and respond. Custom rapid delivery is a part of this world. It's putting you in touch with the customer like you've never been in touch before. The hands of the whole value chain are surrounding and touching the customer. When they ask for something, they want it in a certain way, at a certain time, in a certain place, at a certain price, for a value. The manufacturing company in our business that figures out how to do that better than anybody else will win. This is the world that we are now moving towards.

Interestingly, even as the profits of the giant make-and-sell enterprises confirmed the validity of the Industrial Age business model, a sense-and-respond model developed in the professional services industry. Systems integrators such as Bechtel, Fluor, EDS, and IBM's Federal Systems Division (the forerunner of today's Global Services organization) demonstrated as early as the 1950s that responding flexibly to unpredicted, individual customer requests could fuel profitable growth. Rather than *schedule activities* to produced predetermined offerings, these firms *dispatch capabilities* to produce unique responses to one-off requests for proposals. Customer requests, not a predetermined business plan, determine what they do and how they deploy their resources.

Thinking Customer-Back, Not Firm-Forward

Sense-and-respond firms operate from the customer-back, not from the "firm-forward." Individual customer wants or needs constitute the engine driving the company's operations; they set the firm in motion. Custom Foot, for example, makes shoes to order using thirteen precise, individual measurements of each customer's left and right feet. Custom Foot cannot make a single shoe until some customer provides it with this information. Florsheim, in contrast, does not need a customer to make its shoes: It needs only a forecast and a plan. The customer occupies the center of the sense-and-respond universe. In make-and-sell companies, the plan comes first, driving operations from the firm forward. Most make-and-sell companies do invest in market research aimed at fine-tuning their products and gathering requirements for new offerings, but such research relies heavily on predictions, focusing on what is common among many customers rather than what is different about individual ones. Individual needs become homogenized as market segments, and new products target the most attractive segments. The firm, its plans, and the efficiency of its productive processes remain at the center of the make-and-sell universe.

Ultimately, of course, all companies are customer-dependent. If potential customers choose not to buy what a firm sells, the firm will eventually fail. But when customer needs are stable, predictable, or controllable, businesses can afford to look inward, focusing on what they do to meet those needs and how to do it efficiently. As long as their targets move slowly enough, these companies can refine a precision mechanism that will hit bull's-eyes over and over again.

When customer needs become *unpredictable,* firms, to survive, must move their center of attention to understanding those changing needs. Adaptive organizations require, first of all, a systematic ability to search out, capture, and interpret clues about emerging and as yet unarticulated customer preferences. They must employ equal vigilance both in sensing developments that might enable new capabilities and in anticipating environmental changes, such as regulatory or political dynamics. Like athletes in the ready position, sense-and-respond firms must excel at sensing subtle change earlier and in responding to it faster than do their competitors. Such firms can establish reinforcing cycles of success that provide profit and drive change at a pace rivals can't match.

Sense-and-respond does not always mean *listen-and-comply.* "No bid" should be the response to a customer request that, even after negotiation, is not a good fit of customer's needs with the firm's capability to respond profitably. Sense-and-respond can also mean *anticipate and preempt,* to use Adrian Slywotzky's term for its proactive form. In this case the firm invests in gathering and interpreting contextual data about changes in customer preferences. Businesses that get very good at doing this, as the on-line grocery company Peapod or the bookseller amazon.com seek to do, may come to know more about their customers' preferences than the customers themselves do.

The Make-and-Sell to Sense-and-Respond Spectrum

A business has only two options: to make offers to customers or to respond to their requests. This essential difference separates make-and-sell from sense-and-respond organizations. All businesses, of course, do some degree of both, and many institutionalize (or intend to) a hybrid form. Nevertheless, at the enterprise level, the two functions require fundamentally different organizing principles. The make-and-sell company is conceived as an efficient machine for making and selling offers, the sense-and-respond company as an adaptive system for responding to unanticipated requests. The make-and-sell company concentrates on mass production, making and selling as much of the same thing as possible to achieve economies of scale. The sense-and-respond company focuses instead on modular customization, allowing it to economically produce what its customers ask for. Such companies realize economies of scope by reusing modular assets to reduce the costs of customization. The make-and-sell company excels at planning and control: Orders cascade down a chain of command to be carried out by those "below." The sense-and-respond company consists of dynamic teams making decentralized decisions based on a shared understanding of organizational purpose. The make-and-sell company schedules activities; the sense-and-respond company dispatches capabilities. Make-and-sell stresses efficiency and predictability; sense-and-respond prioritizes flexibility and responsiveness. Table 1.1 summarizes these distinctions.

RESOLVING THE STRATEGY PROBLEM: STRATEGY AS STRUCTURE

The concept of business as an efficient machine is disappearing. One clear sign of its abandonment has been the disbandment of large central planning departments. As these staffs struggled unsuccessfully to keep up with unanticipated change they created more burden than benefit and were gradually dissolved.

The vacuum left by the demise of central planning and control staffs has not been filled, but it has led to prescriptions for employee empowerment. Companies now hope distributed decision-making—guided by leaders' vision statements—will produce strategic behavior. Some proponents of applying complexity theory to human social systems have argued, in fact, that, left to themselves or given only a few simple rules, organizations will self-organize. But neither logic nor experience support the assertion that large, complex corporations can self-organize to produce *purposeful strategic* behavior. Managers at all levels, left free to decide in isolation how to respond to local conditions, will make appropriate local decisions. But a collection of decisions that make only local sense will not cohere into a purposeful enterprise strategy.

So neither strategy-as-plan nor strategy-as-emergent-behavior address the overriding issue presented by discontinuity: how to adapt systematically. The sense-and-respond alternative implies a different way of expressing strategy. Once a company organizes or reorganizes itself to recognize current customer needs and respond to them, it no longer operates from a strategic plan. Now, the *design* of its systematic capability to respond to unanticipated customer requests expresses its strategy. When Westpac Bank executives, for example, recognized that they could no longer predict future customer needs and could not, therefore, develop a traditional strategic plan, CIO Alan Hohne and Chief General Manager Peter Douglas implemented a sense-and-respond solution. They developed the ability to rapidly implement whatever strategy became necessary, rather than determine *the* strategy in advance.[4] Using a modular design, they created a *structure* that expressed their sense-and-respond *strategy*.

TABLE 1.1

COMPARING MAKE-AND-SELL TO SENSE-AND-RESPOND

MAKE-AND-SELL	CONTINUUM	SENSE-AND-RESPOND
	⬍	
Business as an *efficient mechanism* for making and selling *offers* to well-defined market segments with predictable needs.	**Mind-set Behind Strategic Intent**	Business as an *adaptive system* for responding to unanticipated *requests* in unpredictable environments.
Embedded in products. The expertise of designers, engineers, or actuaries is captured as a new braking system, style innovation, insurance policy, or . . . that is incorporated in an offer.	**Know-how**	*Embedded in people and processes.* Expertise is codified in processes or identified by individual. It is applied on demand to respond to a customer request.
Mass production. Emphasis on repeatable procedures, replaceable parts, and standard job definitions to efficiently make a high volume of the offers *defined by the company.*	**Process**	*Modular customization.* Modular products and services, produced by modular capabilities that are linked to create customized responses to requests *defined by customers.*
Efficiency and predictability. Control company's destiny by accurately forecasting changes in market demand, and *scheduling* the production of offers at low cost.	**Organizational Priority**	Invest in capabilities and a system for rapidly and dynamically *dispatching* them into the processes required to respond to an individual customer request.

Profit margins on products, and economies of scale. Make and sell as much of the same thing as possible to reduce the fixed cost per unit of production.	**Profit Focus**	*Returns on investments and economies of scope.* Reduce cost of customized responses by re-using modular assets over a wide range of product components and customers.
Functional and sequential activity. Centralized planning and follow-up by a specialized planning staff. Cascade orders down the chain of command in accordance with a pre-defined value chain.	**Operational Concept and Governance Mechanism**	*Networked and parallel activity.* Dynamically formed teams making decentralized decisions within a shared enterprise context. Use of a common commitment management protocol to coordinate the production of customized value chains in accordance with the business design.
Functionally managed, and optimized. Each function creates its own view of "what's going on out there" and has its own processes for "how we do things around here." Focus on providing the information needed to execute the business plan.	**Information Architecture**	*Enterprise management* of essential information to create a unified view of the environment and key processes. Support decentralized decision-making. Focus on providing the information needed to determine what the business response should be for a specific request.
Host-centric. Shadowing the hierarchical top-down command and control management system.	**Information Technology Architecture**	*Network-centric.* Shadowing the dynamic network of people and teams.
Share of offering market. Share of mid-sized vehicles sold, personal computers sold, full-life policy premiums, etc.	**Market Leader Criterion**	*Share of customer spending* on a class of needs. Share of spending on personal transportation, information and knowledge management, financial security, etc.
Strategy as plan to aim defined products and services at defined markets.	**Articulation of Strategy**	*Strategy as adaptive business design* to sense earlier and respond faster to unpredictable change.

Even after an organization has structured itself for sense-and-respond, of course, important strategic issues remain. Foremost, it must settle what to sense, what response capabilities it will invest in, and what will be its defining organizational purpose and the boundaries of organizational behavior. But those issues follow from the basic decision to address the puzzle of formulating strategy in the face of uncertainty by building the capacity to adapt. This ability comprises two essential elements: a specific way of processing information and a modular organizational structure.

THE ADAPTIVE LOOP

A four-phase adaptive loop defines the crucial behavior of sense-and-respond organizations. Both adaptive individuals and adaptive organizations first *sense* changes in their environment and internal states. They next *interpret* these changes in the context of their experience, aims, and capabilities, separating threats from opportunities and discarding irrelevant information. Next, they *decide* how to respond and, finally, they *act* on their decisions. The progression from sensing to interpretation to decision to action becomes an iterative loop as the adaptive system monitors the results of its previous actions and picks up environmental changes that have occurred since the previous cycle.

Organizations of all kinds, including make-and-sell firms, follow these basic steps to adapt their behavior. Even make-and-sell firms change over time. But they try to stay in the *act* phase as long as possible, relying on learning curve effects to increase their profits by improving efficiency as they do the same things over and over again. This motivates make-and-sell firms to resist change. They behave like closed systems, only responding to environmental change when it becomes too great to ignore. Sense-and-respond organizations, on the other hand, are aggressively open systems. Rather than ignore environmental change, they probe for new signals, cycling through the adaptive loop as quickly as possible to leverage the changes they sense into new and profitable responses.

No organization, of course, can interpret, let alone respond to, more than a fraction of the flood of signals that pours in from the environment. *Where* organizations choose to place their sensory probes and *how* they distinguish meaningful signals from random "noise" determines whether they will be sufficiently aware of what is happening "out there." Once aware, they must dispatch capabilities from their repertoire. Although information technology plays an essential role in this process, human skill in recognizing patterns and thinking creatively about unanticipated challenges will continue to mark the difference between successful firms and unsuccessful ones.

THE SEARCH FOR COHERENCE

Command-and-control governance is a signature characteristic of classical make-and-sell organizations. Using the resources of large central planning staffs, senior management decided what employees should do and told them when and how to do it. The staff orchestrated the decision-making process and monitored compliance. In well-run companies, the command-and-control system ensured coherent organizational behavior by cascading instructions down the organization's hierarchy. The plan determined interactions among organizational units. The linear sequence thus created, aptly termed the value *chain,* required minimal communication among functions. From the planners' point of view, it didn't much matter that development never talked to marketing. Their relationships were predetermined. The system's inherent inflexibility—the industrial equivalent of a military machine—ensured coherence.

Such systems no longer work. The central planning groups that capably formulated and followed up on plans in a stable environment proved unable to do so when faced with rapid change in an increasingly unstable environment. When their efforts to keep up with unforeseen change created delay and bureaucratic burden rather than meaningful direction, most large organizations dissolved them. Moreover, leaders could no longer see clearly what actions employees should take. To cope, they began distributing decision-making power to units and groups more in touch with "what was happening out there." Some leaders communicated policy decisions to mid-level managers, leaving them to develop appropriate actions. Some communicated only the company's vision and values, trusting the empowered groups to figure out, somehow, how to turn that vision into reality.

But communicate-and-hope, even when supplemented by a financial model, does not constitute genuine governance. Broad directional statements by leaders, without a central staff to interpret them and monitor organizational behavior, are unlikely to produce the coherence needed by large, complex enterprises. No wonder that recent interviews of senior executives in two of the world's largest companies revealed dissatisfaction with "lack of accountability," "too many visions," "lack of synergy," and "poor execution." It could hardly be otherwise. When hundreds, even thousands of managers throughout large, complex global organizations are empowered to make their own decisions and interpret their leadership's vision in their own way, the failure of these organizations to achieve coherence should come as no surprise. In their efforts to become more flexible, many organizations have simply become more chaotic.

Leaders of successful sense-and-respond organizations must skirt these pitfalls. How can they govern their organizations to ensure both coherent organizational behavior and responsiveness? A few business thinkers who believe complexity theory provides the answer argue that leaders have no substantive role. These theorists point to the many natural systems that self-organize to achieve important results. Large flocks of birds, they note, behave in a strategically coherent manner, migrating thousands of miles without benefit of an avian CEO to develop a strategy and issue instructions. But some important differences between complex social systems known as human organizations and the natural systems studied by complexity scientists undermine this conclusion. For now, it is sufficient to note that the few large self-organizing businesses that do exist exhibit an underlying simplicity that distinguishes them from most large corporations. Though interesting, these examples tend to disprove rather than to support the idea that large, complex firms can self-organize to carry out a specified purpose.

Leaders of sense-and-respond organizations can ensure flexibility and coherence through a new approach to governance I call *context and coordination*. Sense-and-respond leaders must first create,

promulgate, and enforce an unambiguous organizational *context.*
Second, they must develop a system of *coordination* to govern—but
not dictate—individuals' behaviors to ensure they are consistent
with the organizational context.

THE LEADER'S ROLE: PROVIDING
CONTEXT AND COORDINATION

The word *context,* popularly taken to mean information providing an explanatory background, has a much more specific
meaning in the sense-and-respond model. *Organizational context*
encompasses three basic parts: the organization's reason for being,
its governing principles, and its high-level business design. Unlike
typical mission and vision statements, which propose a (sometimes inconsistent) mix of goals and principles, a reason for being
statement unequivocally defines the organization's primary purpose—the one outcome that justifies its existence. It also identifies the primary beneficiary of that purpose and any absolute constraints on how it is to be achieved. Governing principles set forth
the organization's unbreachable limits of action, including what its
members must always do or never do in their pursuit of the firm's
purpose. A high-level business design is a system design of the organization's essential structure. It illustrates the relationships
among elements both inside and outside the organization in terms
of the outcomes they owe one another—the outcomes essential to
achieving the enterprise reason for being. Together, these three
components of context tell accountable, empowered people where
the organization is headed, the boundaries on their actions, and a
picture of how what they do relates to what others do and to organizational purpose. A well-articulated context provides an unambiguous framework for individual activity, aligning and bounding
organizational actions without dictating what those actions should
be. It leaves empowered individuals free to choose the best responses to unanticipated requests within a unifying framework of
unambiguous purpose, principles, and structure.

Developing and adapting organizational context is the primary
responsibility of leadership. This creative process differs consider-

ably from the problem-solving activities that many senior managers still consider their principal work. It calls for dramatically different skills. The rigorous intellectual exercise of context building depends on leadership's ability to develop viable conceptual business models—an ability rarer than talent for putting out fires. Creating an effective context also requires establishing a degree of clarity that some senior managers may prefer to avoid. Ambiguity defeats purposeful and coherent organizational behavior. Without clarity about purpose, bounds, relationships, and measurements, people throughout the organization who must make tough choices about trade-offs will have to make their own interpretations, thus increasing the chances that these choices will be inconsistent both with one another and with organizational purpose. Whether equivocation stems from leaders' own uncertainty about the purpose or from their fear of offending a constituency, ambiguity about purpose, boundaries, and essential structure all but guarantees incoherence. As difficult as it may be to achieve, the creation of organizational context is an absolute requirement for coherent, flexible, and, ultimately, viable performance.

Leaders' responsibilities do not end with creating context. They must go on to ensure that organizational behavior accords with it. This requires tracking the important commitments negotiated among accountable, empowered people. Defining organizational roles in terms of commitments made to deliver particular outcomes to particular internal or external customers puts appropriate emphasis on the *interaction* of system elements, not on their actions. It also emphasizes the system-defined outcomes required of these roles, that is, their contribution to organizational purpose, as opposed to the procedures required to produce that contribution. People in roles defined this way come to understand that they are not accountable for their actions but for the *consequences* of their actions.

Coordinating commitments, rather than supervising activities is the proper concern of sense-and-respond leadership. This is a crucial distinction. Activities are the focus of make-and-sell management, whose function is to keep the organizational machine running smoothly by making sure that people perform specified tasks at or above specified levels of productivity and quality.

In a sense-and-respond organization, roles are not defined in terms of activities, because responding effectively to unanticipated customer requests requires the continual invention of new ways of doing things. Sense-and-respond leaders must manage the interlocking sets of commitments required to marshal a response consistent with the enterprise context. Deciding *how* those commitments are met—the processes used to produce the outcomes—falls to those making the commitments, within the limits established by the governing principles.

As sense-and-respond organizations adapt to changing conditions and reconfigure their capabilities to meet new customer requests, new commitments will be negotiated and some old ones renegotiated. Later, I will describe a commitment management protocol for tracking the complex shifting patterns of interdependent commitments—who owes what to whom. This rigorous and universal protocol specifies a particular way for people to define, negotiate, and execute commitments with each other. It is especially applicable to modular organizations because it gives any two organizational roles a way of interfacing—even if they have never worked together before. Using the protocol, commitments can be tracked by software, the only feasible way to manage dynamic commitments in a large or complex organization.

MANAGING BY WIRE

In the Information Age, more and more knowledge and more and more ways of creating economic value are being abstracted into symbols that can be combined, transformed, and sent around the world at electronic speed. Our ability to manipulate this dematerialized reality drives both wealth creation and the discontinuous change that makes sense-and-respond organizations necessary. To be adaptive, however, organizations must meet an essential criterion for processing information from the environment: They must translate apparent noise into meaning faster than it arrives.[5] As both noise and potentially meaningful data arrive faster and faster, complex organizations in complex environments need help to sense and interpret events quickly.

Managing the consequences of using information technology requires more information technology. The abstraction and electronic manipulation that have increased the speed of change can be used manage it. In the mid-1980s, far-sighted managers at Westpac concluded that they could improve the speed of the bank's adaptation to change by first modularizing and then codifying core functions, policies, and knowledge in an electronic system. Linking this system to current information about their environment, they were able to reduce their time to market with new products, meeting changed market conditions in weeks or months instead of months or years. Although successor executive teams did not use the technological initiative to support a complete sense-and-respond transformation at Westpac, the effort established the feasibility and benefits of running an organization by managing its electronic representation.

The term for managing a business by managing its information representation is *managing by wire,* an expression meant to draw an analogy to modern aviation's fly-by-wire systems.[6] When jet engine technology arrived, airplanes became so fast that unassisted human pilots could no longer sense, interpret, and act on information quickly enough to fly them. So computer systems were developed to present pilots with concise displays of essential information and then to translate pilot responses into the myriad actions needed to execute the pilot's decisions. This technology mediated and accelerated the pilot's adaptive loop, making it possible to fly a plane traveling at several times the speed of sound. Managers needing to "fly" modern, fast-moving businesses will increasingly find similar systems both technically feasible and necessary.

MANAGING THE SENSE-AND-RESPOND TRANSFORMATION

Some executives have already begun to adopt the sense-and-respond model. Analysis of their experiences demonstrates just how fundamental a change it entails. These pioneers reconceived their organizations from top to bottom, developing new roles and structures and educating their organizations' members about new ways of thinking about their responsibilities. Not content with looking for better ways to continue doing what they have always done, they are striving to change their corporate DNA. Having recognized the imperatives of a new economic world, they strive to become the type of organization that can thrive there. They have discovered, as well, that changing from the make-and-sell to the sense-and-respond model requires transformation, not merely reformation.

Transforming a system involves changing both its purpose and its structure.[7] Leaders must anticipate the effects on the whole system of each change they make to any part of it. A system cannot be improved, much less transformed, by making isolated adjustments to individual capabilities. The transformation from make-and-sell, however, should not, and probably could not, happen all at once. Individual decision-makers must nonetheless maintain a constant awareness of the larger context and take it into account when weighing options.

Organizations will find the journey to sense-and-respond challenging; most make-and-sell organizations will evolve into hybrids of make-and-sell and sense-and-respond, developing sense-and-respond capabilities only as these create value for their customers. General Motors, in an effort I will describe more fully in a later chapter, has developed a strategic framework for moving systematically from a make-and-sell to a predominantly sense-and-respond enterprise. The competencies required to create and manage large, adaptive organizations are rare, and will have to be developed. Many firms will nevertheless undertake the transformation because, in the long run, they have no alternative—their survival in our age of discontinuity depends on it.

An increasingly unpredictable marketplace is the premise of the sense-and-respond model. For large enterprises, this model promises systematic and successful adaptation without sacrificing the benefits of scale and scope. Between acceptance of the premise and realization of the promise lies a new way of thinking about strategy, structure, and governance.

Sense-and-respond is not a universal prescription, since some firms will find and exploit a decreasing number of important niches for predictable products and services. Furthermore, the rate at which organizations become information-intensive will vary, allowing some more time than others to manage the transition. Because the transformation to sense-and-respond will require fundamental change in the way people lead and work, leaders must accept and internalize the premise as a first priority. For this reason, Chapter 2 is dedicated to an investigation of why we should expect an increasingly uncertain future, and what this implies for business.

CHAPTER 2

We cannot overcome the problem of unpredictability.
[It] represents the fundamental and universal
situation of life on earth.

—PER BAK, *HOW NATURE WORKS*

UNPREDICTABILITY

The Only Sure Thing

IN THE EARLY 1980S, IN AN EFFORT TO PREPARE FOR DEREGULA-
tion and the opening of Australia to foreign banks, executives of
Australia's largest and most profitable bank consulted extensively
with colleagues in major financial institutions around the world to
determine what financial products and services the industry
should offer over the next five years. Expectation of deregulation
and foreign competition had already led to the creation of Westpac
in a 1982 merger in which the Bank of New South Wales, Australia's oldest bank, acquired the Commercial Bank of Australia.
Combined, the firms enjoyed a 20 to 25 percent market share of
most retail and corporate banking segments in Australia. Westpac
executives now sought greater understanding of the world in
which they would be operating.

They found, much to their surprise, that none of the executives to whom they spoke believed reliable predictions of new
products and services were possible even one year into the future,

much less five. The variety and pace of new product introduction in the financial services industry made a mockery of forecast assumptions. The "continuous discontinuity" of marketplace change made it impossible to place strategic bets on new product development with any confidence.

Deregulation alone did not explain this state of flux in a once stable industry. More fundamental was a radical change in the products themselves. Traditionally, the wealth handled by financial institutions had been embodied in precious metals. These could be physically shifted from vault to vault and represented by certificates and banknotes. By 1980, both wealth and the conditions for its exchange could be represented electronically. Financial products were coming to exist only as symbols in cyberspace. And because computers can manipulate symbols very rapidly, new products could go from concept to launch in weeks or even days. More than anything else, the uncertainty faced by Westpac and other banks was driven by the possibility of creating almost instant new products on computer workstations.

The first of these products—examples of what became known as financial derivatives—were mortgage-backed obligations introduced in the United States by the Federal National Mortgage Association (Fanny Mae) a few years before Westpac asked its questions about the future of the industry. Fanny Mae did so to transfer some of its mortgage loan risk to buyers and sellers in the securities market. Banks developed their own version of this innovation: the so-called interest rate mismatches that later developed into interest rate swaps and still later into swaptions. These and other derivatives have a purely electronic existence, with all the dynamic potential for rapid change that implies. They can be almost as varied as the imaginations of their creators. By the early 1990s, financial derivatives had become a $30 trillion global market. Their spectacular success came even though no one ever has seen or ever will see a financial derivative.

We often hear repeated the adage that we live in the Information Age, yet rarely do we stop to ponder what that really means. But one symptom we all experience is this: Not only are we swamped by unprecedented amounts of information, but, increasingly, we work with and generate wealth from information rather than from things. Financial derivatives provide only one of many examples.

THE MOTHER OF ALL DISCONTINUITIES: CODIFIED INFORMATION AND KNOWLEDGE

In a speech given in 1989 at an IBM Process Industry Conference, Wharton professor and former Assistant Secretary of Commerce Bruce Merrifield reported that 90 percent of the world's codified information had been produced since 1960. (See Figure 2.1.) Merrifield went on to project that the then current amount would double in the next fifteen years. As a result, he predicted, more change would occur during the next quarter century than humanity had seen in the entire span of its history.

Merrifield's curve started its almost vertical climb in the early 1960s, when solid state computers were first introduced for com-

FIGURE 2.1

MERRIFIELD'S CURVE

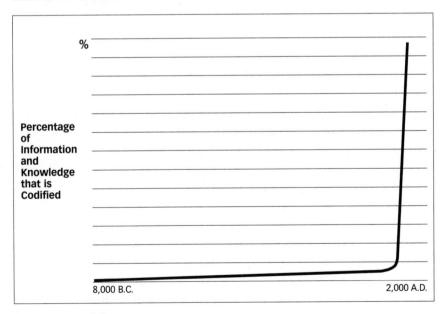

Source: Bruce Merrifield.

mercial use. Many people, seeing such evidence, assume that information technology alone brought about the Information Age. The role of computers such as the IBM 1401 (1959) and the IBM S/360 (1964) did play an undeniable role in the explosion of information, but technology is at most half the story. Equally astounding, but often overlooked, has been the improvement in our ability to create rich symbolic representations of real world objects and actions. Building and using these representations may *depend* on the capacity of computers to store and rapidly manipulate vast quantities of data, but the representations derive from efforts of human thought and imagination. The advent of the Information Age required more than the collection of ever larger quantities of data. It required the abstraction of real entities and behaviors into symbols, and the use of that codification of reality to change reality.

In the late 1950s, limitations imposed by the eighty-column IBM card restricted computer representation of the entity *customer* to a very few attributes, such as name, address, amount of transaction, and so on. Today, an MCI database contains rich abstractions of up to 10,000 items of information each on 140 million households. Technology made such a database feasible, but humans determined the essential information elements of what *customer* means to MCI. Abstractions of behavior have developed to a similar degree. In 1960, cutting a payroll check could be represented symbolically with sufficient rigor to automate that process. Today, the design, virtual construction, and testing of something as complex as a Boeing 777 can occur entirely in cyberspace. The 777 prototype was an electronic abstraction; the first physical 777 built went into commercial service. Symbolic abstractions, which can be manipulated at electronic speeds, can be created, modified, and moved much faster than can their physical counterparts. In this lies their principal source of economic advantage. Behaviors thus codified have yielded over the past four decades a 25 percent *annual* improvement in productivity.

These changes have put intangibles at our culture's economic center. In 1979, Harvard sociologist Daniel Bell wrote that, just as capital and energy had replaced land and labor as the basic wealth-creating economic resources, "codified information and knowledge are replacing capital and energy as the primary trans-

forming economic resources."[1] He supported this assertion by cit-
ing Marc Porat's research on changes in the distribution of work.
(See Figure 2.2.)

The information and knowledge economy not only moves
faster than the capital and energy economy, it works differently.
The economic properties of information differ from those of the
material resources that fueled the agricultural and industrial ages.
Traditional capital assets have maximum value before they are
used. *Until* used, however, information has no value at all. Land,
labor, capital, and energy are appropriable, that is, once given
away, they are no longer possessed by the giver. Moreover, their
value generally increases as they become scarcer. These economic
laws do not govern information. Those who give information to
others still have it, and the value of knowledge tends to increase
rather than decrease with sharing and use.[2]

Bell points out that an economic value theory of information
does not currently exist. By this he means that, as yet, no one can

FIGURE 2.2

DISTRIBUTION OF WORK IN THE U.S. ECONOMY

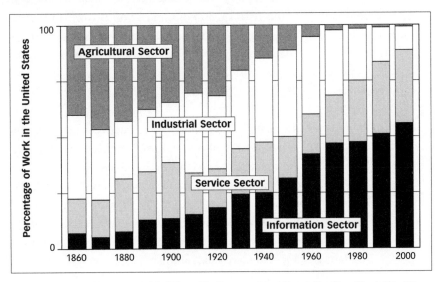

Source: From Michael Dertouzos and Joel Moses, *The Computer Age: A Twenty Year View* (Cambridge, MA: The MIT Press, 1979) Figure 9.2.

predict how a given change in information input will affect the output of a productive process.[3] Without a theoretical basis for measuring the economic value of knowledge, databases costing billions of dollars as well as most of the knowledge in employees' heads cannot and do not appear on corporate balance sheets. Though many executives like to say that "people are our most important assets," these particular assets are marooned on income statements as expense and cost. Because the value of knowledge cannot be measured, the term *knowledge management* remains more a wish than a reality. Without such valuations, in addition, uncertainty over company worth increases. What is happening when the stock market values a company at many times the value of its capital assets? Is the market reflecting the underlying value of the company's intellectual assets? Or is it manifesting the kind of speculative exuberance that drove tulip bulb prices to astronomical, unsustainable heights in seventeenth century Holland?

Similarly, the theory of decreasing returns to scale, another so-called law of classical economics, does not always apply in the Information Age. The theory holds that the finite size of the market, the entry of competitors, the limited availability of resources, and similar factors limit a firm's profitable growth. Growth of even the most successful company will eventually be curtailed by negative feedback, driving it toward economic equilibrium. Industrial Age experience has largely borne out the theory, but economist Brian Arthur says that the theory of *increasing* returns with *positive* feedback cycles is more likely to apply to knowledge-intensive firms.

> If one product or nation in a competitive marketplace gets ahead by "chance," it tends to stay ahead and even increase its lead. Predictable, shared markets are no longer guaranteed. . . .
>
> [T]he parts of the economy that are resource-based (agricultural, bulk-goods production, mining) are still for the most part subject to diminishing returns. Here conventional economics holds sway. The parts of the economy that are knowledge-based, on the other hand, are largely subject to increasing returns.[4]

Arthur uses the metaphor of a gambling casino to describe the experience of knowledge-intensive companies competing in an increasing-returns economy. Imagine you want to enter a new, high stakes game, digital communications. The ante is a few billion dollars. You begin to play, even though you don't know who you will be playing against. The rules won't be established until all players join in, and they will be subject to change during the game. You won't know what new technologies will be developed or how the government might decide to regulate play. But you cannot stay out of the game until you have this information because only those in it from the start have a reasonable shot at winning. You play, trying to make sense out of what happens and acting accordingly, but other players' actions and sensemaking efforts affect and alter the way the game proceeds. Pure chance usually determines who gains sufficient initial advantage to ride the positive feedback cycle. If you are dealt a losing hand, you have to get out quickly and cut your losses. Even if you're a winner, you must quit while you're ahead, moving on to the next game, and the next after that.[5]

This vivid, unsettling, but very apt metaphor captures the unprecedented challenge firms face in trying to conduct business in an information economy.

Consider once again these historic, irreversible developments of the last few decades.

- The quantity of information and knowledge has increased explosively.

- To an ever greater extent, information and knowledge consist of symbolic representations of reality subject to high-speed manipulation by technology, a process that both reflects and exacerbates rapid change in the real world.

- Information and knowledge have become primary economic resources but remain difficult to measure, with economic behavior differing vastly from that of traditional capital assets.

These changes underlie the discontinuity recognized by the banking executives Westpac consulted and by the executives surveyed at the Advanced Business Institute. They characterize the Information Age, and they have created a new economic world. The organizations that thrive in this world will be as different from those of today as the factory was from the farm in the nineteenth century.

THE NEED FOR A NEW ORGANIZATION

For an organization to work as an efficient making-and-selling machine requires above all a clear understanding of how things should be done, a specification that should not change frequently or unexpectedly. Frederick Taylor, the famous pioneer of machine-like efficiency in the work place, unequivocally assumed that this kind of certainty was not only necessary, but possible. These two quotations reveal how Taylor and his followers thought about the conduct of business:

> The high-priced man does just what he is told to do, and no back talk. When [the foreman] tells you to walk, you walk; when he tells you to sit down, you sit down.

> It is necessary in any activity to have a complete knowledge of what is to be done and to prepare instructions. The laborer has only to follow instructions.[6]

As dated as this now sounds, the approach works extremely well if leaders have "a complete knowledge of what is to be done." If not, it breaks down. Make-and-sell firms clearly lack the agility to play successfully in Brian Arthur's increasing-returns casino, where even a moderate chance of winning requires sensitivity to the game's changing complexion and sufficient creativity to make sense out of unexpected events.

Westpac began to perceive the changes overtaking the banking industry at much the same time that new technological developments were redefining the computer industry. Westpac was not ready for a world of discontinuity and rapid change. When it acquired the Commercial Bank of Australia, the Bank of New South Wales had been an innovator for thirty years, introducing private savings banks, automated check clearing, bank investment services, credit cards, and ATMs to Australia. In 1985, however, Westpac was taking eighteen to twenty-four months to develop new financial products, a dangerously long time, given the impossibility of knowing what the industry would be doing in twelve months. Westpac's competitors, on the other hand, had development cycle times of less than a year.

The acquisition, meanwhile, intended to increase the bank's competitiveness, had created its own problems. Integrating the banks proved difficult. Each bank had its own product lines, and each product line had its own processes and IT applications. Developing a new product thus required developing a new IT system. When Merrill Lynch, a non-bank competitor, arrived with its sweep function that integrated information about all products utilized by individual clients, Westpac could not respond in a timely way. The bank's management saw the need "to get IT off the critical path." IT contributed significantly to Westpac's 15 percent competitive disadvantage in structural costs and to the growth penalties associated with being chronically late to market.

The strategic challenges facing Westpac in 1985 boiled down to these: impending deregulation, new offshore niche competitors, an unpredictable market for financial services, an uncompetitive cost structure, and a two-year product cycle time. Despite its size and past success, Westpac was unprepared to compete in the Information Age that was now transforming banking. CEO Robert White characterized the trend and magnitude of the transformation: The industry had been "banking in the 1960s, became financial service in the 1970s, was becoming financial intermediation in the 1980s, and would mature into information intermediation in the 1990s."[7]

In other words, Westpac needed to learn how to participate in a new game; the old one was not being played any more. The new game would move faster and would be more unpredictable. Westpac's executives came to realize that unpredictability was no longer a problem: It was *the* problem.

That unpredictability was due to the growing importance of information. Why does information as the basis of wealth creation wreak such havoc on market predictability? In the 1980s, Berkeley professor Rashi Glazer developed principles that provide important insights about the answer to this question.

GLAZER'S LIST

At a time when little empiric evidence was available, Glazer derived his principles directly from the economic properties of information. He published them as logical implications of doing business in information-intensive environments. Experience now corroborates Glazer's insights, as information-intensive organizations increasingly come to resemble his predictions. He addressed both the nature of the conditions firms face in the Information Age and the necessary responses to those conditions. His definition of information intensity captures the connection between information and change.

> [A] firm is information intensive to the degree that its products and operations are based on the information collected and processed as part of exchanges along the value-added chain. Whereas traditional products and operations are relatively static, information-intensive products and operations *change* as new data from the environment become incorporated into them.[8]

Because the information component of products *can* change faster, it *will* change faster. Because information *can* be rapidly disseminated, it *will* be rapidly acquired by others. As a result, product life cycles will continue to shrink, and the pace of change will continue to accelerate.

Glazer has more recently described interactive commerce using electronic media, the result of a transition from what he calls dumb (that is, not interactive) environments to smart environments, in a way that also puts rapid change at center stage. He identifies four basic types of change for Information Age commerce.[9]

- Frequent turnovers in the stock of knowledge or information

- Flexible, adaptive roles and boundaries that change as information is exchanged

- Smart products that change as users interact with them

- Smart prices that change through negotiations, auctions, and yield management techniques

Taken together, the following hypotheses about information-intensive organizations point toward a markedly different way of doing business than that of traditional make-and-sell firms. Glazer emphasizes the following key transitions.[10]

- **Product life cycles will shorten**
  As products become more information intensive and as information technology accelerates the rate at which information changes and spreads, product change becomes easier and more necessary. Given the short economic shelf life of most information, product life cycles shorten as their information component increases.

Where speed, flexibility, and variety are possible, they become necessary. If you don't offer them, your competitors will, and your customers will disappear.

- **Markets and industries will be defined in terms of customers rather than products**
  Interactive transactions will give businesses more current information about their customers' wants and needs. Businesses will use this to discover more opportunities to create customer value.

- **Market power will shift from suppliers toward customers**
  As customers become the main source of information about value, shorter product cycles and customer-defined markets will give consumers more options and lower switching costs.

- **More reliance will be placed on flexible, customized marketing and intangible elements of the value proposition**
  Customer-specific information will lead to more varied, targeted marketing and the embodiment of that information in products and services better tailored to customer needs.

- **The need to choose between a high volume/low cost strategy and a niche/differentiation strategy will disappear**
  Flexible, modular marketing systems, informed by increased customer knowledge and complemented by modular, information-driven manufacturing systems, will make possible

systematic, low-cost customization. Sometimes called "mass customization," this development will allow companies to pursue both high volume/low cost and niche/differentiation strategies simultaneously.

- **Maximizing the number of transactions with the same loyal customer by offering a diverse array of products and services will become increasingly important**
  As market power shifts to customers and modular production and marketing systems become more important, products will cease to be the basis of lasting differentiation.

- **The most productive business strategies will be cooperative, not competitive**
  Because it changes rapidly, customer information has most value if it is acted upon quickly. By sharing it with firms with complementary competencies, a business can more rapidly bring appropriate offerings to market, to the benefit of all. Hypercompetition for customers thus increases the need for collaboration among competitors.

Competition in the Information Age will become situational rather than institutional. Quick and flexible response to ever-changing customer needs will require businesses to form multiple simultaneous cooperative relationships.

- **Organizations will rely more on decision teams and parallel information processing and less on individual decision-making and sequential information processing**
  Parallel processing—different brains working simultaneously on different elements of a problem—can more efficiently and naturally extract meaning from data than can sequential processing. Because organizations make meaning out of huge quantities of diverse data, parallel processing will become essential.

Glazer's propositions of the 1980s are rapidly becoming the realities of the 1990s. CIBC Insurance, a fast-growing and very profitable Canadian company founded in 1993 is one example.

It sells all of its property and casualty insurance and 80 percent of its life insurance directly to clients by telephone. CIBC representatives completely customize all term-life policies, building each from modular components to meet individual customers' needs.[11]

WHAT WILL REPLACE MAKE-AND-SELL?

Some of the changes described by Glazer were already affecting the banking industry in 1985, when Westpac was trying to develop its future strategy. Notable were shorter product cycles and increased choices for consumers. Banking was on its way to becoming an electronic business, with products and services existing more in the world of information than in the world of things.

As the century ends, Glazer's hypotheses now read like a prophecy of many organizations' initiatives. Modular customization, customer relationship management, rapid product development, responsiveness to customers, strategic alliances, and parallel information processing (another way to describe the distributed, collaborative decision-making known by the rubric *empowerment*) have become central to business conversation and—to a lesser extent—to business action. Glazer's description of interactive, electronic commerce summarizes the way some of his earlier hypotheses are now playing out on the World Wide Web.

But these innovations, when attempted, are often adopted piecemeal. If taken together, Glazer's insights about information-intensive businesses constitute more than a description of initiatives and improvements that can help make-and-sell businesses survive in the Information Age. They imply the need for a radically new business model—the sense-and-respond model.

Consider once more this question: What can planning and strategy mean when unpredictability becomes the norm? This chapter covered some of the disruptions created by the Information Age. The center of gravity of economic value creation shifts from tangibles to intangibles. Information arrives in an ever-increasing flood. New economic rules arise and old ones mutate. The relationship of companies to both their customers and their competitors alters dramatically. Strategy, clearly, must be flexible and adaptive. The next chapter will look at the effect these changes should have on the concept of business strategy. Does *strategy* have any meaning at all in the casinos of the Information Age?

CHAPTER 3

It is our future that lays down the law of our today.
—NIETZSCHE

STRATEGY

Past and Future

PAUL GADDIS, A PROFESSOR OF CORPORATE STRATEGY AT THE University of Texas at Dallas, has described the history of strategy as an oscillation between "proactive purposefulness" and "reactive powerlessness."[1] The make-and-sell era can be characterized as an age of proactive purposefulness. Corporate leaders prescribed broad courses of action in advance of events, confident that they could control their companies' destinies. These leaders often believed that they could not only *predict* the future but *create* it as well, by influencing their customers' behaviors. A comment frequently made by T. Vincent Learson, president of IBM in the late 1960s and chairman in the early 1970s, encapsulates this view: "I don't worry very much about making the right decision. I worry a lot about making the decision right." IBM's success during Learson's executive career appeared to justify this approach.

Learson's leadership exemplifies a familiar, traditional view of strategy: A group of corporate "generals" survey the territory they want to capture or protect (their customers), study the capabilities of the enemy (their competitors), develop a battle plan to achieve their objectives, and, finally, direct the troops who carry out the plan. The origins of the word *strategy* support this image. *Stratēgos* refers to the responsibility of an army commander to decide what the troops should do and then make sure they do it. This image of top-down leadership and unquestioning obedience closely mirrors the hierarchical leadership model of classic make-and-sell firms and the kind of strategic planning they used. Bruce Harreld, IBM's senior vice president for strategy, calls this the "we know, you do" theory of management.

To succeed, traditional strategic plans must meet two basic conditions. First, critical opportunities and threats must be sufficiently predictable. Every strategic plan includes a list of the assumptions on which the strategy's effectiveness depends. Westpac executives, for example, were unwilling to invest in the assumptions underlying 1985 product forecasts, but they were willing, ultimately, to invest $100 million in an assumption of generic unpredictability about product demand. For most other large companies, too, rapid technological innovation and new sources of competition eroded or eliminated the kind of control that Learson describes. The sheer complexity of managing such large enterprises further undermined that control.

Second, successful strategic planning requires an effective mechanism for translating plans into action. In large make-and-sell firms, the planning process typically began with senior management setting the company's financial goals. These goals and the plans developed for achieving them were built on assumptions about future customer demand and competitors' offerings, along with expectations about economic growth, technological change, and geopolitics. In many firms, a large central planning staff was responsible for the management system, whose purpose was to ensure machine-like efficiency in forecasting, developing, making, selling, and distributing the kinds and quantities of products called for by the plan. Most staffs did this by overseeing internal *dependencies*—the actions, product components, or information owed by each unit to the others. The staff tracked these dependencies, following up on the fulfillment of each unit's commitments to carry

out their part of the plan. Again, success depended on a sufficiently predictable business environment. When unanticipated
events made it impossible for a unit to meet one or more of its
commitments, the planning staff managed an escalation process to
reallocate resources, adjust schedules or revise objectives to resolve the problem with the least possible disruption to the annual
plan. Although managers talked about "the constants of change"
as early as the 1960s, the central staffs of many large companies
successfully managed the relatively few unwelcome surprises that
came their way in those years.

Beginning in the early 1970s, however, many firms experienced a rate and discontinuity of change great enough to overwhelm the ability of their ever-growing staffs to coordinate the
many interdependent adjustments needed to modify the plan as
its assumptions were proved wrong. In 1973, for example, IBM's
planning bureaucracy had grown to three thousand people and its
"annual" planning process approached an eighteen-month cycle
time. At IBM, as elsewhere, the centralized staff that had once
served company needs so well, was now creating more delay and
problems than it did value. *The Economist,* reporting on a 1997
finding that business executives expect strategy to be the most
pressing issue they would face over the next five years, connected
the demise of the central planning staff with the increasing speed
of change.

> Back in the 1970s most firms still relied on an annual "strategic
> plan" produced by a specialist department. This has not lasted. Del-
> egating decisions about direction to people who belonged neither in
> the engine-room nor on the bridge was a bad way to generate new
> ideas in fast-changing industries.[2]

One after another, IBM, Kodak, GM, DuPont, GE, Xerox, and
other industrial giants dismantled their central staffs. Yet, for all
their problems, these staffs had provided the essential control
mechanism in the command-and-control management system.
Their elimination led to a coordination vacuum. By the mid-
1980s, consequently, a number of large firms, including American
Express, announced that they were abandoning attempts to

achieve synergy, the additional value derived from having two or more units work cooperatively as parts of a system. The need for coordination has not gone away, however, and later we will discuss a new coordinating mechanism appropriate to a sense-and-respond world. But most policy executives didn't focus on this issue when they abandoned central planning.

Management's willingness to eliminate the planning staff signaled, above all, that the very *idea* of a strategic plan was losing viability. In truth, the track record of strategic plans over the past thirty years has been dismal.[3] Russell Ackoff estimates that no more than 2 percent are ever successfully executed.[4]

In short, radical uncertainty about the future washed away the foundation on which traditional strategic planning rested. Pervasive uncertainty about customer preferences calls into question the usefulness of both strategic plans and the business structures designed to carry them out. If you *cannot* know what your customers will want or your competitors will offer next year—or even who your customers or competitors will be—you cannot develop an effective plan for achieving targeted levels of sales and profits.

Some companies have found scenario thinking useful in recent years, because it does not depend on predictions about the future. Scenario development helps identify the most relevant areas of uncertainty and the future events that might signal an unfolding in reality of a given scenario or combination of scenarios. Such exercises help organizations prepare themselves for a wider range of possibilities, encouraging them to become more effective at sensing "what's going on out there." Arie de Geus, discussing scenario planning at Royal Dutch/Shell, has said that "scenarios act as a signal-to-noise filter," sensitizing observers to what may turn out to be significant environmental signals.[5] Scenarios can help organizations learn what environmental signals to track and how better to interpret them.

De Geus points out that the scenario thinking process involves preparing multiple scenarios, rather than relying on a single "most likely" description of the future. Executives think through in advance actions that would make sense in each scenario and identify strategies that would be appropriate in all of them. With this mental preparation, management can sometimes reduce its reaction time to events it did not predict.

FROM CONTROL TO EMPOWERMENT

When the central planning era ended, management began decentralizing decision-making: The trend toward empowerment had begun. Leaders hoped that giving more autonomy to those closest to the customer and to the company's daily operations would improve responsiveness. Rather than draw up a detailed battle plan, corporate generals authorized lieutenants to take the actions they deemed appropriate to their situations. The idea of high-performance teams took root. But what were these teams to do? How were their efforts to be coordinated? Lacking an overarching plan, and with only mission/vision/value statements to navigate by, the newly empowered people were left to decide for themselves what to do. As a result, decision-making became more local and less consistent. Management would intervene occasionally, settling conflicts and establishing priorities for the various units. But with every change in the business climate, new conflicts arose and old priorities became obsolete, leading to yet more sporadic interventions. Situational problem-solving dominated. But without a consistent context, these piecemeal solutions failed to add up to coherent behavior at the enterprise level.

Strategy all but disappeared from the landscape. Financial plans and communications about priorities replaced strategic plans. Even if a strategic plan *were* created, at most companies no mechanism would exist for turning it into action. A bemused observation by Robert Hendry, CEO at Saab, summarizes very well the state of strategy: "These days, strategic thinking is all about tactics."[6] Hendry finds this state of affairs uncomfortable, but for others, it affirms that top-down planning never was a very good idea. Given the right chance, they think, strategy will emerge.

EMERGENT STRATEGY

Can strategy arise from the spontaneously autonomous decisions and actions of empowered groups within an organization? Some theorists would answer "yes," but distinguish emergent strategies from the "reactive powerlessness" described by Gaddis.

They maintain that an enterprise has a latent capacity to behave as a coherent system—even when its leaders can't determine in advance what actions are needed to achieve that coherency. The concept of emergent strategy implies reactive rather than proactive behavior. Its supporters believe that complexity and uncertainty render organizational leadership powerless to chart an effective course of action.

A few "emergent behaviorists" believe that scientific theory about complex adaptive systems can be directly applied to human organizations. They argue that coherent behavior can evolve without any intentional shaping or even direction-setting, as hurricanes sometimes emerge from tropical depressions formed by the autonomous actions of sea currents and shifting winds. Gaddis associates this view with the concept of a "*super-organization* that can continuously develop, increment by increment, its own strategic direction to a prosperous (undefined) future." Long term direction is not needed from the top of the organization—only day-to-day support of the on-going efforts of the superior organization.[7]

Less doctrinaire believers in emergent strategy hold that it requires conscious direction, but only in the limited form of statements about common goals or values. In this view, once leaders formulate and articulate the signposts, the autonomous behaviors of groups within the organization will create collective behavior that is both coherent and responsive to the changing environment. Still other theorists maintain that direction is not enough: small numbers of decision rules must exist that apply throughout the organization.

These different viewpoints about emergent strategy stem from the same basic premise: Complex human systems, like some complex physical systems, *naturally* tend toward order rather than randomness. Efforts to direct their behavior—beyond, perhaps, establishing a few basic goals and rules—is not only unnecessary but probably destructive, because anything more would impose an unnatural rigidity on an organic system that "wants" to thrive in its changing environment. In other words, a system can instinctively know how to act purposefully and strategically.

If the theory of emergent strategy actually works, it will go a long way toward solving the problem of strategy in discontinuous environments. Emergent strategies will predominate in turbulent times and planned strategies in periods of relative stability. If the actions of empowered groups, free to respond to the environmental changes they sense, naturally cohere into useful, purposeful behavior, a benignly neglectful strategy *is* the best strategy.

The logic supporting this hope, unfortunately, is fundamentally flawed. Human organizations are not like flocks of birds or hurricanes or wolf packs. Human organizations are *social* systems; that is, not only the systems but the elements *of* the system can make decisions about the system's purpose and rules.[8] This is precisely why coherency is an issue. People can and often do make conscious choices that are inconsistent with the system's purpose. Humans can think outside the system; they can change the rules and even the function of the system of which they are part. They can also decide whether or not to cooperate with others in the system. At a minimum, research needs to be done to understand the behavior and principles of complex, adaptive *human* systems whose elements are capable of conscious decision-making. Pending a theory, we hear more about poor execution, lack of synergy, and people working at cross-purposes than we do about successful emergent strategies.

Nevertheless, successful emergent strategic behavior has been demonstrated by a few large organizations. The following brief examples provide insight into what emergent strategy means and how adaptive systems work. The organizations described, however atypical they may be, can contribute to a better understanding of sense-and-respond organizations. They also suggest why most corporate leaders would do well to remain cautious about the promise of applying complexity theory to achieve emergent purpose and strategy in human organizations.

The Merchants of Prato

One very impressive case of large-scale emergent strategy is most definitely not an Information Age exemplar. For seven hundred years, the textile merchants of Prato, a city about twenty-five miles northwest of Florence, have been operating as a virtual corporation, in which a large number of small groups, acting autonomously, cohere into a purposeful, productive, and very adaptive system.

In Prato, approximately 8,500 small firms, half employing fewer than ten people, form a dynamic network producing custom fabrics for the middle and upper end of the fashion industry. The single largest agglomeration of textile manufacturing facilities in Europe, with annual revenues of more than $5 billion, Prato merchants work together to respond to specific customer requests. Most of these go first to independent master brokers, called *impannatore,* who interact with customers and dispatch work to individual firms. The *impannatore* has no authority and exercises no control over these firms, and the whole system works without formal contracts. Kuldeep Kumar, a professor at Erasmus University, describes this coordination as "achieved by horizontal communication between adjacent parts [of] the [dynamic value] chain. It is very common for the *impannatore* to communicate only with the first and last actor in the chain."[9] Because there are only about half a dozen *types* of specialty manufacturing operators, sequencing the steps for a given order is not a complex task. Individual business units need not be connected to a very large number of other units to respond with the product variety and production capacity any given order requires. In theory, every order could give rise to a different chain of firms, each chain ceasing to exist once the order is filled. Surprisingly, but aptly, Kumar likens Prato to a slime mold, a collection of single-cell organisms that aggregate to form a mold that can move to search for food. For slime molds, mobility is the emergent strategy and finding food the emergent purpose. When the mold locates food, it disaggregates again.

Prato collectively exhibits successful organizational performance in the face of unpredictable demand. No part of this virtual enterprise attempts to forecast aggregate demand or even predict the next customer request. Like the adaptive systems of complexity theory, its relatively simple local behaviors create a systematic ability to respond to complex, changing demands from the environment. Simple, tacit, and unambiguous rules govern behavior within the network, rules very analogous to those that govern the behavior of birds in flocks. Units in the Prato network must deal only with other units in the network, do what they say they will, stick to what they know how to do, and incrementally improve the way they do it. The penalty for not adhering to the rules is shunning, resulting in economic—and probably social—death for the offending unit. These rules do not constitute a strategy in any usual sense of the word, but taken together, the behavior of Prato's textile merchants is evidently both strategic and adaptive: It has successfully met changing demands for fabric for seven hundred years. So, it seems, emergent strategy can work, and work on a large scale.

An element clearly essential to Prato's success is a high level of trust, trust that has been centuries in the making. Because of this trust, the Prato system defies the economic theory that networks have lower production costs but higher transaction costs than do vertically integrated organizations. The merchants of Prato enjoy both low production *and* low transactions costs. Like information, trust reduces uncertainty. In fact, trust eliminates the need for certain kinds of information—contracts and due diligence reports, for example. The member firms in the Prato network trust each other's competence, honesty, and mutual interest in preserving the network. Severe penalties follow rule violations, because the system survives on mutual confidence that other members will observe the established conventions.

The importance of trust is one of the major elements we should take from this example. The overall effectiveness of any system depends on the *interaction* of its elements, and mutual trust makes possible the collaboration of humans to fulfill common purposes, without bogging down over complex, rigid contracts or in lengthy negotiations. The Prato system also illustrates the modularity on which sense-and-respond organizations depend.

The Emergent Strategy of Taxi Fleets

The strategic behavior of taxi fleets—for instance, clustering at hotels and airports in the morning and evening—results not from a master plan scheduling particular drivers to be at specific places at appointed times. It emerges from the individual behaviors of fairly autonomous individual drivers. Some writers assert that this coordination can be produced by having all taxi drivers follow two simple rules: Do not get into any line that has more than five cabs in it, and bid on every call the dispatcher broadcasts (with the closest cab getting the fare).[10] Personally, I have not met a cab driver who admits abiding by these rules or even being aware of them. Nevertheless, distribution of taxi cabs over the course of a day does tend to be predictable and strategic, in that cabs usually show up where they are most needed, without being told where to go by any planning staff. The cumulative result of thousands of decisions made by empowered individual cab drivers—most of them in competition with each other—is a purposeful system, even though no one in the system has consciously designed or managed the interactions between taxis.

Taxi fleets thus provide another example of emergent strategy. Individual cab drivers apparently (and perhaps unconsciously) follow emergent rules that trigger behaviors from which a successful strategy emerges. As in the case of Prato, the system works much better to accomplish its ends than could a centrally organized one. No top-down plan could produce a system of remotely comparable efficiency and flexibility for a city the size of Boston, for example. Further, a centrally controlled system would almost certainly fail to be as robust. In Boston, more than ten percent of the taxi fleet can be out of service without noticeably degrading the system's ability to handle a normal day's demand.

Visa

The number of large organizations *intentionally* designed to foster emergent strategic behavior remains quite small. Probably the most famous example of one is Visa. Dee Hock, founder and first CEO of Visa International, claims that "Like the body, the brain, the biosphere, [Visa] is largely self organizing." Hock describes Visa as a system that works effectively as a whole but leaves members free to make their own decisions and to develop their individual strategic initiatives.

> Authority, initiative, decision-making, wealth—everything possible is pushed to the members. This design resulted from the need to reconcile a fundamental tension. On the one hand, the member institutions are fierce competitors: they—not Visa—issue the cards, which means they are constantly going after each other's customers. On the other hand, the members also have to cooperate with each

other: for the system to work, participating merchants must be able to take any Visa card issued by any bank, anywhere. . . .

Members are free to create, price, market and service their own products under the Visa name. At the same time, in a narrow band of activity essential to the success of the whole, they engage in the most intense cooperation.[11]

When Hock left Visa in 1984, the venture was clearly successful, although he estimated that he had achieved no more than 25 percent of what he had wanted to do. By consciously establishing a system-level purpose and a prescribed mechanism for coordinating certain behaviors of otherwise autonomous units, Hoch created an important variation on the Prato and taxi-fleet models of emergent behavior. The crucial issue of how system-level purpose and coordination can co-exist and connect with lower-level autonomy will be discussed later in the chapters on organizational governance.

THE LIMITATIONS OF EMERGENT STRATEGY

The examples above demonstrate that emergent strategic behavior does exist in the real world. Visa is clearly a success story. Both taxi fleets and the Prato merchants show how individual behaviors can cohere into a system that effectively handles the demands of unpredictability about what the next customer will want. It therefore appears that, in some situations, emergent behavior governed by a clear goal and few rules can succeed better in dealing with uncertainty than can centrally-planned systems. It is difficult to even imagine a plan that specifies all the movements of all the taxicabs in Boston.

All three of these systems, however, are inherently simple. They are all flat, slime-mold organizations, to use Kumar's term, or *swarms,* in the vernacular of complexity theory. In each system, the only vertical communications required are those with the dispatcher or coordinating mechanism. None of these networks consists of multiple layers of subsystems, thus limiting coordination problems. Also, the constituents of the system perform a very limited number of different functions: only one, in the case of the taxi fleet, and only a few in the case of Prato (such as cutting, dyeing, and pattern design) and Visa (for example, credit checks, issuing cards, clearance).[12]

Not surprisingly, most large corporations remain skeptical about the applicability of these examples to their own organizations. General Electric, AT&T, Royal Dutch Shell, Westpac, and General Motors have structures much more complicated than do Prato, taxi fleets, and Visa. They consist of multiple layers of many subsystems performing a wide range of tasks to generate a host of products and services. Logic suggests that, given the size and complexity of these organizations and the multiplicity of behaviors, goals, and conditions that characterize them, the likelihood that coherent strategic behavior will spontaneously emerge from their millions of individual decisions must be near zero. In this particular instance, logic and reality coincide. Synergy no longer seems an attainable goal in most large organizations. The less lofty aim of simply doing appropriate work consistently well has also come to seem beyond the reach of well-intentioned employees, as well as of executives who feel frustrated by poor operational execution and confusion over priorities.

Henry Mintzberg, an influential authority on business strategy, argues that strategy *emerges* in the sense that it can only be described after the fact by inspecting the decision chain that led to a particular result. But hindsight does not explain how the thousands of dynamic decision chains that characterize large organizations managed to align themselves with one another, especially if each chain was comprised of a separate, autonomous unit. Even if it were possible to analyze each chain to discover its inherent strategy, how could those many micro-strategies possibly add up to an effective organizational strategy?

THE FUTURE OF STRATEGY

We have looked at two closely related themes. First, we examined the idea that strategy, whether planned or emergent, is evidenced by behavior that meets environmental challenges to achieve an organizational purpose. Second, we discussed the importance, especially in large organizations, of *coordinating* behaviors to ensure that the parts of a system work together to produce *coherent* behavior.

Strategy-as-plan has ceased to be a viable option for most large organizations because creating an overall plan of organizational behavior requires the ability to predict or control the future, an ability that, according to our premise, no longer exists. Coordinating behaviors from the top down is also no longer possible: There is no mechanism for doing so when the required responses are not predictable. Strategy-as-emergent-behavior does not appear to be a promising alternative for complex organizations that require unplanned, yet coordinated, behavior by many groups to produce a wide range of potential outcomes.

If strategy is neither a purposeful plan to make and sell offers nor a naturally emerging phenomenon, what is it? Westpac's strategy of the mid-1980s answers the question for large firms operating in highly unpredictable environments: Strategy is *a design for an adaptive structure*. I argue that this is the *only* strategy that makes sense under such conditions. The future of strategy, therefore, lies in expressing it as a design. The next chapter, describing the sense-and-respond alternative to both make-and-sell and emergent strategies, explores the idea of strategy as structure. It also explains how a strategic organizational structure can solve part of the coordination problem, though only part. Later chapters on governance deal more fully with the coordination issue.

CHAPTER 4

We have learned that . . . the past will be a poor guide
to the future and that we shall forever be dealing with
unanticipated events. Given that scenario,
organizations . . . will need individuals who delight
in the unknown.

— CHARLES HANDY

THE SENSE-AND-RESPOND
ALTERNATIVE

WESTPAC'S STRATEGY FOR DEALING WITH DISCONTINUOUS
change established this Australian bank as a prototype of
large sense-and-respond organizations. By 1985, Westpac executives had come to grips with the unprecedented uncertainty they
faced. They were experiencing many of the changes predicted by
the Glazer hypotheses (described in chapter 2). Information and
information technology were increasing the speed of change. Financial products in the form of electronic abstractions could be
created and changed quickly. Product life cycles were shrinking.
Continual innovation and rapidly changing customer needs had
left even the savviest professionals unable to predict the future offerings of their own industry.

Like other banks, Westpac had always had to take chances
and make important choices without knowing, for example,
whether interest rates would go up or down, what competitors
were really up to, or how intermediaries would react if the bank

started selling through a new channel. For years, Westpac addressed much of this unpredictability, as similar institutions did, by preparing alternative plans for different plausible situations and by hedging its bets with investments in a variety of promising areas. Mostly, the bank relied on its experienced managers to deal with unanticipated events as they occurred. When uncertainty becomes endemic, however, contingency plans and situational problem solving will never be adequate to deal with the steady stream of surprises. The increasing pace and degree of change will at some point overwhelm these traditional ways of dealing with moderate change. This happened to the central planning staffs of most large corporations, and it happened at Westpac.[1]

Westpac CEO Robert White asked Peter Douglas (chief general manager of management services) and CIO Alan Hohne to work on the problem. Believing unpredictability to be no longer *an* issue but *the* issue Westpac faced, Douglas and Hohne came to a fundamental conclusion. "Change can be managed," they concluded, "even if it can't be predicted." They believed it possible to deal with unpredictability systematically without developing specific plans for an expected future. The key, according to Hohne, was the "ability to rapidly implement whatever strategy is necessary, rather than determine *the* strategy in advance." Hohne and Douglas envisioned a new form of strategy for their organization: a sense-and-respond structure and the computer system needed to represent it. Their solution embodies the concept of strategy-as-structure as opposed to strategy-as-plan. As White remarked at its initiation, "The greatest strength of the system is the extent to which it will be able to adapt to changes not even contemplated at the present time." To do this, the system would have to effectively *sense* what is going on "out there"—both what is happening in the industry and the changes in what customers want—and *respond* by providing appropriate products and services. Further, this sense-and-respond behavior must be fast enough to satisfy customers and efficient enough to be profitable. In this case, sense-and-respond meant *dispatching* Westpac's capabilities to meet unexpected current customer needs, rather than *scheduling* its responses to predicted future needs.

This was a radical concept, but White saw no other way to deal systematically with the unpredictability that confronted the bank. Thanks to his backing, the board's respect for Douglas and Hohne, and the lack of a plausible alternative, Westpac invested $100 million in a six-year project to embody this sense-and-respond concept in a new information technology system. The system, called CS90, would codify the essential functions and processes of the bank, including management policies regarding risk, market selection, and other essential considerations.

The first challenge was to create an enterprise model of Westpac's retail and commercial banking businesses. The business functions selected and the description of their interdependencies were crucial design choices. Large scale adaptiveness requires modular disaggregation of the functions in the value chain. Choosing which functions (modular capabilities) to include and how granular the disaggregation should be were among the most important decisions of the entire project. At Westpac, business professionals, not IT experts, made these decisions. System architects had then to faithfully represent the modular business design in CS90. This provided a software abstraction of the bank, enabling it to respond at electronic speed to particular customer needs. Instead of requiring assumptions about a particular future, Westpac's CS90 was designed to prepare the bank for any future.[2]

SENSING AND RESPONDING AT WESTPAC

Westpac felt it had to be continuously aware of its changing environment, capturing and evaluating information about customers and industry developments and staying alert for potential opportunities and threats. Information about customers' entertainment preferences, for example, might suggest new services, such as facilitating electronic ticket purchases from home. New technological developments might trigger changes in how the bank could and should transact business or share information with customers, as happened in the case of the sudden growth and popularization of the World Wide Web. The possible impact of regulatory changes would be constantly evaluated. And so on.

Each of Westpac's market segment managers identified the environmental signals required to support their decision-making in every segment. Employees assumed explicit new responsibilities for picking up and interpreting these environmental signals and for deciding if, when, and how to change the kind of signals that were captured. CS90 management information tables incorporated all potentially significant signals, providing, in today's terminology, the equivalent of a data warehouse. According to Hohne, these tables constitute "the total information resource of the enterprise." The tables are refreshed at different rates, depending on content. Updates occur daily for tables showing attributes of clients' net positions with the bank, for example, weekly for product performance tables, and monthly for client demographics tables. The data in these tables and the relations among tables define at any given moment Westpac's perception of its changing environment.

But understanding events in a rapidly changing environment serves little purpose if it takes eighteen months or longer to create a new product, as had typically been the case at Westpac before CS90. Westpac executives saw that the key to quick and appropriate responses to change lay in representing electronically the principles, processes, and other criteria that guided development of the bank's products. Despite its own considerable technological capability, Westpac engaged IBM's Federal Systems Division to provide the systems integration skills the project demanded.

The heart of CS90 was the Product Development Application, which represented Westpac's retail and commercial business as a set of relationships among more than two thousand modular software objects. Some objects were activities, such as *negotiate, pay, refund, add customer, receive, charge,* and *sell,* that could be reused for any client or product. Others were organized as a hierarchy of product types. Loans, deposits, investments, and transactions were subdivided into more specific products. Loans, for instance, were broken down into term loans, revolving loans, and overdrafts; term loans were further subdivided into farm loans, personal loans, home loans, and so on. A module at any level inherited all the attributes of the modules above it on its branch. The system's designers thus created a robust representation in software of what the bank did. Using it, loan officers could readily dispatch capabilities to create customized responses consistent with Westpac's current business rules.

The Product Development Application (PDA) captured the know-how of Westpac's best professionals in an expert systems repository. The repository also contained abstractions of current management policies, the logic underlying banking activities (including such basic concepts as crediting accounts with interest only *after* they are opened), and relevant government regulations. Applying the expert system's rules to a customer request made in a branch office, PDA determined the range of allowable values for variables such as interest rate, frequency of repayment, and payment amount. Using the system, loan officers could assemble a new product in the presence of the customer, confident that the result would be consistent with bank policies and practices. Credit instruments, for example, could be tailored to the client's personal requirements for amount of credit, term of loan (or deposit), type of collateral, payment frequency, accounts to be used for payments or repayments, interest rate type (fixed or variable), and so on. Information on variables such as whether the client already does business with the bank, the nature and amount of other products held, and the client's credit rating could be obtained directly from PDA databases or by interviewing the client at the time of application. The loan officer would then immediately enter the request into PDA for verification of consistency with current policy. Upon verification, PDA entered the customized product into the transaction system, which executed the transaction and notified the loan officer that confirmation could be given the client on the spot.[3]

When clients began to request a product function for which no generic PDA capability existed, software engineers were called in to build it, incorporating into the system any new rules required. Because only new functions, rather than entire products, had to be developed, Westpac realized a tenfold improvement in time to market.

The earliest substantial return on the investment in CS90 came from the system's ability to ensure institutional integrity. It was able to make sure that the bank's commitments to its clients were consistent with its own policies and with regulatory constraints. In 1992, Westpac's auditing department estimated that this improvement in consistency was "worth around $100 million per year in interest and fees previously forgone due to poor negotiation [with clients] and compliance."[4]

One key design decision was how detailed the business model should be. If the modular decomposition of the bank's value chain was not granular enough, the system would not give Westpac the flexibility it needed to respond to unanticipated requests. Too many requests would be special cases, outside PDA's capacity. Speed of response would suffer, and managers would be overwhelmed by the demands of constant change. If capabilities were too detailed, however—too granular—unproductive effort would be invested in building seldom used modules. The economic advantages of modularization depend on reaching a sufficiently high level of reuse. CS90 also needed an appropriate variety of product functions and the capability to rapidly add new modules.

Thanks to PDA, every and any transaction can create a new Westpac product. Customer requests that fall within the scope of what a loan officer is empowered to decide can produce new product responses on the spot. If fulfilling the request exceeds the officer's authority, modifications by the product manager may require hours or days. If the request calls for a development of an entirely new function, the response time may stretch to weeks or months, but even this worst case represents a dramatic improvement in Westpac's previous response time.

Adaptation occurs at multiple levels. Loan officers adapt to customer requests within the context established by product managers; product managers adapt their products within the context set by the business design; and the business design itself is systematically modified to reflect the interpretation of environmental changes by functional management. The bank's current business policies constrain all of these adaptations. The system automatically propagates changes to these policies to all levels, ensuring consistent behavior.

By using information technology to model their entire business as a modular system, Westpac succeeded in getting its information technology department off the critical path of product development and introduction. In the past, new products could not be launched until the appropriate applications had been constructed. This meant creating each essentially from the ground up. The extensive programming required accounted for much of the bank's lengthy product development time. With CS90, most new products could be created by clicking together existing modules or by varying existing products in a manner consistent with the system's embedded policy constraints. New product development became the province of loan officers and product managers working directly with customers, requiring no IT mediation.

THE IMPACT OF CS90

CS90 came on-line in stages, becoming fully operational in December 1993. The bank had experienced many changes since 1985, when the project began. Peter Douglas and Robert White had retired in 1987. Hohne had left in 1991. White's successor, Stuart Fowler, and Eric Neal, the new company chairman, chose to expand internationally by making commercial loans to firms in the exploding Asian economy. Many of these loans proved to be bad, leading to a two-year loss of around $3 billion. Neal resigned in 1992, as did Fowler's successor, Frank Conroy. By the end of 1992, Westpac's executive team was two generations removed from the team that had formulated the strategy-as-structure concept embodied in CS90. The project had continued but its original sense-and-respond premise had been lost in the twists and turns of corporate history.[5]

The new 1992 executive team saw the PDA as a powerful speed-to-market weapon for make-and-sell offers, not as an abstraction of organizational structure for a sense-and-respond approach to customer requests. But the system quickly produced clear benefits. The head of product management reported that PDA had delivered more new and changed products in its first ten months of operation than the bank had generated *in total* over the previous six years. Late in 1994, for example, Westpac introduced new mortgage options that allowed clients, at their own discretion, to accelerate payments and generate payment-reducing credits, a first for Australian banking. Because these products were built almost entirely from new combinations of existing software objects, they required only a small amount of new programming. As a result, the total time from concept to launch was ten days. Some other banks that eventually offered similar products required more than a year to do so, because IT was still very much on their critical paths.

PDA's modularity paid off in another way, as well: Only two IT people are now needed to support the thirty-member product management team. Previously, twenty-five IT professionals had worked full-time to handle systems maintenance and peck away at a backlog of new product applications that would have taken many years to complete. CS90 also made possible the elimination of about one thousand people from the "day two" post-processing of checks, an efficiency over and above the already cited $100 million a year savings from enhanced institutional integrity. In announcing 1997 year-end results that included a 14 percent net profit improvement over the previous year, CEO Bob Joss said, "Our customers are enjoying better pricing and greater choice in products than at any previous time in the 180-year history of the bank."[6]

But the ability to design and *offer* new products quickly does not guarantee having the products people want. When brush fires ravaged large areas of Sydney one Friday in January 1994, Westpac used the PDA to develop special mortgage offerings for victims of the fire *over the weekend.* The bank's response to the fire was immediate, but they predicted what customers would want; they did not negotiate and respond to individual customer requests. Despite their seventy-two hour speed to market, bank officials were operating from a make-and-sell rather than a sense-and-respond mindset. They sold only three of the special mortgages, because their three-day forecast of customers' needs was poor.

Even a complete sense-and-respond system, of course, cannot guarantee successful adaptation. A bank's rapid response capability can customize bad loans as quickly as good ones. Westpac, however, has been recently successful, thanks not only to its system, but to good business decisions made by talented people. Large enterprises may find the sense-and-respond model necessary in the future, but they will continue to rely on capable professionals to cope successfully with the challenges of an unpredictable environment.

IMPLICATIONS OF THE WESTPAC EXPERIENCE

Even though White's successors departed from his strategic vision, its operational feasibility was ultimately demonstrated by the successful implementation of CS90's design. As a sense-and-respond prototype, Westpac's contributions stem as much from how its leaders thought as from what they did. Out of this combination of thought and action came empirical evidence supporting the following assertions:

- Large organizations can use technology to cope systematically with marketplace unpredictability.

- An adaptive strategy can be achieved by the modular design of organizational structure.

- Large organizations can robustly represent their structure and policies in software.

- When customer preferences are unpredictable, adaptiveness requires a shift in emphasis from planned offers to customized responses.

- Companies can leverage an ability to respond to unpredicted change by causing more of it.

Although Westpac was an important early prototype, it is not currently an exemplar of sense-and-respond. Nevertheless, the bank's experience provides a valuable case history for exploring the sense-and-respond idea. First, the main problem Westpac faced—a radical inability to predict future customer demand for offerings—drives the need for sense-and-respond. Second, the solutions envisioned by Hohne and Douglas incorporated several of the most important elements required for systematic adaptation to change. They sought to create institutional capability for managing uncertainty by sensing and responding to customers' current needs, rather than by trying to predict them. They relied on a responsive structural design rather than a strategic plan. They focused their design efforts on developing and dispatching modular capabilities for rapid, low-cost custom responses. And they invested company resources to sense a continuing stream of information about individual customers.[7] We can use a comparison between bus companies and taxi companies to clarify the distinction between make-and-sell scheduling and sense-and-respond dispatching.

MAKE-AND-SELL BUSES VERSUS
SENSE-AND-RESPOND TAXIS

Bus companies are essentially make-and-sell businesses. Using forecasts about where most people will be at different times of the day and where they will want to go, company planners decide the routes buses will take, the stops they will make, and how frequently they will run. Like make-and-sell companies drawing up strategic plans, production schedules, and marketing strategies, bus companies schedule operations that offer the services they expect their customers will need and pay for. Like any good make-and-sell worker, bus drivers must carry out the planners' schedules as accurately and efficiently as possible. Drivers are evaluated on how closely they adhere to the schedule and, perhaps, on how few complaints riders make about them. Their job entails taking the prescribed route and getting the bus where it is supposed to be, when it is supposed to be there.

Bus drivers do not need to know where their passengers are going. In fact, they don't need passengers at all to do their job well. They merely have to execute a plan. Like corporate planners relying on sales forecasts to judge the potential of future products, bus company planners review historical information about numbers of passengers carried and adjust routes and schedules on the assumption that the patterns of the past will hold in the future. To maximize productivity and avoid the costs of retraining passengers and drivers to a new schedule, bus companies tend to stay with an existing schedule until they see overwhelming need for change. Certainly, any bus drivers who leave their routes to search for additional passengers would be punished, not praised, for their initiative.

Taxi companies, on the other hand, share many essential characteristics with sense-and-respond organizations. They hire drivers based on their expectations of how many people will have unpredictable transportation needs. They also establish and enforce geographical boundaries, a rate structure, and a compensation scheme. Within that context, however, drivers use their own knowledge, skill, and initiative to get passengers where they want to go. The company dispatches a customer-moving capability. Customers making requests and drivers empowered to fulfill those requests do the rest. Unlike bus drivers, without information from customers about what they need—"I have to be at the airport in half an hour"—taxi drivers cannot perform their service. Only after that request is specified can cabbies put their driving skills and knowledge of city streets and traffic patterns to productive work.

If the travel needs of people in cities changed every day in drastic, unpredictable ways, bus companies would fail. Bus drivers would be paid and buses fueled and maintained to drive empty along once popular routes. Angry crowds would wait for buses to appear on last week's low-volume routes, or they would give up and take a cab. Bus company attempts to adjust schedules would be foiled by further unanticipated changes. Taxi companies, however, could adjust to the situation. Their drivers can cruise until they find customers and are empowered to take those customers wherever they want to go. If customer destinations changed every day or even every hour, it would make no difference. Company policies would, of course, establish boundaries, prohibiting out-of-state trips, for example (with management perhaps granting an occasional exception). Taxi drivers function somewhat like the Westpac loan officers who tailor new products with and for customers—as long as they do not overstep the established boundaries. Having customers decide "where to go" is the hallmark of sense-and-respond organizations.

The bus versus taxi metaphor echoes some of the fundamental distinctions made in Table 1.1.

- The make-and-sell bus company emphasizes *efficiency* and *predictability*. The sense-and-respond taxi company emphasizes *flexibility* and *responsiveness*.

- The make-and-sell bus company employs *centralized operational decision-making,* and cascades procedural instructions down to the drivers, who carry them out. The sense-and-respond taxi company relies on *distributed decision-making;* its employees respond independently to customer requests and changing conditions, within the context established by the company.

- Information from a company *plan* determines the activities of bus drivers. Information from *customer requests* establishes what a taxi driver does.

- Bus companies function as *mechanisms* for efficiently generating unchanging (or gradually changing) products and service. Taxi companies function as *adaptive systems* for responding to unanticipated requests.

A New Relationship with Customers

Most of the differences between bus companies and taxi companies reflect different relationships with customers. The traditional relationship between taxi drivers and their passengers characterizes the new ideal of the "customer-back" company. Whatever the ultimate aim of a sense-and-respond company—making money for stockholders, providing meaningful employment, producing great products and services—it accomplishes its purpose only by responding effectively to individual customers. Glazer predicted this dynamic. As market power shifts toward the customer in information intensive businesses, companies will increasingly be defined in terms of their customers, rather than their products. Firms will increasingly find learning how to collaborate *with* customers, suppliers, and even competitors more valuable than getting better at competing *against* other firms.

All businesses, of course, want to know what their customers need. Many spend a great deal of money and time trying to find out. Make-and-sell organizations gather data on customer reactions to current offerings. They test market new products to help predict what customers might buy later on. Such market research helps them chart what they hope will be a profitable future course. If pertinent and well interpreted, the research can help ensure that any retooling of their productive machinery will pay off. The research investment will be worthwhile, however, only if enough people want the new products for a long enough period. This approach differs fundamentally from that of designing the entire company to respond to customer needs as they arise.

Collaboration with Customers

Customers will provide suppliers with information about themselves only if they anticipate value from doing so. When this is the case, both parties benefit from the information-for-value exchange, fostering the development of customer-supplier *relationships* in place of periodic transactions. If a significant amount of additional value is created, suppliers will be increasingly interested in taking equity positions in customers' outcomes. They will no longer simply sell things to them. This dynamic explains why, in the future, more attention will be paid to games with customers than to games against competitors, and why collaborative skills will become more important than competitive skills.

Knowing fully what individual customers want and providing a quality response to those requests can occur only in relationships built on information exchange. This opens the door to a shared stake in the customer outcome. When suppliers become greater contributors of value to their customers, they are drawn to invest in the customer outcome and trade off immediate transactional profit for a stake in a long-term mutually profitable relationship. Relationships based on a common objective tend to endure, and the potential profit tends to become greater.

An increasing number of company-customer relationships may involve *only* the exchange of information, where that information has sufficient value for both companies and customers. The better the information available to a firm, the more readily it can respond to current customer requests and anticipate future requests. It develops new capabilities for meeting as yet unarticulated customer needs. For their part, customers increasingly need information to make choices among the numerous and ever-changing products and services available to them. In parallel, their need for knowledge itself, as well as goods, continues to grow. This shared hunger for information suggests a new dimension in the relationship between companies and customers. Both benefit more from information exchange than from goods-for-money transactions.

Westpac, for example, benefits from information about consumers' financial needs even if they are not and never will be Westpac customers. Producers of tangible products should consider making the same kind of investment. Firms skilled at capturing and interpreting information about customers can build an enlightening context around specifically stated needs and requests. Just as doctors and other professional experts do, such informed companies can, in certain cases, use this context to understand

customers' underlying needs better than do customers themselves. If the firm succeeds in identifying and satisfying those
needs, it will produce greater value for the customer. In addition,
these deeper needs, once known, often prove more stable than
those for a specific product or service.

A few years ago, attendees at an Advanced Business Institute
seminar examined Goodyear Tire's Internet home page. At that
time, visitors to the site could answer questions about preferred
tire characteristics and receive an ordered list of the Goodyear
tires that best matched those preferences.[8] The visitor could also
request the location of the nearest dealer who carried the tires
named at the top of the list. Someone in the class asked, "Why
don't they show the best match with Michelin and Bridgestone
tires, too?" Another attendee responded immediately with the obvious answer: "Because Goodyear is not in the business of advertising competitors' tires, that's why!" But perhaps they should be.
If Goodyear were to establish its home page as the best source of
information on tires and the most accurate product-to-need
matches, regardless of manufacturer, consumers would check
there first to find the product they needed. The company would, in
turn, learn earlier than its competitors about current needs and
about changes in individual patterns of preference. With enough of
this contextual information, Goodyear might find a profitable way
to be first to market with superior value propositions, including
maintenance, financing, and other services that reduce the total
cost and hassle of tire purchase and ownership. Quite possibly, the
costs of maintaining the site and of lost sales due to recommend-
ing competing products would be more than offset by advantages
of having more and earlier information about individual consumers. This knowledge would be of value not just to Goodyear itself, but also to its dealers and car-manufacturing customers.

Unfortunately, but very characteristic of assets that have no
value until used, Goodyear cannot determine what it will learn
without first making the investment to capture and interpret these
information assets. But return-on-investment calculations with a
question mark in the numerator are not a popular feature of make-
and-sell business cases. For this reason, many companies today do
not invest in continuous collection of data about individual cus-

tomers. Yet this kind of investment will have to become business as usual for information-intensive companies hoping to make effective decisions about the next game to play in Brian Arthur's increasing-returns casino.[9]

Once again, the question boils down to whether or not unpredictable customer preferences are the strategic issue. If they are, sense-and-respond and customer-back behaviors become imperatives, rather than options, and several strategic business design choices must change. Adrian Slywotzky and David Morrison have identified four strategic decision types that, taken together, profile a company's design for staying in what they term the *profit zone*. This zone changes every few years, sometimes quite unpredictably. Slywotzky and Morrison argue, with many examples, that successful firms sense these moves earlier than do others because they are customer-centric. In other words, the search for the profit zone begins with continuous and thorough exploration of the customer value zone. Table 4.1 captures the evolution of firms from make-and-sell toward sense-and-respond, using Slywotzky and Morrison's strategic choice categories.[10] Consistent with the discussion above of Goodyear's possible use of its Web site, notice the shift in control point from *product superiority* to *dominant share* to *information gateway* to *exclusive* (or at least prior) *knowledge* of current individual customer preferences and behaviors.

MODULAR ORGANIZATIONS

A widely accepted precept of business strategy is that companies can succeed *either* through differentiation, for example, by customizing products, *or* through a high volume/low cost strategy—but they should never try to combine the two. According to Michael Porter, no company could do both well.[11] Research by Michael Shank, however, has revealed that many companies do, in fact, pursue both strategies simultaneously and successfully. Using a framework developed by Bart Victor and Andrew Boynton, Shank established that the dynamics of change in the *processes* that produced products, as well as in the products themselves, were important determinants of appropriate organizational struc-

TABLE 4.1

CHANGING STRATEGIC CHOICES

		Migrating from **MAKE-AND-SELL**			to **SENSE-AND-RESPOND**
	Migration Zones	ZONE 1	ZONE 2	ZONE 3	ZONE 4
Strategic Choices*	**Customer Selection**	Mass markets for product attributes with broadest appeal	Segmentation of markets by product attributes	Segmentation of markets by customer attributes	Fundamental, individual customer needs
	Scope Definition	Markets and products	Market segments and offerings	Personalized offerings	Personal needs and firm response capabilities
	Value Capture	Product program margins and economies of scale	Margins and ROA	Customer profitability (to firm)	Equity position in customer outcome
	Strategic Control Point	Superiority of offering	Dominant offering market share	Gateway for customer access to information and services	Exclusive awareness of customer behavior and preference patterns

*As defined by Slywotsky and Morrison.

ture and business success. Shank discovered that a large number of successful companies simultaneously operated in not only two but four distinct ways. Boynton and Victor had labeled these *invention, mass production* (Porter's two choices), *continuous improvement,* and *systemic* (or *modular*) *customization.* Each of these operating styles requires different strategies, organizational forms, skills, management systems, and information systems. Shank presented empirical evidence showing that successful companies first develop standard processes and then continuously improve them before disaggregating them into modular components.[12]

A business that dispatches modular capabilities to create specific responses to customer requests can achieve large-scale, rapid, low-cost customization—a fundamental requirement for sense-and-respond organizations. With this structure, mass customization does not require *inventing* from the ground up a great number of extraordinary efforts to please many customers. Customization can be achieved by a stable dispatching process that the organization carries out over and over again. This is how sense-and-respond organizations work.

We should distinguish between product modularization and organizational modularization. Make-and-sell firms sometimes develop modular *products* that can be customized in a number of ways, for example, by plugging in a variety of certain components such as chips or dashboards to modify computers or automobiles. By doing so, they broaden their product lines, increasing the number of choices they provide their customers.

Sense-and-respond organizations operate differently. They modularize their business *functions* to create capabilities that, in combination, can respond to a much broader (exponentially greater) spectrum of possible customer requests. The make-and-sell firm that offers modular products still focuses inward on its production processes. The sense-and-respond firm focuses on customers, standing ready to bring together the capabilities needed to meet their requests.

Some systems integrator companies provide good examples of how modular organizations work and good lessons about the skills required to operate successfully in environments of unpredictable change. At one large systems firm, for example, an RFP (request for proposal) arriving from a potential customer is assigned to a program manager accountable for the profitability and successful execution of systems integration projects. The program manager must first decide if the firm should bid or not and, if so, produce a proposal. To diagnose the issues raised by the RFP, the program manager dispatches specific organizational capabilities, such as pricing, technical risk assessment, schedule risk assessment, and business risk assessment. The results of this work help determine whether a profitable bid with a reasonable chance of winning can be made. If the answer is yes, a proposal is prepared through the dispatch of technical, business, and project management capabilities. If the customer accepts the proposal, the program manager dispatches a project manager who is accountable for completing the project on time, to specifications, and within budget.

Most large integration projects that fail do so for one or both of two reasons: The integrator promises more than can be delivered or the customer changes the specification in midstream. These events themselves, however, do not cause failure. Such changes are the rule rather than the exception in the systems integration business. Over the course of a long project, the customers's situation often changes and many times some of the supplier's assumptions will turn out to have been wrong. Failure occurs when the agreement cannot be adapted in a manner satisfactory to both parties. Good project managers are nothing if not adaptive. They expect the unexpected to happen. To compensate, they negotiate in the *original* contract a framework that will apply to any later renegotiations initiated by either party. In other words, they agree in advance about how they will deal with future change. A later chapter will deal with the importance of negotiating authentic agreements that are not only sincere, but that accurately reflect both parties' uncertainties about what will be needed and what can be provided. Authenticity in negotiating and renegotiating agreements is a critical trait for both project and program managers.

The project manager dispatches yet other organizational capabilities, such as industry specialists, technical specialists, design engineers, architects, and so on. The entire company thus operates as a pool of different types of talent to be dynamically allocated by program and project managers in response to customer requests. In most large projects, furthermore, a bidding firm will partner with other systems integrators to gain access to skills not in its own repertoire of response capabilities.

The leadership of a modular organization has made several crucial organizational design decisions. It has specified and invested in a particular set of response capabilities. It has determined how granular these capabilities will be. In considering logistics, for example, it has decided whether to have one large module, or two more specialized inbound and outbound logistics modules, or even smaller subdivisions (such as cross docking). As we saw in the earlier discussion of Westpac's business model design, these choices require balancing flexibility with degree of reuse. Choices in modularization will determine how profitable and competitive the firm will be.

After defining capabilities, leadership must decide which capabilities to own and which to outsource. In addition to the normal criteria used in making outsourcing decisions, modularization requires consideration of an additional factor. With how many internal capabilities will a particular outsourced capability interact? The greater this number, the more likely that the outsourced capability will be required to sacrifice its own local interests to maximize the total performance of its customer. In such cases, acquiring or creating the capability in-house may be preferable to contracting for it with a supplier. In structuring outsourcing deals, avoiding the perils of fragmented suboptimization becomes an important issue.

This is because modular organizations must be managed as systems. Systems produce synergy. How much synergy they produce depends on how effectively the *interactions* among capabilities are managed. Modules function as interacting pieces that snap together easily to make something new. Coordinating these elements is an important challenge for sense-and-respond organizations. Groups with different capabilities must speak the same language, understand their common goal, and use a common linking mechanism to define, deliver, and evaluate the contributions they make to fulfilling customer requests. As we saw in the merchants of Prato example, success depends on trust. In Chapter 8, I will discuss how effective linking can be accomplished and what other issues leaders must address to achieve coordinated behavior in large enterprises. Appendix A contains a more detailed treatment, with several examples, of the issues associated with creating modular organizations.

HYBRID ORGANIZATIONS

As Table 1.1 shows, make-and-sell and sense-and-respond represent endpoints on a continuum. For companies moving from make-and-sell to sense-and-respond, a transformation occurs somewhere along that continuum. The orientation of the enterprise as a whole becomes predominantly sense-and-respond. This phase change is determined not by the number of organizational subsystems that have been transformed, but by the extent to which the company's customer value proposition consists of responses rather than offers. The bulk of individual capabilities in a large sense-and-respond organization may actually be make-and-sell because the *internal* requests made of them are highly predictable. They respond directly to their internal customers, but in the same or similar ways over and over. Conversely, a make-and-sell company might invest in sense-and-respond capabilities to increase its speed to market with new make-and-sell offers. Westpac eventually used its adaptive structure in this way.

Large, complex businesses face the unavoidable problem of accommodating discontinuous change in some parts of their customers' range of needs while maintaining a make-and-sell model for dealing with the predictable or stable elements of customer demand. The IBM PC Company's introduction of SystemXtra in 1997, for instance, was a step toward sense-and-respond by a traditional make-and-sell business (personal computer systems). The PC Company invested in an expanded value proposition incorporating additional value elements derived from a better understanding of the context surrounding its customers' product preferences. The program expanded on earlier efforts at modularizing products to allow dealers to assemble custom system configurations for individual consumers. With SystemXtra, IBM, through its dealers, offers to assume responsibility for managing any part or all of the customer's total cost of acquiring, financing, learning, using, maintaining, and upgrading the system purchased. This creates the basis for an ongoing relationship with customers based on their total cost of personal computer ownership—including non-IBM systems. This expanded context of customer needs amounts to about $13,000 per year per computer, compared to the earlier $3,000 value proposition of replacing products every few years in a series of transactions.

By providing these services, IBM can sense changes in customer usage patterns as they occur. The company gains valuable information about the kinds of service capabilities its customers want. If the PC Company invests in continuous collection and interpretation of new signals about changes in individual user activity, it will evolve from a make-and-sell organization with some sense-and-respond capability to a sense-and-respond organization with some make-and-sell capability. The above statement is qualified to emphasize that sporadic updating of a company's customer files does not amount to sense-and-respond behavior. Ongoing sensing of customer signals must take place if companies are to systematically detect and anticipate changes in what their customers value.

THE TRANSITION TO SENSE-AND-RESPOND MUST BE SYSTEMATIC

Hybrid organizations will be the norm, but this should not obscure the fundamental differences between the two organizational models. The essential difference, as I have said, lies in organizational design. Is the company designed to make offers to its customers? Or respond to their requests? That difference implies many others. The make-and-sell focus on efficiently carrying out production plans emphasizes efficient repetition of established input-process-output procedures. Little sharing of information is needed beyond the predetermined description and timing of handoffs from function to function. The sense-and-respond focus on new and flexible responses to customers depends, instead, on a constant stream of communications among modular capabilities. These communications make it possible for them to coordinate their dynamic interactions into coherent enterprise responses.

Becoming a sense-and-respond organization requires systematic effort in two related ways. First, the leaders guiding the change must maintain a focus on the whole and on the interactions of the parts. Second, leaders must make sure that all aspects of the organization align behind the same purpose: Information systems, employee abilities, reward structures, communication practices, and organizational culture must all be treated as parts of one coherent system. Simply encouraging people to be more responsive or bolting on a new sensing function without making sure it meshes with the rest of the organization will not suffice. Consider, for example, the experience of one company attempting to graft customer focus onto an organization with a strong make-and-sell product orientation.

One January a few years ago, after an intensive analysis of strategic options and a two-month effort to articulate a new mission statement, the leadership of a very large company proclaimed a new, customer-centric mission and vision. In speech after speech, management exhorted employees to focus on "solving the customers' problems, not ours." Employees, and the sales force in particular, responded to this new approach with great enthusiasm. When client representatives cut through red tape to fulfill customer requests, they received bonuses. Their accomplishments were touted in internal communications and featured the following spring at sales recognition events. Reengineering, quality, and customer delight training received top priority, leading to measurable improvements in customer satisfaction over time. Accompanied by suitable fanfare, customer satisfaction was included in the top five balanced scorecard measurements reviewed monthly by the company chairman. Every department was required to develop quality priorities and plans and to have them ready for executive inspection at any time.

Within six months, however, all of this new customer-centric vision, rhetoric, and action came up against an important reality and was defeated by it. The company had not changed in any fundamental way. Its old plan-make-and-sell structure, processes, accounting systems, business case methodologies, and measurement and reward systems remained firmly in place. This deeply embedded corporate DNA, and the processes built on it, was not customer-centric; it focused inward, on the firm. Furthermore, the firm was organized as a semi-autonomous collection of functions and units, a fragmentation justified in the name of empowering local decision-makers. So, six months after the mission was announced, when one of the company's largest product divisions reported it was running seriously behind projections for volume, revenue, and profits, the message from leadership changed. They told the sales force, in effect, to "solve your customers' problems, but solve them with this division's products." In other words, "tell them they need what we need to sell." A simultaneous and substantial change in the sales incentive plan reinforced the message.

Given the size of the financial shortfall involved, management had little choice. The real problem was not the decision to push certain products, but the earlier attempt to create and communicate a direction incompatible with the organization's rigid procedures, its fragmented design, its scorekeeping accounting conventions, and its reward systems. The decisions first to create and then to change the message arose from the conviction that there wasn't time, in the company's fast-moving business environment, to think through carefully all that had to be done to put the customer first. Company leaders also explicitly rejected the idea that anything as abstract as measurement and accounting systems could scuttle the noble and sensible imperative of serving the customer. They did not see that a genuinely customer-centric company and a product-centered company implied different kinds of organizational designs. It is not possible, as company leaders found out, to shift focus to customer needs while leaving everything else the same.

The damage done within the company was severe. Because the "customer-first" message, so attuned to what employees believed right and wanted to hear, had come with such energy and consistency from so high in the organization, extreme disillusionment and bitterness followed its later retraction. Months and even years later, seasoned field managers said openly that they would not take at face value any future directional statements from company leaders. A rich fund of employee trust, built and nurtured over decades, had been squandered. In the end, management lost not only the confidence of their employees but that of the board as well.

SENSE-AND-RESPOND AS STRATEGY

We have seen several illustrations of information-seeking, customer-back, sense-and-respond behavior in this chapter. What do these examples tell us about sense-and-respond as a *strategy?* It is clear that the response strategy for every new opportunity is indeed emergent, in the Mintzberg sense of that term. Only in retrospect can one describe the ad hoc courses of action taken to respond to each customer-specific opportunity. At the enterprise level, however, strategy is not emergent. It is expressed as an a priori systems design for dispatching modular capabilities. In the case of Westpac, CS90 codifies the bank's adaptive system design, and both the design and the capabilities are represented by symbols residing in information technology.

In large enterprises, modular organization provides the flexibility needed to adapt in time to a range of different opportunities. But structural modularity is not the only requirement for systematic adaptiveness. Equally important is the ability of people in key roles to adapt in unprecedented situations. As we will see in the next chapter, this ability requires a specific talent for processing information: making meaning out of apparent noise.

CHAPTER 5

*In the old economy, the challenge for management is
to make product. Now the challenge for management
is to make sense.*

— J O H N   S E E L Y   B R O W N

You can observe a lot just by watching.

— Y O G I   B E R R A

ADAPTIVENESS

Finding Meaning in

Apparent Noise

THE ADAPTIVENESS OF SENSE-AND-RESPOND ORGANIZATIONS
stems from two sources: the modularity of its capabilities and
how people accountable for those capabilities process information. In earlier chapters I discussed the flexibility that comes from
dispatching modular capabilities in response to current requests.
Now we will consider ways of enhancing the adaptiveness of the
individuals accountable for creating those responses.

Every adaptive system, whether an individual living creature,
a computer virus, or a large organization, survives by making sense
out of its environment and responding with an appropriate action.
It then repeats the cycle, factoring in the results of the previous
one. In this circular and continuous process, the adaptive system
senses its environment even as it acts. The distinguishing quality
of individual humans and human organizations is their ability to
make *conscious* decisions about what things to sense, how to interpret them, and how to respond to the interpretation.

The generic adaptive loop shown in Figure 5.1 presents a schematic view of this process that applies equally to all adaptive systems. An adaptive system must first *sense* what is going on in its environment. Different systems have different capacities in this regard. Dogs, cats, and people, for example, hear, feel, and smell different signals. They are therefore aware of different realities. As a system, each must *interpret* the data it has registered, separating meaningful signals from noise, the flood of random stimuli with no relevance to its survival or success. It discovers meaning in the data by looking for patterns related to some previous experience or known concept. The system must then *decide* what do in response. Finally, it must *act* on its decision. This sequence may be automatic and reflexive or conscious and reflective. Once a cycle is completed, a new one begins, in which the system incorporates the outcomes of the previous cycle with any newly perceived environmental signals.

Complexity scientist Seth Lloyd has derived an important principle about the sensemaking requirements of adaptive systems. His insight can be paraphrased as: Successfully adapting sys-

FIGURE 5.1

THE ADAPTIVE LOOP

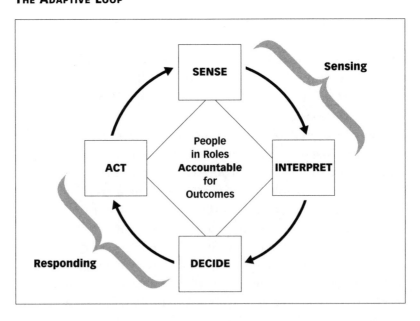

tems have the property of translating apparent noise into meaning at a faster rate than the arrival rate of apparent noise.[1] Lloyd's principle about the primacy of sensemaking as an adaptive competence is echoed by Brian Arthur in his prescription for survival in increasing return economies.

> [T]he challenge to management in this game is not so much to optimize . . . or to lay their bets just right. Instead, the challenge is to make better sense out of the situation than the next guy. . . . The strategic challenge here is a cognitive one. . . . [W]hat frameworks do they wheel up to understand the situation? . . . A system that is to [adapt] successfully . . . must adapt by constructing models that allow it to decide what information to get, and how to act on it.[2]

The distinction between *real* noise—pure randomness, against which no strategy can prevail—and *apparent* noise is very important. Data with no meaning in the existing framework, or context, may have meaning in some other context. This is where people come in. Our capacity to invoke meaning by drawing on analogous experience in other contexts is an enormous advantage when making sense out of new signals from the environment. Flatworms, computer viruses, chemical clocks, tornadoes, and other complex adaptive systems cannot do this. Humans, it seems uniquely, can consciously adapt the context itself as well as adapting within it. The hierarchy of adaptive contexts within which Westpac's loan officers, product managers, and system designers worked illustrates this. Adapting organizational context is the key to keeping a business viable in discontinuous change. It is a critical leadership competence in sense-and-respond organizations.

The adaptive loop begins with and is fueled by data. The system must transform this data into information and knowledge before it can take action. Adaptive organizations possess the survival trait of making rapid and continuous iterations around this loop. Make-and-sell companies cycle through this loop, too, adapting gradually to gradual change, but in a different way. A bus company, to return to the previous chapter's example, will do market research to sense people's transportation needs, and will use models to interpret what this data mean for bus utilization rates. Its analysts will interpret the data, looking for patterns useful for predicting new customer needs and company opportunities. Then the company's leadership will decide whether or not to buy new busses, hire more drivers, or modify their schedules. Finally, they will have to act on those decisions. The bus company, like other make-and-sell companies, resists change and tends to rationalize or ignore signals that suggest its necessity. They find it very advantageous to stay in the act phase as long as possible, because the efficiency of tightly integrated make-and-sell operations depends on stability. Change is disruptive and undermines efficiency. Such companies are, therefore, predisposed to seal themselves off from their environment. They act as if stable conditions prevail—until the environment changes enough to confront them with a crisis, such as the one that forced Westpac, out of desperation, to adopt a radically different strategy. Make-and-sell organizations attempt to act like closed systems. As noted earlier, they focus on internal information, investing attention and energy in making their procedures more efficient rather than in looking for signs of change. In so doing, they risk getting better and better at doing the wrong thing.

In contrast, sense-and-respond organizations are open systems. Instead of resisting change, they actively seek out the slightest hints of it. They do this not only to improve their reaction time, but to detect as soon as possible meaningful *differences* in individual customers' needs. They equip themselves to exploit the value of differences, as well as similarities, between customers. At the same time, and just as systematically, they look for early indications of new capabilities that would enable them to respond better to the needs identified. Once sense-and-respond organizations become good at cycling rapidly through the adaptive loop, they experience the increasing returns effects described by Brian Arthur. Companies that take longer to cycle through the loop fall farther and farther behind.

SENSE

In a competitive sense-and-respond world, sensing the obvious is not enough. Rapid listen-and-comply is responsive, but anticipate and preempt is decisive. Successfully proactive, adaptive systems must register implicit and tacit signals as well as explicit ones. Sometimes customers literally do not know what they need. Their articulated responses to market research questionnaires will be wrong, incomplete, or both. One researcher has estimated that as much as 80 percent of human communication is nonverbal.[3] Context, inflection, body language, and other behaviors often convey more meaning than do the words they accompany. To understand as early as possible the customer's underlying, unarticulated request, organizations must invest in collecting signals that may not appear to be requests at all.

Several years ago, for example, automobile manufacturers placed video cameras in parking lots to record people as they got in and out of their cars. In airport parking lots, researchers repeatedly saw travelers straining to lift heavy suitcases over the high lower lips then typical in trunk design. Cameras in mall parking lots recorded the expressions and body language of the many shoppers who arrived at their cars with drinks in hand. A significant number of drinks were spilled, evoking, most of the time, unequivocally negative reactions. These signals, previously hidden in the noise of the world around us, were subsequently interpreted as implicit requests for lower trunk lips and for drink holders. Now these features are standard equipment on virtually every automobile manufactured.

Making Meaning Out of Apparent Noise at Red Lobster

A few years ago, the management at Red Lobster, then a General Mills' restaurant, confronted a problem familiar to firms in many industries: Its high-volume product had become a commodity, rather than a differentiator. The shrimp on Red Lobster's menu was indistinguishable in quality and price from the shrimp on competitors' menus. As a result, period profit on this product ranged from minuscule to negative. Because shrimp accounted for a substantial percent of revenue, Red Lobster's bottom line suffered.

Management came up with a surprising answer to the question, "What should we begin sensing that we haven't been?" They decided to invest in satellite technology to sense, twenty-four hours a day, the salinity, acidity, and temperature of streams flowing into the Gulf of Mexico. Why? Perhaps because someone found, in an obscure scientific journal, a model that could use this data to produce accurate predictions of Gulf shrimp yields. Those predictions, fed into a good trading model, would allow GMR to take positions in the shrimp futures market that, when executed, would reduce their shrimp cost by up to 15 percent. The savings could go either in GMR's pockets or on the menu.

Management probably did not arrive at their unusual conclusion this way. A more plausible explanation starts with the problem to be solved and the two alternatives available: raise prices or reduce costs. The debate may have been similar to the following: "Raising prices will lead to an unacceptable loss of share, and there's no more fat in operations." "How could we reduce the cost of shrimp?" "Well, if we got lucky on the futures market, we could buy at lower prices than our competition." "We're managing restaurants, not gambling casinos; how could we make the risk acceptable?" "Find a good forecasting model for shrimp yields."

The *directed* search for good models that would follow has a greater likelihood of turning up that obscure but highly relevant journal article. Once GMR found, and validated, the model, its investment in satellite equipment to scan, twenty-four hours per day, the salinity, acidity, and temperature of streams flowing into the Gulf of Mexico begins to make much more sense.[4]

This example illustrates the process of making meaning out of noise. Red Lobster is not offered here as an example of sense-and-respond behavior, because GMR's orientation was make-and-sell. But two important points emerge from this hypothetical decision-making process.

- Thinking "backwards" through the loop can narrow and give direction to a search for apparent noise and the patterns that can make it meaningful.

- The probability is very, very high that data on the salinity, acidity, and temperature of streams flowing into the Gulf of Mexico remains nothing but noise to every other restaurant chain on earth. But at Red Lobster, these signals translate into cost savings.

Turning the Adaptive Loop
into a Learning Process

The Red Lobster example also illustrates the point that adaptive loops may or may not be *learning* loops. (See Figure 5.2.) Let's say that GMR makes its manager of operations accountable for menu profitability. From technology, this manager receives data on the price of shrimp futures and the salinity, acidity, and temperature of streams flowing into the Gulf. Two models then translate those signals into an interpretation of advantageous buying opportunities on the shrimp futures market. The manager makes decisions to execute a specific futures contract, and then to reflect some or all of the resulting savings on the menu.[5]

FIGURE 5.2

THE ADAPTIVE LOOP APPLIED AT GENERAL MILLS RESTAURANTS

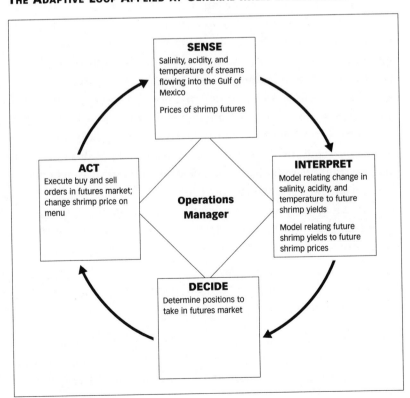

GMR's ability to respond earlier than its competitors can to changes in wholesale shrimp prices stems directly from its ability to anticipate these changes. This ability is based on the signals it chose to capture and by the models it chose to turn that data into decisions and rapid action. The managers' adaptive loop, illustrated in Figure 5.2, is certainly a learn*ed* process. It reflects learning by the company about how to adapt to changes in the salinity, acidity, and temperature of streams flowing into the Gulf. But it is not a learn*ing* process. Why not? Because the adaptation described above occurs within an unchanging context about what is going on in the environment.

If unpredictable events—such as oil spills or red tides—cause discontinuities in shrimp yield, the manager will need a greater capacity for adapting than the existing models support. To *learn* how to adapt to new variables, the business design must include another accountability (perhaps named *shrimp yield model maintenance*), assigned to another role (for example, Manager of Models), that iterates through a different adaptive loop to decide whether and how to update the models in current use. Systematic learning requires more than adaptation within a given context, it requires adaptation of the context itself. This important type of organizational learning often remains unrecognized as a distinct process. Most discussions of adaptive organizations focus on learning and creative problem-solving within a given context. But humans and human organizations have the capacity to consciously and intentionally reframe their contexts. In environments of discontinuous change, thinking outside the box is not sufficient: It is also necessary to think about changing the box.

The following techniques can help firms increase the probability that they will find the meaningful signals hidden in today's flood of real and apparent noise.

- Place more probes in the environment and sample them more frequently.

- Use probes that pick up nonverbal signals—the tastes, smells, sights, sounds, and feel of the total customer experience. By gathering and interpreting clues about the tacit and

emotional preferences of its customers, a firm can differentiate itself from competitors who continue to dismiss these signals as noise.

- Use analogies from other systems that seem to adapt well.
  Some are obvious, such as the best practices of companies in
  the same or other industries. Others will be less obvious
  metaphors from biological and natural complex adaptive systems. To discover relevant analogies, firms will need people
  with demonstrated intuitive and perceptive skills.

- Focus decision-making processes on the unknown and highly
  uncertain influencers of organizational success. (Appendix B
  describes a powerful method for doing this.)

Capturing all of these signals will result, of course, in data
glut. It is, nevertheless, the necessary first step to finding the
meaning in apparent noise. Strategic choices must be made about
how many and what kind of probes to deploy. Too few, and the organization will suffer from sensory deprivation. It will fail to register signals about developments, knowledge of which is essential to
its survival. Small advantages in organizational sensemaking can
become powerful strategic advantages.

INTERPRET

The next step in the adaptive loop, *interpret*,[6] involves applying context to data, giving it meaning and transforming it into information.[7] The context comes from filters that impose patterns on
raw data. (A good definition of an expert is someone who can impose a relevant pattern on a problem.) Humans are very good at this.

For large organizations, transforming data into information
involves a great deal of data reduction and abstraction. Financial
models, forecasting models, pricing models, procedures, simulations, reports, experimental designs, blueprints, data models, and
enterprise models are all filters designed to abstract the essential
from the mass of detail. This entails making choices about what

things are important, what qualities of those things are important, and what relationships among them are important.

These decisions, if well made, yield insight and understanding. If made poorly, they contribute to institutional delusions and hallucinations. Yet responsibility for these choices usually falls to specialists in the market research or information technology departments. Someone with a title such as database architect interviews business people about their expected information needs and then defines the entities, attributes, and relationships that give meaningful structure, or pattern, to data stored in databases or information warehouses. To a large degree, decisions made by the database architect determine how the organization interprets the signals it collects. These decisions reflect the predictions of business people about the questions that will need to be answered.

If the right questions are known and incorporated into data systems, operational performance can improve. But new questions constantly arise in an environment of rapid change, increasing the odds that database designs costing millions of dollars to implement will quickly become obsolete. The unpredictability inherent in information economies is nowhere more difficult to manage than in the IT department, where extraordinarily important strategic decisions determine how the institution makes meaning out of its data.

Data warehouses can contribute great value to an organization if they meet two criteria. First, they must structure information to answer questions that are, in fact, predictably important. Second, they must be exploited as repositories of unstructured "apparent noise." Predefined data architectures address the first condition, and a class of technologies called *data mining* addresses the second. Data mining technologies include a collection of tools and methods ranging from mathematical algorithms to so-called neural networks. Their common function is to find patterns in large aggregations of data. Only humans can determine if these patterns have meaning or not.[8]

Thinking of apparent noise as hidden patterns reveals the importance of data mining technologies for adaptive organizations, whose very survival depends on the systematic translation of apparent noise into meaning. The following two thumbnail sketches of successful data mining applications illustrate this point.

Fingerhut

Fingerhut, a $2 billion midwestern retail catalog company, uses data mining algorithms to customize its catalogs. Customers receive personalized catalogs containing only products that meet three criteria. First, they are of likely interest to the recipient. Second, the customer is likely to order the items immediately. Third, the customer is likely to pay for the products ordered. The patterns Fingerhut uses to make these inferences are created by applying data mining techniques to databases containing more than five hundred types of information about more than fifty million actual and potential customers. The data include name, address, social security number, last purchase, marital status, number of children, household income, payment history, family member birthdays, hobbies, language spoken, and willingness to accept telemarketing calls.[9]

Fingerhut reportedly enjoys a spectacular sixty-day response rate to its catalog mailings of 47 percent, as compared to the 6 percent achieved by the typical successful catalog. It may be the only retail catalog company making a profit from households with less than $25,000 annual income. Fingerhut customizes catalogs, not products. The important question for Fingerhut's management is: What specific products should we offer to what specific customers? They use the answers provided by their system to improve forecasts about what products will sell in volume, and to identify the individual customers who will make that volume profitable. Because of the way it interprets customer information, Fingerhut can deal profitably with customers that their competitors lose money on.

Kraft Foods

In early 1993, Lorraine Scarpa, then the senior vice president of marketing for KGF (Kraft General Foods), commissioned a trial application of neural net technology. She engaged Michael Rothman, who had successfully applied neural nets to increase chip manufacturing yields at IBM's East Fishkill plant, to help KGF extract meaning from a marketing database it had bought in 1992. The database contained a year's worth of consumer panel data on millions of purchases of food categories by twelve thousand U.S. households. Thinking of KGF's customers as *households* was a relatively new notion. For the most part, Kraft had marketed brand by brand to each individual in a household. But as Scarpa realized, "This strategy walks away from two kinds of efficiencies in marketing: selling more cases by promoting brands that are *bought together* by the same household; and amortizing promotion costs across as many brands as possible."

Rothman's skill and intuitions about the potential significance of relationships among disparate types of data enabled him to rapidly transfer his manufacturing experiences with CMOS chips to the domain of cold cuts and Jell-O. He showed Scarpa and her colleagues sixteen natural household segments that cut across existing category and brand segmentation schemes to produce startling insights into buying patterns. In each of these natural segments, a small percentage of households consistently accounted for between 40 and 80 percent of the total sales in a given product category. Scarpa, immediately grasping the import of these findings, had some questions for her colleagues. "Can anyone here tell me why we should continue to do national brand advertising? And can anyone explain why we organize ourselves by brand, rather than by household segment?"

No one present could answer those questions, but by mining the household data they found answers to these:

- Which households are the biggest users of Kraft's brands? Which are heavy users of more than one of Kraft's brands? How many and which?

- What clusters of brands do each segment of households consistently buy?

- What is the signature profile of a household that buys a Kraft brand (for example, Jell-O) in one category and a competitive brand (such as Folgers) in another category in which KFG has a franchise (for example, Maxwell House).

In this case, data mining not only translated apparent noise into meaning, it also helped Kraft recognize that some apparent meaning was really noise! Scarpa analyzed the findings this way.

> We *assumed* when we began our analysis that the breadth of the product line [sixty food and beverage categories] would mean that a relatively low percent of households would be heavy users across categories. We *thought* our categories acted independently, with different households being important to different categories. *Wrong!* Twenty percent of households account for a significant percentage of all Kraft volume, and the *average* number of categories a Kraft heavy user household buys is thirty-three. That means that these households are worth over $600 [in annual sales, compared to the average of $250].[10]

Examples of surprises produced by data mining abound. A West Coast supermarket chain discovered a strong relationship between the sales of beer and diapers on Thursdays and Saturdays in certain of their stores. Tokyo's Marui department store discovered (by looking for patterns in more than eight years of sales and credit data) that women between the ages of 25 and 40 who bought expensive tennis rackets were much more likely than others to buy fur coats in the next eighteen months. And so on and so on. They are testimony to the potential of this technology to assist businesses make meaning out of apparent noise. Because data mining can require large investments, management should find reassurance in the many examples showing that this capability can pay off handsomely in the short term.

It is worth repeating that data mining *complements* other ways in which database technologies provide information. The answers to some questions are, indeed, of predictable, enduring value. Good relational database architects provide essential data views, affording perspective about "what's going on" using variables and relationships known to be important. Data mining helps to identify new variables and new relationships that have—or could—become important determinants of success.

DECIDE

Decisions transform knowledge into action. At least, they do if "decision" is taken to mean *allocating resources,* as opposed to simply arriving at conclusions. Given an interpretation of a particular situation, decision-making involves choosing a course of action and investing in it. Some decisions are *reflexive* (such as removing one's hand from a hot stove). Some are *conditioned* (such as taking an umbrella along on cloudy days with rain in the forecast). Some are *reflective* (such as imagining multiple possible futures and actions and thinking through the implications of several combinations of them).

This book, of course, focuses on the latter. It is specifically concerned with *strategic* (as opposed to tactical and operational) *decision-making* (as opposed to "decision *support*") in large, complex organizations operating in environments of substantial uncertainty. Decision-making processes, if managed as described in appendix B, can systematically help organizations achieve the following important results.

- Making decisions with a customer-back orientation.

- Gaining insights about ways to create additional value.

- Discovering what data must be sensed and how it should be interpreted, and understanding what kinds of signals and models will increase the firm's ability to turn apparent noise into meaning.

- Aligning internal decisions by assessing alternative choices in terms of a common, extra-system criterion. For customer-back, sense-and-respond firms, the appropriate criterion will be impact on customer value.

- Identifying essential outcomes, thereby identifying key roles and accountabilities that should be included in the organization's design.

As Kusnic and Owen point out in appendix B, a sense-and-respond application of collaborative decision-making should emphasize *customer* value. This will highlight relevant areas of uncertainty and suggest what new signals not currently included in the business model should be included.

If a firm had to choose a single core competence, a good case could be made for decision-making. It may sound strange, in an action-oriented culture, to nominate a fundamentally intellectual process as the preeminent competence. But decision-making is necessarily a theoretical exercise because, to quote Kusnic, "There are no data about the future." We can formulate assumptions, trends, predictions, and dependencies, but we can gather no facts about anything except history.

As a result, good decision-making involves thinking *backwards* through the adaptive loop. Decision-makers must start with the desired outcome, define alternative courses of action that might achieve it, select among alternatives by interpreting their relative potential value, and capture the historical data needed to make those interpretations.

Act

Once strategic choices have been made about how resources should be deployed, the time has come to put them to work—to act. Action may mean communicating the decision as a command, or suggestion, or blueprint that commissions activity by others. Or, as in the case of Westpac, the decision may be automatically tested for conformance with relevant firm policies before being linked directly to an automated transaction system.

Each phase of the adaptive cycle has been presented here in terms of information management choices and the strategic consequences of making them well or poorly. Because total organizational cycle time is the sum of time spent thinking about decisions and time spent acting on them, integration of information choices in each of the four phases with information technology decisions becomes extremely important. Managing-by-wire implementations, described in chapter 9, use technology to speed up each phase of the adaptive cycle for key accountabilities in the organization. Each of these accountable roles, be it policy-maker or research team or channel manager, will require role-specific adaptive-cycle information support to create the outcomes for which they are accountable. The key accountabilities, in turn, will be linked to a high level design that codifies the essential structure of the organization, thereby expressing its strategy. This process will be described in chapter 8.

Proactive Capability Development

Customer and environmental signals are not the only sources of proactive behavior in the sense-and-respond model. Information about new capabilities under development outside a firm's traditional research framework can be just as important as sensing environmental change in customer preferences and competitor actions. A case in point is Xerox, once accused of "fumbling the future" because other companies regularly preempted it in commercializing its own innovations. In response, Xerox in the late 1980s established two internal venture capital companies. Though subject to the profit measurements of any venture capitalist, their primary role was to act as new technology sensors, finding outside investors for Xerox innovations that its own divisions did not want to pick up. They invested as well in new technologies developed by others that might have potential applications at Xerox.

Sense-and-respond firms do not forecast demand for products and services. But they do place selective bets on the stability of fundamental customer needs and on what capabilities should be in their modular response repertoire. Those accountable for new capability development must adapt to unpredicted innovations, some of which may at first seem mere noise, irrelevant to the enterprise's purpose. The steam engine, the computer, and the Internet provide good examples of capabilities looking for problems to solve when they first appeared.

Replying to customer requests is a reactive application of the sense-and-respond concept. *Inferring* customer requests—and acquiring the capabilities needed to respond to them profitably— is a preemptive approach. In the latter case, vigilant sensing of signals about emerging capabilities can trigger directed searches for the fundamental customer value attributes the firm could address—if it acquired those capabilities.

People accountable for keeping an enterprise on the cutting edge of new capabilities and technologies must be every bit as adaptive as the individuals accountable for marshaling capabilities into customer-specific responses. They will need different probes and frameworks. Their decisions and actions will determine the extent to which the firm drives change, rather than being driven by it.

LEADERSHIP AND THE ADAPTIVE CYCLE

Chapter 6 examines the role of leadership in sense-and-respond organizations. Their adaptive loops must be tailored to the special needs of their role.

Organizational leadership can be seen as a role accountable for the creation and adaptation of a viable organizational context—the enterprise's purpose, policies, and essential structure. For this role, adaptiveness entails timely changes in policies and business design, and, in extreme cases, of organizational purpose itself. Leadership's adaptive cycle must be tailored to support decision-making on these issues.

For example, organizations operating in environments of great uncertainty might choose scenario development to structure leadership's adaptive loop. This approach requires continuous monitoring of signals about trends and change rates for the dozen or so uncertainties most important to the firm.[11] One typical way of using scenario development to extract meaning from data about key uncertainties involves a simple two-by-two model, the dimensions of which are two of the uncertainties that capture a broad range of possibilities. The vertical axis might be labeled *laissez faire* at one end, for example, and *re-regulation* at the other. The horizontal axis might be labeled *high rate of technology change* at one end, and *evolutionary technology change* at the other. Plausible stories would then be created to characterize the nature of each of the resulting quadrants. The *high technology change* and *laissez faire* quadrant might be labeled *Pandora's box,* with an accompanying scenario text that suggests how the other key uncertainties might plausibly resolve themselves in such an environment. With these four scenarios, an analysis can be made of the applicability or robustness of alternative decisions across all quadrants. The development of the two-by-two grid, the stories, and the analysis constitute an *interpretation* by the leadership of "what's going on out there." Another set of signals and models would make explicit leadership's assessment of how well current organizational policies, strategies, structure, and competencies match each scenario. Together, these interpretations constitute the leadership's "heads-up display."

Decision-making involves making choices based on the issues surfaced by the scenarios. Which should be addressed? What policies should be created or abandoned? What structural changes are required? Action entails establishing accountabilities for implementing the strategies and transferring resources to the accountable roles. Continuous updating of the environmental uncertainties, scenarios, and operational capabilities makes this a learning process.

How can large, complex organizations cope systematically and successfully in a changing, unpredictable world? Increasingly, companies today can't know what they will be called upon to do next and must therefore express their business strategies as designs for adaptiveness, rather than as plans for efficient operation. Two essential requirements must be met if a large, complex enterprise is to be adaptive. First, its people in key roles must possess an aptitude for finding meaning in apparently irrelevant, noisy signals. Second, it must establish a modular organization, the capabilities of which can be dispatched to provide the most appropriate response to the meanings discovered. Now it is time to consider the implications of these requirements for the role of leadership.

*I must go now, for there go my people, and I am
their leader.*

—GANDHI

THE ROLE OF LEADERSHIP IN SENSE-AND-RESPOND ORGANIZATIONS

ONE EFFECT OF OPERATING A BUSINESS IN AN ENVIRONMENT
of discontinuous change is that leaders can no longer know
as well as followers how to get things done. A leader's role cannot
be, therefore, one of devising battle plans and issuing orders down
a chain of command to coordinate their execution. In sense-
and-respond organizations, leaders have very different responsibilities, the nature of which will be this chapter's focus.

A useful starting point will be to think of the organization as a
pool of modular capabilities. People occupying various roles are
accountable for using these capabilities to produce specific deliverables. To turn this collection into a successful enterprise, the
outcomes produced by the capabilities (including those external
to the enterprise) must be orchestrated into a coherent system.
This use of the word *coherent* has two aspects. First, it implies that
the purpose and scope of the business are clear to everyone. Second, it means that the contributions of all organizational capabili-

ties will be coordinated, allowing the business to achieve its purpose. The leadership role is accountable for declaring a viable purpose and scope for the organization, defining the capabilities it will have, and ensuring their coordination.

In the sense-and-respond model, leadership's accountability for coherence is carried out by providing *context and coordination*. These two deliverables are owed by leadership to the other roles in the organization, without which their decisions and actions will not be coherent. *Context* consists of an unambiguous definition of the organization's reason for being, its governing principles, and its high-level business design. *Coordination* combines the high-level business design with a commitment management system. In sense-and-respond organizations, context and coordination replace command and control.

THE DECLINE OF COHERENCE

The old make-and-sell organization could behave coherently by acting as a machine designed to create a stable, known set of products and services. Leaders could and did decide in advance what those products and services would be. Aided by their planning departments, they developed and oversaw a detailed, linear, sequential game plan for achieving their defined results. They enforced coherent behavior by telling people, as specifically as possible, what to do. Command-and-control was the name of the game, and it was the game to play as long as leaders could work from reliable predictions about what offerings their customers would buy. When they no longer could, command and control broke down. Strategic planning departments, overwhelmed with unforeseen exceptions to their plans, became increasingly ineffective. Eventually, they were disbanded or given new missions, such as developing alternative ways to think about the future. When the planning and follow-up staffs disappeared, with them went the control part of command and control. As an instrument of corporate governance, the central staff was crucially important to coherent behavior. Without it, leadership was left with little else than a financial model, directives, exhortations, and mission, vision, and value statements. But this is not governance. This is replacing command and control with communicate and hope.

Many leaders recognized that empowering groups and individuals to make their own decisions could help the organization recognize and respond to change more quickly. People on the front lines saw what was happening "out there" sooner than their leaders did. If they had to pass their observations and recommendations up a hierarchical chain of managers and then wait for leadership approval to come back down the chain, the opportunity they had seen would be gone. But if troops closer to the front line had power to act autonomously, they could respond quickly, before continuing change made the response obsolete. Experience and logic both argue, however, that simply giving hundreds or thousands of managers decision-making authority and a vision statement results in a multiplicity of local actions. This approach is very unlikely to produce coherent organizational behavior, even when leaders try to guide the company using mission and directional statements. The Visa and Prato merchants examples described in chapter 3 show that coordinated strategic behavior *can* emerge spontaneously from independent actions—but only given special conditions. In large, complex companies, communicate-and-hope management will not work.

WHEN PROBLEM-SOLVING CAUSES PROBLEMS

Consider the following too-familiar example of organizational incoherence. In this case communicate-and-hope, along with fragmented problem-solving by local managers, fostered uncoordinated and self-defeating behavior.

In the mid-1980s, a large industrial company had seemed to be doing almost everything right. A list of their successful management initiatives at the time can serve as a virtual guide to contemporary thinking on best management practices. The company had become a recognized leader in a number of key areas.

- Quality, as certified by a Baldrige award.

- Process orientation and core competence identification, having undertaken two rounds of company-wide key process improvement.

- Lean manufacturing, with some of its logistics systems ranked as industry benchmarks.

- Customer orientation, with billions of dollars invested in integrating products and services into customer "solution" offerings.

- Empowerment, having decentralized into a dozen quasi-autonomous business units.

- Teaming, with established cross-functional teams having developed and launched several new products that captured the largest market share in multi-billion dollar industries.

- Outsourcing, to the extent that less than 7 percent of the value added to their third most important product line was generated in-house.

Despite these impressive internal accomplishments, severe competition from niche players was eroding the firm's margins and markets around the world. Top management chartered a series of world-wide task forces to study the competitive threat and to devise a response. After spending millions of dollars and decades of employee-years on the effort, the teams presented their joint recommendation: Invest in recruiting and training highly-skilled experts to compete head-on with the company's chief rivals in each region. The executive committee accepted the group's analysis. It was pleased with the executability of the proposed plan and approved the investment needed to carry it out.

Less than ten days later, the same executives met to review the company's quarterly financial performance. The news was not good. Faced with lower-than-expected revenues and profits, they decided to cut headcount across the board.

A week after that decision was made, the financial vice president of the company's U.S. operating subsidiary found two executive committee directives on her desk. One instructed her to increase the divisional sales force by 150 to carry out the new competitive initiative. The other told her to reduce total divisional headcount by 375 to compensate for the profit shortfall. Such mixed messages appeared frequently, and she followed her normal practice in dealing with them. She made the subtraction and spread the pain to subsidiary units in proportion to their size and contribution to the U.S. company's local priorities. Work related to some existing commitments abruptly stopped. Managers of other autonomous units made different trade-offs. The uncoordinated executive committee decisions gradually dissipated into dozens and then hundreds of small, isolated choices about how to allocate resources. Operations managers applied intelligence and logic— but very local logic—to the choices they faced. Not surprisingly, action on the new competitive initiative proved incoherent and in-effective. Some months later, a frustrated member of the executive committee, angry about spotty implementation of the competitive initiative, called it yet "another example of lousy execution of a good strategy."

In perhaps the most remarkable aspect of this sequence of events, none of the executives involved seemed to think that send-ing essentially contradictory directives to lower-level management was dysfunctional or even unusual. It was their job to solve prob-lems, and they had solved two nasty ones in ten days. Lower-level executives were also paid to solve problems and were empowered to make trade-offs. It would have taken far too much time for the executive committee to track down all of the highly interdepen-dent repercussions of each individual decision, much less the combined impact of both. The phrase *paralysis by analysis* was frequently invoked to dismiss that approach. Even had they wanted to, these executives could not have carried out such an as-sessment. No mechanism existed to reflect the impact of a corpo-rate decision on the thousands of lower-level activities set in mo-tion by earlier decisions and commitments. The top-down plan and central staff that once defined and tracked such interactions no longer existed, and no new coordinating mechanism had taken its place.

In fact, lack of coordination meant that the impressive list of initiatives cited above were all managed as stand-alone projects. The costs and benefits of each were analyzed in terms of its partic-ular aims, with little or no attention given to how they might sup-port or conflict with one another. Each was carried out with intel-ligence, skill, and hard work, but they were not interested in a coherent design of how the organization should function. They were parts of a *system,* the elements of which affected one another and the performance of the whole, but this was largely ignored. That lack of coordination makes it less surprising that so many successful, but fragmented, initiatives did not prevent the company from losing market share to its competitors.

This example highlights some of the problems that large, decentralized corporations face when trying to achieve coherence in an era when command and control no longer work and empowerment consistently generates uncoordinated, even contradictory actions. Several senior executives from two Fortune Ten companies expressed some common frustrations in recent internal interviews and speeches.

> "We agreed we needed new strategies, and we created them, but we didn't implement them. All our problems were the result of a failure to do what we knew we had to do."
>
> "Because everyone is perceived as being 'in charge,' no one is perceived as being in charge or accountable for anything."
>
> "There is a lack of strong leadership that sets boundaries and makes sure that there is compliance, or that there are consequences for non-compliance."
>
> "Anyone can say 'no' at any time for any reason, even when that is dysfunctional to the organization."
>
> "Aren't there too many people here with different visions of what should be?"

The same sentiment is often expressed more colloquially at lower organizational levels: "We don't have our act together." Establishing coherence means just that: getting the enterprise act together.

CREATING ORGANIZATIONAL CLARITY

Comments such as those above suggest the solution to the problem they describe. Ineffective, incoherent organizational behavior results from confusion about corporate mission, or over which of two conflicting corporate principles represents a higher priority, or over the extent and limits of individual authority and accountability. When any of these conditions develop, leadership has failed to deliver on *its* accountability to establish clarity about institutional purpose, scope, and accountabilities. The solution lies in creating an unambiguous organizational context.

The late Vittorio Cassoni, former CEO of Olivetti, understood the importance of organizational clarity. Cassoni believed that reducing ambiguity and confusion was a corporate leader's most important job. Asked to describe his primary responsibility, Cassoni once said, "I absorb uncertainty."[1] He knew that clarity and consistency about corporate purpose, policies, and structure enabled others to act more effectively. When leaders are *not* clear and do not shield their organizations from mixed messages, organization members waste time and energy trying to understand the context. They try to make sense out of ambiguous statements and situations. Employees will, in fact, impose their own sense on the ambiguity. They have to, if they are to relate their own work to company goals. Inevitably, these many interpretations will diverge, and the decisions based on them will be incompatible. The result: incoherent action and fragmentation. The system will fail to work *as* a system. The corporate executives cited above who criticized their companies' poor execution and multiple visions were complaining, in part, about the effects of ambiguity. They were concerned about having to act while unclear about their shared aims and the common constraints on their actions.

Ensuring coherent organizational behavior requires more than replacing muddled thinking and speaking with straight talk. It requires developing, communicating, and enforcing a clear, consistent, systematic definition of organizational aims, behaviors, and responsibilities.

IN SEARCH OF COHERENCE: ALFRED SLOAN ON GOVERNANCE

It may seem odd to turn to an Industrial Age leader for guidance on how to govern a sense-and-respond organization in the Information Age. Alfred Sloan presided over a make-and-sell firm that we sometimes think of as *the* prototype of a successful twentieth-century industrial corporation: General Motors. GM under Sloan was designed for and thrived in a more stable era, now left far behind. Nevertheless, his conception of the role of corporate leadership continues to be valuable, perhaps more so today than ever. His leadership approach provides basic lessons about how to manage a large, complex company in a rapidly changing world.

Sloan came to General Motors in the early 1920s, convinced that his first priority was to establish and maintain a clear organizational context. He believed, in other words, that his role was one of defining GM's purpose, principles, and structure as clearly as possible. He spent most of his time and energy on concepts, policies, and principles because he thought it crucial to provide people under him with the right framework for making their own decisions. In *My Years with General Motors,* Sloan affirmed "the paramount importance, in an organization like General Motors, of providing the right framework for decisions." He went on to state that "We all felt [a need] for ground rules, that is, for first principles."[2] Sloan knew that senior management had responsibility for establishing these principles and building the framework. He wrote, "The activity of the Executive Committee should be establishing policy in clear-cut and comprehensive terms to supply the basis of authorized executive action." For Sloan (but not for his rival Henry Ford), it was this conceptual work—not telling others precisely what to do—that constituted executives' primary duty: "The Executive Committee should confine itself to principles rather than constitute itself [as a] group management."

In 1921, a committee of senior executives under Sloan's leadership began to develop the framework that would govern future decisions at GM. Although the executives were comfortable with conceptual thinking, they had not previously developed a comprehensive concept of their own business. "GM had no clear-cut concept of the business," Sloan said, and he emphasized the need to develop a conceptual model. "We started not with the actual Corporation but with a model of a corporation, for which we said we would state policy standards."

GM's Unambiguous Purpose, Circa 1930

The committee's first task was to make GM's purpose explicit. They came up with an unambiguous statement of General

Motors' reason for existing: "The primary objective of the corporation," they declared, "[is] to make money, not just to make motor cars." This may seem an obvious statement for a large, profit-making corporation, but, in fact, it is one of several possibilities and represented something of a shift in the company's sense of purpose. Sloan felt that "the idea of the revolutionary car was very much entrenched in the Executive Committee." In other words, GM's earlier implicit reason for being, perhaps never clearly articulated, had been (in part at least) to make revolutionary new motor cars. In the minds of some leaders, that goal outweighed the aim of making money or (because the company's purpose had not before been unequivocally defined) was muddled up and sometimes conflicted with the goal of making money. It is easy enough to see how striving to develop "the revolutionary car" could lead to decisions incompatible with maximizing profit. Ambiguity about which one purpose should be a firm's primary purpose unavoidably increases the probability that operating executives will make inconsistent trade-offs.

Sloan and his executive committee emphasized the preeminence of GM's money-making purpose by clearly describing the consequences for endeavors that failed to make money: "The strategic aim of a business is to earn a return on capital. [If the] return in the long run is not satisfactory, the deficiency should be corrected or the activity abandoned."

GM's Ground Rules

Because it was unambiguous, the reason for being devised by Sloan and his group could serve GM as the cornerstone of organizational coherence. No large business can work consistently toward a goal if its members are unsure what that goal is or if different groups in the business have different ideas about it. The clearly articulated goal, making money, provided an essential criterion for decision-making. It told GM managers, for example, that certain efforts towards developing a revolutionary car, though possibly interesting and satisfying in themselves, would be acceptable only if they became profitable within a defined timeframe.

By itself, however, a clear statement of purpose does not provide enough context to ensure coherent decision-making throughout the company. Boundaries also need to be set. These are expressed by clear statements of the constraints imposed by other constituencies, by the values of the organization, or by the factors critical for success. From these comes an understanding of the boundaries on empowerment. Policy-makers thus impose certain enterprise-wide limits to foster behaviors consistent with their concept of "what kind of company this is." The second sentence in the executive committee statement above is one such directive: It constrains all business ventures by defining the condition (satisfactory return in the long run) of their continued existence.

Sloan formulated a number of these principles, which he called "ground rules" to govern GM's organizational behavior. They were not suggestions or guidelines, but laws. They could not be violated with impunity. They did not tell managers precisely what to do, but they established unambiguous boundaries for their actions. The lists below contain some of Sloan's ground rules, rephrased as *always* and *never* statements to emphasize their obligatory nature.

General Motors will *always*

- Abandon a business if its long-term rate of return is not satisfactory.

- Deploy capital and operate in the best interests of GM as a whole.

- Hold the head of each sector absolutely responsible for its outcome.

- Offer cars at least equal to the best of the competition in each line.

- Purchase items or services if GM cannot do better.

General Motors will *never*

- Leave wide price gaps in the line.

- Get into the fancy price field with small production.

- Have duplication in the price field by automobile line.

That Sloan understood the rationale for outsourcing ("Purchase items or services if GM cannot do better") fifty years before it was called that illustrates his visionary brilliance. Today, the company is still trying to deal effectively with this issue. Similarly, GM executives ignored Sloan's constraint on duplication in the 1970s, and consumers had difficulty distinguishing among the many similar models of Chevrolets, Oldsmobiles, Buicks, and Pontiacs.

CREATING A CONTEXT FOR COHERENT SENSE-AND-RESPOND ACTION

Sloan clearly understood that the essential job of organizational leadership is not to solve business problems but to establish a shared context for the thousands and tens of thousands of decisions made throughout large corporations. He and his executive committee sharply defined the organization's primary purpose (to make money, not just motor cars). They also set clear boundaries—including behavioral imperatives and taboos—constraining action taken in pursuit of that purpose (Sloan's *always* and *never* principles). Because of Sloan's dedication to clarity, managers in the company had a solid basis for decision-making.

Governing adaptive organizations requires a context for behavior, not a means for *dictating* it. In sense-and-respond organizations, context consists of three elements:

- A reason for being

- Governing principles

- A high-level business design

A *reason for being* statement articulates the organization's essential purpose. The equivalent of Sloan's organizational purpose, it differs from most vision and mission statements in that it precisely defines what an organization exists to create—its function—as opposed to what it must do in order to exist. *Governing principles* resemble Sloan's ground rules. They set the boundaries on allowable behavior, constraining how members of the organization may act to achieve the reason for being and defining the always to be observed limits on their behavior. Finally, the *high-level business design* represents the organization's essential structure. It specifies how critical elements of the organization interact to fulfill its reason for being. This concept of *system* design has no direct equivalent in Sloan's General Motors, although his holistic approach in starting with a top-down conceptual model of the organization demonstrated his understanding that every part of the company should relate to GM's purpose. We will consider these three essential components of organizational context in detail in the next chapter.

WHAT DEFINES SENSE-AND-RESPOND LEADERSHIP?

Establishing context is a creative, conceptual act. It is not to be confused with problem-solving. As the example earlier in this chapter shows, problem-solving alone tends to deal with the situation of the moment, at the expense of the wider context. Narrowly focused problem-solving can lead to contradiction and confusion. In fact, developing an effective new concept can dissolve many of the problems that once seemed so important. The problem of sailing off the edge of the earth simply evaporates when one understands that the earth is round.

In many companies, though, the best problem solvers rise to the top; their most noted and rewarded ability is putting out fires. This skill can be compatible with that of conceptualizing the context in which problems must be solved. But the latter remains the crucial competence, even though it has not always been a criterion for entry to the top echelons of business.[3] It should be. Context-creation is the leader's foremost responsibility. In fact, sense-and-respond enterprises *define* leadership as the creation, propagation and enforcement of organizational context. Leaders alone are responsible for absorbing uncertainty and generating certainty about three crucial questions: Why are we here? How do we relate to one another? What limits our discretion to act?

The leadership of any organization is responsible for delivering the results it has promised its external constituencies. In sense-and-respond companies, leadership is accountable for three, and only three, *internal* outcomes.

- Creation and continuous adaptation of a viable organizational context.

- Establishment of a commitment management system to coordinate the behavior of people in accountable roles.

- Population of roles with the right people.

These accountabilities must be carried out competently if the organization-as-system is to realize its purpose. The reason for being and the governing principles may fail to provide an adequate compass. The high-level business design may not comprehend the current reality. The company's people may be unable to carry out their commitments without specific direction. If so, leadership is failing to deliver the outcomes for which it is solely accountable. Every time leaders intervene in operations they step out of their leadership role. They are also receiving a signal either that the context needs changing or that important roles are not filled by the right people.

The operational experience, problem-solving talent, and specialized knowledge of individual leaders, of course, are important resources that should be made available to the firm. But these talents and skills should be tapped either through solicitation of advice (not directives) or by assigning these skilled individuals to additional roles.

REDUCING AMBIGUITY

Ambiguity about purpose or principles undermines coherent action. It leaves unanswered questions about which of two or more possible meanings should apply in a given case. Ambiguity can never be eliminated in the real world, but organizational leaders must strive to keep it at a minimum.

To a very important extent, ambiguity is a language issue. Leaders express organizational purpose and principles—organizational context—in words. The words they use must be clear and clearly understood if the purpose and principles they embody are to be understood. We often object to what seem time-wasting arguments about "semantic differences," as if those differences were insignificant. But the word *semantic* comes from a Greek word that *means* significant. A semantic difference is a difference in meaning. A disagreement about the meaning of words used to define organizational purpose constitutes disagreement about the purpose itself. Leaders developing organizational context must use language that expresses their meaning as precisely and unequivocally as possible. A Chinese proverb captures the importance for leaders of finding the right words: "The first work of governance is the rectification of names."[4] Confucius himself laid out the consequences to coherency of failing to do this well.

> If names are not rectified, then language will not be in accord with the truth. If language is not in accord with the truth, then things cannot be accomplished. . . . [T]he people will not know how to move hand or foot.[5]

Good system design takes as a principle the importance of reducing ambiguity. Ambiguity increases system incoherence and limits effectiveness. In particular, four kinds of ambiguity affect the design and governance quality of sense-and-respond organizations: ambiguity about purpose, ambiguity about boundaries, ambiguity about essential structures, and ambiguity about the metric of progress.[6]

Ambiguity about Purpose

Consider this hypothetical mission statement: "We will strive to provide the highest return to shareholders and offer the highest quality products and services, while achieving the highest customer loyalty and the highest employee job satisfaction." This company intends to be all things to all people, and its statement offers no clues to employees about ordering priorities. When the need to compromise and make choices arises, as it inevitably will, the statement will give employees no clear basis for making decisions and no help in determining how to make the necessary trade-offs. What option should a manager choose, for example, when a decision to improve product quality would reduce shareholder return and employee satisfaction? Which should be the primary outcome and which the constraints on achieving it? The organization's primary function is ambiguous, being three or four possible things at once. This is as unacceptable for the design of an organizational system as it would be for a physical system.

Firms sometimes react to unanticipated change by redefining their purposes in mid-stream. Managers sometimes simply change their minds. New and old purposes (and new and old trade-offs) blend into a messy stew of cross-purposes that often leads to failure. Professor Gary Lynn's research on successes and failures of Apple and IBM in the personal computer market shows how ambiguity or clarity of purpose can produce dramatically different results.[7]

Randy Battat, one of the managers of Apple's Lisa project, a precursor of the wildly successful Macintosh, attributes its commercial failure to "tackling [too] many fundamental things all at the same time." The problem, he says, was exacerbated by management generosity: "There was so much resource thrown at the thing that one did not have to make trade-offs."

IBM's initial PC project had a clear, constant purpose throughout, despite a change in project management. When Don Estridge was given approval to launch the PC thirteen months after the project started, he called his predecessor, Bill Lowe, and told him, "What you'd be proud of is that 80 percent of the charts we presented for approval are the same charts you used a year ago." The result was success. The lifetime sales forecast of 241,000 units was exceeded several times over during the first five months after its 1981 launch.

The PCjr. that followed failed dismally, however, largely because multiple senior management interventions blurred its purpose. Originally designed as a powerful home/game system, its performance was intentionally crippled because executives did not want it to cut into business PC sales. In mid-stream it was repositioned from a home computer to a home/business computer, and a new constraint—compatibility with the PC line—was introduced after much of the basic design had been completed. In retrospect, a better scenario for maximizing ambiguity about product design and marketing positioning can hardly be imagined.

Confusion about the purpose of a particular project can spell disaster. Confusion about organizational purpose elevates that dysfunction to the enterprise level. Management maxims about maintaining focus are grounded in awareness of the havoc ambiguity can wreak. But those urged to stay focused on the goal must be given a clear notion of what that goal is. Too many focal points can produce a blur—as damaging as no focus at all.

An unambiguous reason for being that reduces (and as much as possible eliminates) ambiguity about purpose should be the cornerstone of organizational context. As the more detailed discussion in the next chapter will show, its exact formulation has broad implications for the organization.

Ambiguity about Boundaries

Boundaries define the range of permissible action. Rather than providing detailed sets of instructions on what to do and how to do it, they set basic limits, identifying things that must always or never happen. Along with the purpose (reason for being), boundaries largely define the nature of an organization or society. If boundaries are unclear or nonexistent, people will select their own. Coherence and the possibility of cooperation will decline.

Poorly articulated policies and undifferentiated floods of inconsistent policies, principles, guiding principles, imperatives, and priorities increase ambiguity about boundaries. Sometimes this glut of directives reflects disagreement among leaders about how the organization should be run. Sometimes it shows a lack of vision and perspective, the result of a focus on solving current problems rather than seeing the organization as a single system. As in the case described earlier, leaders may not even notice that this week's imperative contradicts last week's priority.

Unambiguous governing principles create clarity about boundaries, defining the field of play within which employees operate. Without telling people what to do on that field, they foster

consistent organizational (and systems) behavior, helping to ensure that everyone plays the same game by the same rules.

Ambiguity about Essential Structure

Clarity about essential structure means understanding how
the elements of a system interact to achieve the purpose man-
dated for the system. Although the word *structure* may seem to
suggest permanence, or even rigidity, the term as used here refers
to defined relationships among an adaptive system's modular
capabilities.

Uncertainty about essential structure sometimes takes the
form of ignorance about the relationship between an individual's
work and that of the organization as a whole. Groups maintain a
local focus, with little or no understanding of how what they do affects others. The degree to which an organization depends on the
matrix concept can indicate the extent of ambiguity about its
structure. People in large organizations play multiple roles and, of
necessity, often have several internal customers to whom they owe
specific outcomes. Matrices attempt to formalize relationships, using dotted lines drawn on organizational charts to represent the
categories of issues for which one individual reports to another.

Matrices fall short not because multiple relationships exist,
but because they are rarely designed as part of a larger system.
Specifically, these multiple relationships are rarely expressed in
terms of outcomes and are often internally inconsistent with one
another. Ambiguity about authority, priorities, and who owes what
to whom leaves people tethered to multiple bosses, any of whom
might yank on the leash at any time with directives or requests
that may or may not conflict with other priorities and responsibilities. Responding to the squeakiest wheel or the most threatening
show of power, individuals may spend time on inessentials, and
they will often knowingly find themselves making inconsistent
trade-offs. In other cases, where many people are held accountable for the same thing and everyone knows that the accountability is dispersed, no one feels really responsible. The work falls between the cracks. Many people will identify with this statement by
Thomas Hout and John Carter about the harmful effects of matrix

management: "The problem with most matrix structures is that they push complexity down into the organization, thus forcing middle managers to make difficult trade-offs between the competing goals of two [or more] bosses."[8]

This captures the real issue with matrix structures. It is not simply that they tend to generate unnecessary conflict, but they also push unavoidable conflict too far down in the organization. Trade-offs become difficult when the relative value of alternate outcomes is ambiguous. "Too far down," means below the level at which the decision logic for a particular trade-off incorporates all the considerations that must be weighed to maximize overall system performance. This problem would be greatly alleviated if matrixed roles were designed in terms of outcomes and customers and if the matrix were designed as a dynamic system of outcomes—rather than as static issue-related management reporting relationships. Issue categorization can be a good analytic technique but it is a poor basis for system design. It is yet one more way to fragment a business.

The cost of failing to manage matrices as a system of dynamic relationships can be significant. A 1998 study of multifunction teams in the sales division of a large company quantified the cost of matrix conflict in terms of deals lost, not pursued, or insufficiently integrated. The research disclosed that the average multi-function team failed to realize more than $10 million in available revenue because of these conflicts—and the division had hundreds of these teams in operation. The root cause was identified as "lack of clarity about roles, accountabilities, and authorities."

A high-level business design provides a map of essential structure. It describes the key outcomes that elements of the system owe one another and must deliver for the system to carry out its purpose. It is not a flow chart showing how key processes accomplish work. Nor is it an organizational chart showing who *reports* to whom. It is a system design that shows who *owes what* to whom. Along with helping to create organizational context by providing clarity about structure, the high-level business design provides a framework for managing commitments and accountabilities. It is a key element of sense-and-respond governance that I will discuss more fully in chapter 9.

Ambiguity about the Metric of Progress

I have already mentioned that emphasizing the importance of certain behaviors while rewarding others creates ambiguity about trade-offs and boundaries. A similar ambiguity results when the performance yardstick measures something other than the real desired outcome. Measuring progress toward an objective of improved quality by measuring the number of defects, for example, may result in fewer defects but no more or even lesser quality in the eyes of the customer. Anyone who has driven a fine automobile, had dinner in a good restaurant, or read a good book knows that "better quality" means more than "having fewer defects." The director of a state agency recently described his organization's goal as "increasing the services provided to citizens." Asked how progress toward that goal was measured, his answer was quality. When prodded further, he explained that the agency measured quality by the "number of citizen complaints."[9] This yardstick, in fact, measures neither quality nor increased services. Furthermore, the director acknowledged that a great deal of organizational energy was spent debating whether a particular communication from a constituent was a complaint or a suggestion, effectively changing the organization's purpose from "increased services" to "fewer complaints."

When rewards are tied to measurements of progress rather than outcomes, measurements usually replace the outcomes as the focus of activity.[10] If the measurement and the outcomes have different dimensions (as quality and defects do) the result is often perverse. Take, for example, the unintended effects of denominator management. A store manager whose performance is measured by sales per square foot decides to improve his numbers by reducing the amount of retail space. But his focus on that measurement undermines the organization's real desired outcome: more profit per store.[11]

Rewarding a metric of progress rather than an outcome, establishes de facto a different purpose, creating ambiguity about which purpose is the real one. When measurements and rewards are inconsistent with organizational purpose, conflict increases and system coherence breaks down.

THE CHALLENGE OF BUILDING CONTEXT

Leadership has responsibility for creating, adapting, and governing a viable organizational context and for populating, with the right talent, the roles defined in it. Establishing the context comes first. This is an inventive, not a problem-solving task, as Alfred Sloan demonstrated. It is a primarily conceptual exercise, relying less on analytical reasoning than on intuitive, creative intelligence and holistic thinking. In sense-and-respond organizations, it will also require a tolerance—if not a preference—for substantial amounts of environmental uncertainty. As the more detailed discussions in the following chapters will show, the process of developing a reason for being, governing principles, and a high-level business design will bring to the surface long-held assumptions and will highlight embedded contradictions long hidden by vague language and ambiguous organizational designs. In most companies, the process will lead to dramatic and often difficult changes in the organization's aims and structure, in the definition and evaluation of people's roles, and in the qualities and skills that will add the most value. The next chapter explains the components of context in more detail and describes some useful approaches to creating it.

The neglected leadership role is the designer
of the ship.

— PETER SENGE

BUILDING ORGANIZATIONAL

CONTEXT

FIRMS TAKE THE FIRST STEP TOWARD BECOMING SENSE-
and-respond organizations by recognizing the need to do so.
As was true of Westpac in the 1980s, the impetus for transformational change often comes from a major crisis that makes unavoidably clear that the current way of doing things won't work any-
more. The early adopters of the sense-and-respond principles
described in this book are executives in information-intensive organizations, operating in business environments becoming rapidly
more unpredictable and increasingly competitive. They see sense-
and-respond as either the best or, in some cases, as the only answer. We have already seen that this conclusion carries with it
some unsettling implications. This and the following chapters will
consider more of them. A considerable amount of this book is devoted to the premises and implications of sense-and-respond precisely because the decision to adopt this model cannot be made
lightly. As Reg Munro of Old Mutual Insurance once said, "Sense-

and-respond will not replace make-and-sell because it is easy, but because it is necessary."[1]

Once they reach this conclusion, many leaders will find that the development of an unambiguous context is their logical starting point. By defining the purpose, boundaries, and structure of the adaptive system they are striving to create, they will establish the necessary foundation on which a sense-and-respond organization rests. Creating a viable design—one both economic and sufficiently adaptive—is no easy task. To explore the issues involved, we need to look carefully at the three key elements of context: reason for being, governing principles, and high-level business design.

THE REASON FOR BEING

A reason for being expresses essential organizational purpose. It states what the organization *exists to do,* as opposed to what it *must do to exist.*[2] It does not list the most important things the organization does or the goals it hopes to achieve. Rather, it defines the essential thing the organization must deliver to justify (rather than ensure) its existence. Unlike many mission statements, a reason for being is unambiguous about the organization's primary constituency and the primary outcome the enterprise must provide that constituency. Later, when difficult trade-offs must be made, this clarity will assist employees in making choices that contribute most to the primary purpose of the enterprise. A clear reason for being serves as the cornerstone of organizational context, providing the reference point for formulating governing principles and the high-level business design.

Let's take another look at Alfred Sloan's statement of purpose for General Motors, rephrasing it slightly, to illustrate the characteristics of an effective reason for being: *General Motors exists to make money by making motor cars.* These ten words unambiguously define GM's primary *purpose,* its primary *constituency,* and its primary *constraint.* These three necessary elements give clarity and specificity to a firm's reason for being, qualities necessary to an effective organizational context. This statement of system purpose tells people, in a straightforward way, what the system exists to do. According to Sloan's reason for being, making money was GM's primary purpose. Its primary constituency was the shareholder, for whom money was made. Its primary constraint dictated that the money would be made by making motor cars—in other words, GM was not in the travel business. Once declared by leadership, these elements are non-negotiable and cannot be modified by any role other than corporate leadership. There is nothing optional about a reason for being.

As we saw in the last chapter, the meanings of words matter. A different phrasing, producing what might superficially seem a very similar reason for being, can, in fact, define a different purpose, constituency, and constraint. Assume, for example, that Sloan had said, "General Motors exists to make motor cars profitably." In this case the company's primary purpose would be making motor cars. Making money would then become a non-negotiable constraint: The cars must be made profitably. In this formulation, the primary constituency becomes not the shareholders, but GM management and employees, the "car guys" who invest their careers and talents in making motor cars. The semantic differences between the two versions define different system outcomes and imply different system designs.

Suppose Sloan and his executive committee believed that the customer should be GM's primary constituency. They would then have developed a different reason for being, such as: "General Motors exists to meet people's personal transportation needs by making motor cars profitably." Making motor cars and making money are now non-negotiable constraints. This formulation recognizes that personal transportation, not cars, is the more fundamental and stable value people seek.

These reason for being alternatives illustrate three different formulations. Each describes a very different business function and calls for a different business design. Mission statements are a form of cheerleading in some companies. They urge employees toward lofty goals, but have little direct effect on business structure or on people's daily work. A reason for being, as a statement of organizational purpose, carries a much more precise meaning. It defines the ultimate priority of all work done for the organization, and it provides a basis for making trade-offs and deciding how that work should be organized. Developing a reason for being challenges companies in several ways.

First, corporate leaders must articulate and choose among contrasting beliefs about organizational purpose. An effective reason for being can have only one primary purpose and one primary constituency—that is what *primary* means. A compromise reason for being, with something for everyone, cannot do its job. It will fail to provide the necessary *unambiguous* statement of what the organization exists to do. Ambiguity can be hard to root out. This is not only because of the intellectual challenge but because ambiguity provides "wiggle room," helping to avoid open conflicts. Is the consumer, the distributor, or the parent company the primary constituency of an appliance maker? Is the primary constituency of a university its students, bill-paying parents, teachers, companies requiring an educated work force, or society at large? Many groups may have legitimate claims that must be met, but the systems designer must know whose interests should be consistently given priority, and whose interests establish constraints on the business design. Singling out a primary constituency may create political, social, or ideological conflict, but in the interests of system coherence, the issue must be resolved.

Second, a reason for being may force leaders to reevaluate how their business works. They may find long-established principles, procedures, goals, and performance measurements incompatible with their newly clarified reason for being. Developing a reason for being should lead to that kind of reevaluation. The point, after all, is business transformation. But fundamental change comes hard. Confronting the fact that an organization needs to work differently to fulfill a new primary purpose requires determination. It also requires a conviction that the new purpose will keep the company viable in the Information Age.

The following example will illustrate the process of developing a reason for being and provide a sense of the challenges and opportunities an unambiguous reason for being presents.

The LaBarr Partnership Creates a Reason for Being

The LaBarr Partnership (the name is disguised) is a midsized midwestern legal firm led by an executive committee of six senior partners. Early in 1996 the committee decided to articulate for the next generation, only one of whom was a committee member, their understanding of what made the firm special and successful. The committee set aside a day in May to formulate a statement of the essential nature and function of the partnership, in other words, its reason for being.

Prior to that session, each committee member was asked to submit a single sentence beginning with the words, "The LaBarr Partnership exists to." They produced the following statements of purpose:

1. The LaBarr Partnership exists to provide challenging and financially rewarding employment to its attorneys in a collegial atmosphere by providing the highest quality service to its clients.

2. The LaBarr Partnership exists to, within a moderate sized firm, provide superior legal services with a financial reward comparable to that at other quality firms in the area.

3. The LaBarr Partnership exists to serve its clients in the most effective fashion while providing a comfortable income to its partners and employees.

4. The LaBarr Partnership exists to provide a vehicle for a group of congenial and highly skilled attorneys to perform sophisticated legal services (in their respective fields, on a parity with those offered by the best law firms in the United States) to clients who, in the main, engage in commerce in some way, and at the same time to give its lawyers an opportunity to earn above-average incomes while engaging in intellectually satisfying activities, so that earning a living is an enjoyment and not a chore.

5. The LaBarr Partnership exists to provide an effective conduit to allow its partners to reap the optimal rewards of practicing their chosen profession.

6. The LaBarr Partnership exists to provide an effective, cooperative, long-term working environment in which men and

women who are highly qualified (in intellectual capacity and technical training), highly principled (in personal and professional moral standards), and highly motivated (in securing both professional and financial rewards) can engage collectively in the professional and business practice of law serving primarily business, financial, and planning needs of individuals, corporations, partnerships, and other entities as attorneys and counselors.

All the partners felt they could easily relate to all six of the statements. Financial reward—a proxy for shareholder return—appeared as a universal theme. Five of the six included the stipulation of providing good legal service. Four mentioned partners or attorneys first. Five of the six committee members had worked together for decades, and the statements did not appear to reveal any dramatic or surprising contradictions in their views of the firm.

Analyzing the statements in terms of implied outcome, primary constituency, and non-negotiable constraints or qualifiers, however, as shown in Table 7.1, brought some genuine differences to the surface.

The six statements identify several different primary beneficiaries and outcomes (or primary purposes), ranging from serving clients to making money for firm members to providing a good working environment. When shown this table, the partners realized that their original statements reflected the three distinct roles they each played at LaBarr: attorney/practitioner, partner/investor, and governing body member. Though not incompatible, each role implied different expectations from and for the firm. Each of those expectations in turn implied a different system design and different trade-offs. Nevertheless, the partners believed that they would not have much difficulty synthesizing these concepts into a single consistent declaration.

One early attempt read, "The LaBarr Partnership exists to provide high quality, financially rewarding legal services." The attorneys are the implied primary constituency. They provide the legal services, listed as the primary purpose, under the non-negotiable constraint that providing these services will be of high quality and financially rewarding for firm members. On reflection,

TABLE 7.1

LaBarr Executive Committee Reason-for-Being Analysis

Action	Primary Beneficiary	Qualifiers	Outcome
1. PROVIDE employment	attorneys	• challenging and financially rewarding • highest quality client service	Challenging and financially rewarding *employment*
2. PROVIDE legal services	clients	• moderately sized firm • parity of financial reward to other firms	Superior legal *services*
3. SERVE clients	clients	• most effective • comfortable income	Effectively *served clients*
4. PROVIDE legal services vehicle	attorneys	• sophisticated • equal to best in U.S. • mostly commercial clients • opportunity for above-average attorney incomes • intellectually challenging activities	Sophisticated legal services *vehicle* for commercial clients
5. PROVIDE conduit	partners	• effective • significant rewards	Rewarding law *practice*
6. PROVIDE environment	attorneys	• effective, cooperative, long-term • highly principled and motivated • professional and business practice • business, financial, and planning needs of clients	Effective, long-term working *environment* for principled and motivated attorneys

however, this reason for being struck the partners as unenlightening, uninspiring, and incomplete.

After a brief discussion, they came up with an alternative: "The LaBarr Partnership exists to make money for its partners by providing high quality commercial legal services." The individual members as *partners,* not attorneys, had become the primary constituency. Making money was now the primary purpose, with high quality services the non-negotiable constraint.

Then someone in the group asked, "Who is going to see this?" After extended debate, the committee concluded that a reason for being must serve as a North Star for organizational behavior. It therefore ought to be something to which both attorneys and clients could relate. Everyone agreed that clients would not be surprised to learn that the firm was in business to make money, but all were troubled that clients were not mentioned in the reason for being. Furthermore, the partners believed that LaBarr's collegial environment constituted an essential part of its special character, and should be featured.

Their next version addressed these concerns. It read, "The LaBarr Partnership exists to make money for the partners by providing our clients with quality legal solutions in a quality working environment." The primary constituency and purpose remained the same, but the non-negotiable constraints had been expanded to include quality legal solutions and quality working conditions. This unambiguous reason for being did not constrain the firm from practicing any type of law. The committee considered this flexibility important in light of rapid changes taking place in their clients' businesses. Some members felt disappointed that the statement did not clearly distinguish LaBarr from other legal firms, but they also felt comfortable with its accuracy.

For the sake of completeness, the partners began to revisit and explore the idea of a reason for being that positioned the client as primary constituency. Like other law firms, LaBarr did some work on a contingency fee basis. This was not a large part of their business, but the partners had seen that the clients involved felt good rather than apprehensive about the amount of time attorneys spent on their cases. This led them to think about what *outcomes* really interested their clients. Was it "good legal work," or a will that sailed through probate? Was it "knowledge that the best legal talent was working for them," or a contract that held up if challenged in court?

The group had taken fewer than ninety minutes to create what they had considered to be their "final" reason for being. Now they talked for a further four hours, developing the logic to support the idea that their partnership should be client-centric.[3] The final version of the LaBarr reason for being makes the client the primary constituency, good legal outcomes the primary purpose, and a collegial environment and fair returns the non-negotiable constraints. It reads, "The LaBarr Partnership exists to achieve, in a collegial and professional environment, high quality legal outcomes for its clients that provide fair returns to the partnership."

Some Implications of the LaBarr Reason for Being

LaBarr's executive committee recognized that adopting this reason for being would lead to substantial changes in the firm. For one thing, attorney skills would be valued differently. Previously, *finders,* attorneys who brought in new clients, were considered more valuable to the firm than *minders,* those who maintained relationships with current clients, or *grinders,* those who did the research, drafted the contracts, and so forth. A client-centric approach implicitly placed a premium on minding talents. Such a change would be far from trivial. Any organization that reorders its list of essential skills and revises its established ideas of where value resides in the firm faces a difficult and potentially acrimonious reaction.

The committee also understood that by specifying high quality legal *outcomes* as its primary purpose (as opposed, say, to "legal work that meets the highest professional standards"), it had significantly affected how the practice would run. The outcomes associated with a contract or will might not become known for years or even decades after the original documents were drawn up. A genuine commitment to high quality legal outcomes would mean that the firm would have to become skilled at tracking changes over time in client circumstances and the law. It would have to be prepared to modify or renegotiate its original work if doing so increased the chances of a favorable outcome. The revised reason for being would also require a new fee structure and new accounting practices. The system could only work if rewards were tied to outcomes, not just to hours worked or tasks completed.

The committee's final reason for being may or may not be the right one for LaBarr. That is not the issue here. More to the point, the LaBarr experience invites several observations that will apply equally to other efforts to develop a reason for being.

- Generating a reason for being brings to the surface tacit understandings about organizational purpose, often highlighting confusion and potential conflicts among the leadership. Where leadership is confused about the primary purpose, how likely is it that employees are not?

- The process generates potentially fruitful insights about firm priorities and possible alternative ways of creating value.

- Similar formulations of a reason for being can specify different primary purposes, constituencies, and non-negotiable constraints. In other words, they can define different organizations. Words matter.

- An unambiguous reason for being requires a reexamination and often a modification or transformation of how the organization works if it is to align with the specified primary purpose, constituency, and constraints.

GOVERNING PRINCIPLES

Alfred Sloan's ground rules for General Motors are a good illustration of what I mean by *governing principles:* unambiguous statements about the boundaries of the enterprise system. Governing principles define what lies outside the system and establish universal constraints on people inside the system. An important class of constraints specify the *deliverables* that must be provided to constituencies other than the primary constituency. If shareholders are specified as the primary constituency by the reason for being, for example, the interests of customers, employees, society, and other stakeholders are represented by governing principles that define the deliverables owed them by the firm, such as quality, safety, personal development opportunities, environmental impact, and so on. Other governing principles may identify specific *behaviors* that are always required and others that are never permitted. Like the Ten Commandments of the Old Testament, this class of governing principles establishes whether a particular type of activity lies in or out of the system. Like the reason for being, governing principles help build a context for decision-making. They clearly and unequivocally describe essential elements of "who we are" and what we are here to accomplish.

Two characteristics of governing principles deserve special emphasis. First, they clearly define the boundaries of action, but they do not tell employees what to do within those boundaries. Old Mutual's Reg Munro says, "The purpose of governing principles is not to relieve managers of their decision-making capability, but to define how far they can go without seeking approval." Telling managers what to do—cascading instructions down a hierarchical command and control structure—is incompatible with the flexibility that sense-and-respond organizations must have. Governing principles define the boundaries of empowerment to ensure that creative, unprecedented responses remain consistent with organizational purpose and policy. They help the system find the balance between freedom and clear direction that coherent adaptive organizations need.

Second, governing principles are not optional. I use the phrase *governing principles* rather than *guiding principles* or *guidelines* to emphasize that the constraints they define are not suggestions, not a wish list, but organizational imperatives. *Guiding* principles tend to be rules of thumb for enhancing the prospect of success within the system. They distill leadership's wisdom and experience in order to help people do their work better. Since they provide important texture to the context, following them may be beneficial. But, generally, compliance with them is not required. *Governing* principles are different. Only people occupying the policy-making roles that created them can change them or authorize exceptions. Violating a governing principle threatens the system's ability to carry out its purpose in a manner consistent with its values and obligations. Because of this, violations should carry consequences for the violators.

Some of Sloan's principles are governing principles; for example, those stating that "GM will always hold the head of each sector absolutely responsible for its outcome" and that "GM will never have duplication in the price field by automobile line." These are clearly rules, not guidelines. As GM's 1970s experiment with "duplication in the price field" demonstrated, this particular principle outlawed behavior that could jeopardize GM's reason for being.

Governing Principles at New Business Development

At one large holding company, supporters of a proposed new business development function developed a reason for being and a set of governing principles to clarify the purpose of the proposed function and the conditions necessary for its success. Their goal was to develop new, synergy-producing businesses for the company. This entailed finding a way to leverage the capabilities in each of the firm's very autonomous subsidiaries to create profitable new opportunities. New Business Development's primary constituency would be the parent company. Its primary deliverable was the creation of viable new businesses. Its non-negotiable constraint would be that the new businesses generate value. Its reason for being read, "New Business Development exists to create new, value-generating business for the parent company."

The group developed governing principles to reflect their understanding of the essential elements of synergy-producing behavior, of what must always or never be done if synergy is to occur. The list below contains some of them, along with the group's brief descriptions of the consequences of violation.

▶ No new business exists until it has obtained a commitment of resources to a specified strategy and has negotiated commitments with the individuals who will have the key accountabilities for implementing that strategy. *Consequence of violation:* The decision to start is neither credible nor actionable.

▶ Every new business architecture will be based on an explicit evaluation of multiple alternatives. *Consequence of violation:* No understanding of the basis for competitive advantage; lack of buy-in from participating business units.

▶ Every new business will increase the value of each of the component business units. *Consequence of violation:* Lack of buy-in by component units.

▶ Every new business proposal will explicitly state its assumptions about the boundaries placed on it by the parent company. *Consequence of violation:* Lack of buy-in by the parent company; lack of coherence in the new business development process.

▶ No new business will be created without an explicitly stated set of its own governing principles. *Consequence of violation:* Incomplete business design; lack of context.

▶ New Business Development's success will be measured by the accumulated net value of the businesses it creates and by the rate of improvement in creating that value. *Consequence of violation:* Lack of enterprise-level measurement of contribution.

The parent company did not approve the proposal for New Business Development, and as a result, the context developed for it never took effect. When the firm's next cross-unit synergy effort failed to get off the ground, an analysis showed that each of the multiple sources of failure could be directly associated with a violation of one or more of the proposed governing principles.

Criteria for Formulating Governing Principles

Because they help define the context for work at individual firms and must reflect and enforce the particular aims, values, and principles of those firms, a generic list of "best" governing principles cannot be formulated. And, for the same reason, there is also no right number of principles. In some cases, the nature of organizational purpose and leadership's style will be such that only a few governing principles will sufficiently establish the necessary boundaries. Other situations may require ten or more. Nevertheless, my experience in helping several manufacturing and service companies develop organizational context has shown that effective governing principles do have a number of common characteristics.

- They establish boundaries for permissible behavior, governing (not dictating) decisions, activities, and accountabilities.

- They are unambiguous and can therefore be formulated in statements beginning "we will never" or "we will always."

- They are usually qualitative rather than quantitative.

- They apply to all groups and units under the authority of the issuing agent.

- They lend themselves to objective tests for compliance.

- They are likely to endure for at least a few years.

- They are devised (rather than just approved) by policy-making executives.

- Violating them results in serious system consequences.

The rationale behind most of these points has already been discussed. Others deserve additional comment. Several reflect the role of governing principles in delineating only genuinely important boundaries, those that make or break organizational purpose and values. A governing principle should have the prospect of remaining valid for years, not months or weeks. It should apply equally to everyone under the authority of the leaders who developed them, because as underlying principles they are intended to foster coherence. They should be devised by policy-making executives for two reasons. First, one of the three primary responsibilities of these executives is to create context. Second, vigilant enforcement is much more likely if the principles come *from* them, rather than to them as the result of a staff exercise. When the leadership of Old Mutual's Employee Benefits division, for example, developed a governing principle stating, "Employee Benefits will always provide learning and growth opportunities that enable our employees to enhance business performance," their personal commitment to doing so became unequivocal.

Some readers may see a contradiction between the statements that governing principles are often qualitative rather than quantitative and that they lend themselves to objective tests for compliance. As a part of the context, governing principles should not be tied to project or period objectives, which can and do get modified in the course of operations. The statement, for example, that "Every unit will provide returns at least equal to the cost of capital, or we will discontinue the business," constitutes a governing principle. The statement that "XYZ unit will return 15 percent after no more than three years," on the other hand, is an operational commitment made within the bounds specified by the principle.

A greater challenge lies in expressing those boundaries that are difficult to measure directly. This gives rise to the danger, mentioned in chapter 6, that the boundary's measurement will *become* the boundary. One way to avoid this is to go directly to the benefiting constituency for an assessment of progress or compliance. One of the governing principles of IBM's Palisades Executive Education Center, for example, states, "The overall Palisades experience will always be maintained at a world-class level, as assessed by our customers." A "world-class overall experience" is a multifaceted qualitative boundary, but direct and systematic feedback from customers about whether their experience was "world-class" makes this principle measurable. This way of quantifying an essentially subjective assessment is more credible than, say, using internal benchmarking results.

Leaders benefit from the process of developing governing principles, as they do from creating a reason for being. In both cases, their own experience and understanding of what the business is about—"who we are" and "what we are trying to do"— shapes and is sharpened by the conceptual work required. Creating governing principles requires making clear distinctions between genuinely critical boundaries and those habits, preferences, or behaviors appropriate only to local or temporary situations. It also implies a willingness to let go of the reins, because, by restricting themselves to the definition of boundaries, leaders establish a distinct space within which people are empowered to act.

THE HIGH-LEVEL BUSINESS DESIGN

A high-level business design is first and foremost a system design. It depicts the relationships among parts of the system. It stipulates the outcomes they owe to one another and to the customer. It does not show who reports to whom, as organization charts do. Nor does it codify the flow of work, as do process maps. A high-level business design originates in the firm's reason for being, the stated purpose the system exists to achieve. All outcomes within the system serve this larger aim. As in any efficient system, all internal outcomes will be necessary but not sufficient to achieve the system's purpose. Sufficiency stems from the way these outcomes are connected.

The fairly obvious point that all parts of a system must serve the system's purpose underscores a basic principle of system design: Design must be done from the top down, not from the bottom up. A high-level business design starts from the reason for being, not from a collection of capabilities. Russell Ackoff warns that efforts to build a system by integrating a collection of existing components are intrinsically anti-systemic.[4] Yet this is common practice in many companies. Designing the system called a wristwatch starts with a purpose—telling time—and uses that function to determine the outcomes required by the next level of subsystem. This cascade of function into subfunctions and then into further subfunctions must occur in conformance with the specifications or constraints given to the designer. It requires, further, an awareness of the interactions among subfunctions. No watch designer starts with a list of parts.

The fundamental unity of systems underlies another principle: System-level performance cannot be enhanced by independently improving the performance of individual elements. To return to the watch metaphor, it would be disastrous to take the watch apart, arrange the pieces on the dining-room table, and benchmark every part against best of breed, with the intention of replacing each piece that didn't measure up with its superior counterpart from another watch. Without a radically new design, one cannot build a RolexMovadoSeiko.

In a small business, the people running it may keep in their heads a shared model of a coherent business design. But as businesses grow and become more complex, working from a purely mental model becomes impossible. The usual response, breaking the system down into smaller, more "manageable" units, will fail. Complex systems cannot be fixed through fragmentation. Not surprisingly, managers overwhelmed by the complexity and multiplicity of the problems they face often embrace simplification by fragmentation. This compartmentalized approach merely demonstrates managers' self-image as problem-solvers, rather than as context builders. The result, unfortunately, contributes to organizational incoherence. Isolating decision-making or problem-solving by process, geographical area, function, or corporate project cannot be effective because those elements do not exist in isolation.[5] The following example will be all too familiar to many senior managers.

Sometimes the System Is to Blame

Recently, an executive excused himself from an Advanced Business Institute seminar because the general manager of his business unit had called, telling him of a crisis requiring his presence at an urgent meeting. The unit was going to miss its quarterly profit targets, and its senior management had to decide what action to take. Before leaving, the executive laid out what he expected would occur.

> Here's what's going to happen. We'll meet this afternoon and tonight to look at the numbers. We'll find the area manager that has the biggest shortfall and haul him or her in for a grilling tomorrow. We'll be told the reason for the missed target—maybe that the service business unit failed to deliver on some huge contracts. Then we'll bring in the service unit executive, who will tell us that the service contract wasn't completed because a product division didn't deliver a key product on time. When the product division president tells us that the delivery date slipped because the centralized world-wide development group was late on a design update, we'll throw up our hands, beat everybody up, and do what we knew we were going to

do all along: cut marketing and administrative budgets by 10 percent across the board.

This may sound like an example of passing the buck, but, in fact, no one person or group was to blame for the shortfall. The system failed, and accountability for systemic results cannot be meaningfully assigned to any one component of the system. Such exasperated resorts to "management by meat cleaver" follow from failing to understand the impact that changes in one part of a system will have on other parts and therefore on the whole.

Foundations of the High-Level Business Design

Alfred Sloan provided us with early examples of a reason for being and governing principles. Because a high-level business design reflects systems thinking that matured after his years at GM, Sloan's GM may not provide a design prototype.[6] Nevertheless, his insistence on building a conceptual model of the business shows that he thought of it as a single entity, not as a collection of productive activities. One of his principles—"Always deploy capital and operate in the best interests of GM as a whole"—also demonstrates his belief in a holistic rather than a fragmentary approach. He focused, too, on organizational purpose, not on situational problem-solving. Pushing too hard on the idea of Sloan as an early systems thinker accomplishes nothing useful, but his creation of a clear purpose and principles for General Motors as a whole clearly points toward the idea of an organization as a single system of interrelated parts.

A context-building high-level business design constitutes the right kind of simplification. It simplifies by highlighting the essential relationships and outcomes that make the system work. It places leaders' focus on the *interactions* while delegating the *actions* to empowered people. These people now must accept responsibility for the *consequences* of their actions, not just for carrying them out. By the same token, elusive problems, apparently no one person's or unit's fault, can now be understood as system design problems. Unnerving as it might be for some executives, this same principle implies that the most important outcomes, those produced at the enterprise level through system synergy, cannot plausibly be assigned to anyone except the leadership itself. None of the parts can authentically be held accountable for a result that does or doesn't happen because of the way in which the system was designed.

Just as no specific number of governing principles is right, no one level of detail or complexity is right for a high-level business design. The design should represent the level of detail that leadership finds it important to specify. The design of lower level functions is delegated to the people accountable for producing the outcomes required of the subfunctions below those specified in the high-level design. Both high-level and lower-level business designs should include only essential outcomes and relationships. In any given case, the complexity of the design will reflect the complexity of the system *and* the level of detail that particular leaders and employees judge to be necessary.

Because a high-level business design must begin with the organization's reason for being, it cannot be created in isolation from the broader process of developing an organization's context. The context-building process carried out by the Employee Benefits unit of Old Mutual Insurance illustrates an actual exercise in building a high-level business design and summarizes the experience of an early adopter of sense-and-respond.

DOWN TO CASES: EMPLOYEE BENEFITS

Old Mutual Insurance has been the major player in South Africa's insurance industry for more than 150 years. It is one of the fifty largest insurance companies in the world, even though 95 percent of its business has been conducted in South Africa. It operates as a portfolio manager of units offering insurance and investment products to three market segments: small businesses, large organizations, and individuals. As its name suggests, Employee Benefits is the Old Mutual division that provides benefits packages to employees (or members, in the case of trade unions and associations). The packages are offered through intermediaries, including employers, trustees, and unions. They are not sold directly to employees or members.

As the whole world knows, South Africa has experienced a great deal of discontinuity and uncertainty for the last several years. Extraordinary political and social changes have been accompanied by dramatic upheavals in the business environment. The lifting of exchange controls is only one of the changes directly affecting the insurance industry. Yet it has been a major one. Because of this change, foreign financial institutions, for the first time, have become important competitors in Old Mutual's market. International companies have introduced new products and distribution channels that eliminate the need for brokers and agents. This new competition threatens Old Mutual's domination of the country's agent distribution system, one of its long-standing strategic advantages. Their agents have traditionally "owned" the clients, but new consumer choices now threaten that hold. Faced with these and other changes, Old Mutual has been changing itself. The company has been developing a new competence as an international money manager, investing time and money in building overseas relationships and revamping business systems to handle multiple currencies.

Reg Munro, general manager of Employee Benefits, was convinced that the social, political, and business changes occurring in the country made it pointless to try to predict what benefits packages South African organizations would need. Like the leaders of Westpac in the 1980s and like those of a growing number of businesses since then, Munro faced a fundamental Information Age dilemma. Making and selling benefits packages would not work in a world where future customer preferences and competitive offerings were uncertain. Munro and others from Employee Benefits were educated on the sense-and-respond model, and they recognized its relevance to their situation. He and his leadership team concluded that they could best cope with the discontinuity they were experiencing by transforming the unit into a sense-and-respond organization.

Employee Benefits' leadership first developed and reviewed plausible scenarios for future regulatory and business environments. They determined that, in each scenario, the benefits providers with the best information about *individual* member profiles would probably have an advantage over their competitors. This conclusion was consistent with the logic underlying sense-and-respond: Companies position themselves to create new value by improving their understanding of individual customers' preferences.

The leadership team invited key employees from each Employee Benefits subunit to a week-long session devoted to creating an organizational context. In an earlier communication to the management and employees of Employee Benefits, Munro had stated the rationale for devoting this amount of time and talent to that session.

> To create a purposeful, adaptive, empowered system that works, it is crucial that we have clarity and agreement about its purpose; its primary constituency; the constraints placed on empowered behavior by our values and obligations to all constituencies; the subsystem outcomes necessary; and the business design that links them to produce the outcomes defined by our purpose.[7]

Reason for Being

Because Employee Benefits is a unit of Old Mutual, Munro's executive group had to be sure the reason for being they developed would be consistent with that of the parent company. But because Old Mutual itself had not gone through a formal context-building process, Munro's team had to use their knowledge of the company to posit one. The group discussed three possibilities at length. The first stated that Old Mutual existed to maximize the return on the assets it managed. According to the second, it existed to enhance the value of a portfolio of businesses that increase the financial security of people. The third held that Old Mutual existed to enhance the financial security of people. The group eventually settled on the last of these, in part because it rendered almost verbatim the purpose articulated by Old Mutual's founder 150 years earlier. They also inferred a set of Old Mutual governing principles from existing policies and practices. Munro, a member of the Old Mutual executive team, accepted responsibility for the validity of these inferences.

Having assumed an Old Mutual context, the Employee Benefits group began consideration of its own reason for being. Some defined the unit's primary constituency as the organizations through which it offered benefits packages. These were, after all, the institutions that paid for the firm's products and services. This logic was expressed as follows: "Employee Benefits exists to provide employers/unions with more financially secure employees/members through the funds with which we contract."

Another option had roughly the same primary constituency but defined the primary purpose as providing benefit plans rather than financially secure employees/members. It stated: "Employee Benefits exists to provide institutions with benefit plans that enhance the financial security of their employees/members."

Others in the group identified the primary constituency as the individual members' beneficiaries: "Employee Benefits exists to enable members of employee groups to achieve financial independence for themselves and dependents through provision of financial products and services."

The group became sensitized to the effects of subtle differences in wording, as well as to the nuances of different definitions of purpose, constituency, and constraints. They discussed at length the likely impact of such differences on organizational behavior. Employee Benefits' existing charter required that it contract with and be paid by intermediaries. It had no direct contact with individual members. The group nevertheless began to generate enthusiasm for making the individual member the division's primary constituency. Even when the apparent contradiction was pointed out to them, the group's preference for this option continued to grow. If, as their scenario exercise had revealed, current information about individuals would be required in any scenario, Employee Benefits' future success would require direct relationships with the ultimate beneficiaries of their products. The reason for being they eventually adopted makes individuals the primary constituency. It establishes enhanced financial security as the primary purpose, with the non-negotiable constraint of achieving this purpose through group arrangements. Their final statement read, "Employee Benefits exists to enhance the financial security of people through group arrangements."

Like all good reasons for being, this one is clear and unequivocal. Furthermore, it zeroes in on the underlying value offered by Employee Benefits rather than on a proxy for that value. Members of the group agreed that the phrase *enhancing people's financial security* was vastly superior to *providing high quality financial products and services.* This was a more fundamental value, and they believed it would make a better touchstone for employees faced with trade-offs and difficult decisions. They recognized, too, that the reason for being they had created called for a different, more adaptive business than the one that currently existed. The statement constituted a challenge, not merely a clarification. But leadership had undertaken this exercise precisely because they saw that their organization had to change in fundamental ways if it was to survive and succeed in a changing world.

Governing Principles

The leadership group then developed a set of governing principles consistent with Old Mutual's implicit governing principles. The Employee Benefits principles reflected and reinforced the elements of its reason for being by requiring that attention be paid to customer needs and assessments. They also spelled out the key external measures for tracking the system's success in fulfilling its purpose. Several of the Employee Benefits' governing principles are reproduced below.

- ▶ We will always enhance our products and services based on feedback about clients' needs and competitor offerings.

- ▶ We will always measure our offerings and responses through client assessment.

One principle reinforced the non-negotiable constraint of "group arrangements" by establishing a specific boundary.

- ▶ We will always observe the limits imposed by the mandate agreed with our principal (the contracting entity).

Another established a relationship between Employee Benefits' responsibility to clients and its obligations to its parent company.

- ▶ We will always present a complete description of a relevant Old Mutual offering in our proposals to clients.

The principles also connect employee success and advancement to the organization's purpose.

▶ We will always have a business-performance-based component to employee earnings.

▶ We will always provide learning and growth opportunities for our employees to enhance business performance.

Finally, they formulated a governing principle that would help define and support Employee Benefits' unique attributes.

▶ We will never outsource, and will always invest in, those competencies and resources designated as distinctive: relationship management, our brand, our capability to construct profitable responses to clients, and our intellectual capital.

High-Level Business Design

The Employee Benefits' leadership had committed its division to significant change. They were determined to become a sense-and-respond organization, and they had embraced a newly defined purpose. They would work to enhance the financial security of individuals through group benefits plans. The high-level business design they developed established the structure of responsibilities and commitments needed to carry out this reason for being. Not surprisingly, it included several important roles that had not previously existed in the organization. A design for carrying out a radically new way of doing business that relied only on rethinking the connections among existing capabilities would be suspect. As I have already noted, the high-level business design needs to come from the top down, from the outcomes needed to accomplish the system's purpose. It cannot emerge from attempts to fit old puzzle-pieces into a new shape.

The leadership first created a new role that they named *integrator*. Integrators would be responsible for diagnosing the clients' needs and constraints and for dispatching product and service components from Old Mutual, third party suppliers, or competitors to create the best possible response. This role would be central to Employee Benefits' sense-and-respond capability. It would be populated by people who knew what signals to look for and who had the talent to translate these signals into an interpretation of the financial security needs of individual client members. Integrators would also need a thorough knowledge of Old Mutual's capabilities as well as those of its suppliers. For this key role, talent would be drawn from Employee Benefits' consulting group.

Other new roles would work closely with the integrators to accomplish the organization's purpose. The Old Mutual *buyer* would be responsible for identifying and acquiring the best external product and service components at the most favorable cost. They would owe these modular outcomes to the integrator. A new *product and service development and delivery* capability would owe new products and services to the integrator. This role would also have two other responsibilities. First, it would deliver the response—the customized product and service package—to client organizations. Second, it would provide individual members with timely information about the effects on their financial security of benefits package performance. Finally, a new *sensing-and-interpreting* role was charged with capturing internal and external signals and providing the integrator and other roles with information and analysis to support their adaptive loop decision-making.

Figure 7.1 presents, in somewhat simplified form, the completed first version of Employee Benefits' high-level business design. In keeping with the aim of such designs, it shows the connections among parts of the system in terms of the outcomes each owes the others. These outcome-relationships define the essential structure of the organization, the network of interactions needed to accomplish the system's purpose.

Strikingly, the four new roles—integrator, Old Mutual buyer, product and service development and delivery, and sensing and interpreting—form the heart of the new system. They are not bolted on to the periphery of an existing organization. They connect intimately to one another in ways dictated by the logic of providing the enhanced financial security demanded by the new reason for being.

FIGURE 7.1

OLD MUTUAL EMPLOYEE BENEFITS HIGH-LEVEL BUSINESS DESIGN

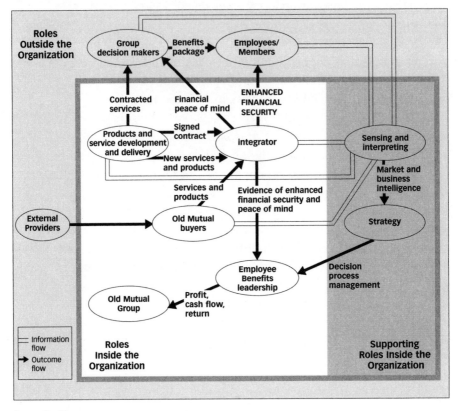

Source: Reg Munro.

Many of the roles identified in the high-level business design are empowered to develop their own lower-level business designs. These roles can specify subsystem designs for producing the functions they themselves are held accountable for in the high-level design. Each lower-level design provides *context* for the groups and individuals involved, absorbing uncertainty by situating their specific responsibilities within the larger web of responsibilities that make up the organization. A context has little value if the individuals involved do not understand where they fit in.

LEADING BY DEVELOPING AND ADAPTING ORGANIZATIONAL CONTEXT

Together, the reason for being, governing principles, and high-level business design define organizational context. Properly formulated, they make explicit and unambiguous the system's purpose, boundaries, and structure, giving employees a framework for empowered decision-making. A clear context that comes from leaders and is backed by their authority takes the sense-and-respond organization a long way towards coherent action.

Building context is a demanding and challenging task, and not only because it requires conceptual skills. As the LaBarr experience and especially the Employee Benefits example show, the process will be an engine of change, not merely an intellectual exercise. It brings spoken and unspoken assumptions and priorities to light and requires leaders to choose among them. It challenges the status quo, testing roles and responsibilities in terms of their contributions to a clarified purpose.

Leadership has exclusive responsibility for developing and promulgating this context because only it has (or should have) enough perspective to see the organization as a whole. But more importantly, only a firm's leaders have the authority to decide what the firm will be. Clearly defining organizational context establishes that identity. Defining context *chooses* an adaptive design for the organization. In most cases, the new design will create new roles and change old ones.

Accountability for context doesn't end with its creation. It can't, given the underlying premise of sense-and-respond. Unanticipated change may render obsolete in weeks a governing principle that was expected to endure for years. Signals from customers about changing preferences may require a new response that would violate one or more principles, making it necessary for leadership to consider relaxing a constraint that now prevents the firm from producing more value. New ideas from anywhere in the organization about how to do things better, or recurring conflicts that require extra-system interventions by leadership, may signal that the high-level business design needs modification. People in adaptive enterprises, most especially their leaders, must be comfortable with the idea that adaptation is a never ending process. A presently successful context does not guarantee its continuing appropriateness. Nor does it predict the nature of the next context. Staying too long with "the context that got us here" can be fatal, and *too long* is becoming shorter and shorter.

Leadership must place the right people in the roles defined by the high-level business design. It also has responsibility for systematic coordination of the dynamics of who owes what to whom as the system adapts to unanticipated events. And it must ensure that these dynamics are consistent with the current context. This crucial governance function was once the purview of the large central staff. The sense-and-respond model's replacement of the outmoded central staff in carrying out this governance function is the subject of the next chapter.

*Until one is committed, there is hesitancy, the chance
to draw back, always ineffectiveness. . . . The moment
one definitely commits oneself, then Providence
moves too.*

— GOETHE

COORDINATION

Keeping Track of Who Owes
What to Whom

ONCE LEADERS ESTABLISH A CONTEXT, THEY MUST PROPAGATE
and enforce it. In sense-and-respond companies, this systematic propagation and enforcement constitute *governance.* Because
the context may change frequently as the organization adapts,
rapid and systematic dissemination of information about change is
vital, and requires the use of technology. This chapter describes a
technology-based governance system that supports the creation
and tracking of commitments among organizational capabilities,
commitments to produce the outcomes required by the high-level
business design. By coordinating the dynamics of who owes what
to whom and detecting breakdowns early on, leadership can manage the *interactions* without interfering with the *actions* of empowered and accountable people. In the previous chapter, we saw
that managing the interactions involves modifying the company's
principles and high-level design, moving individuals in and out of
roles, and establishing a systematic way of coordinating their in-

teractions. Except in the case of critical systemic breakdowns, it does *not* mean establishing local priorities or telling people how to do things.

Many organizations and individuals think of jobs as collections of activities. The typical job description lists activities, sometimes in detail, effectively telling people what they should do during the work day. Such descriptions often provide little guidance about *why* these tasks need doing or for whose benefit the employee performs them. Work is done for managers, who specify the tasks to be accomplished and supervise employees' activities to ensure that they are done well. Everything we know about sense-and-respond organizations and adaptive systems points to another approach.

Organizational responsiveness comes from giving individuals and groups the freedom to behave in ad hoc ways to respond to unforeseen circumstances. Because followers know more than leaders do about how to respond, it makes no sense for managers to define their subordinates' behaviors in advance. It is the ends— not the means—that matter. As the discussion of high-level business designs emphasized, specifying outcomes, rather than the activities undertaken to produce them, is the essence of adaptive system design. In a sense-and-respond organization, roles make commitments to one another to produce outcomes. These inter-role commitments are the interactions that matter most and must be managed. For this reason, organizational roles are defined in terms of accountability for commitments to particular outcomes, rather than in terms of activities.

DEFINING ROLES IN TERMS OF COMMITMENTS AND ACCOUNTABILITIES

In the sense-and-respond governance system, a commitment is an agreement between two parties to produce a defined outcome and to accept that outcome if it meets the agreed-to conditions. One party, the supplier, takes responsibility for producing the outcome. The other party, the customer, must accept the outcome if it meets the conditions of satisfaction. *Accountability* is established by this interaction. It is a personal acceptance of the consequences of making a commitment. Accountabilities exist only in connection with commitments between people. A person must be accountable to *someone,* which means no one can be generically accountable for sales, manufacturing, or quality for the same reason no process, machine, or system can be accountable for anything. Accountability arises from an agreement between two people about who owes what to whom.

Many people find it surprisingly difficult to think about their work in terms of outcomes and commitments rather than activities and plans. When asked to explain their work roles, they almost invariably describe one or more procedures, that is, a sequence of activities, and a set of measurements for evaluating how well they carry out those procedures. Some other individuals, of course, do realize that if they cannot define the outcomes produced by their activities and the customers for those outcomes, they should ask themselves why they do them. Nevertheless, because most people do not think this way about their jobs, many will resist redefining their roles in terms of outcomes owed to customers other than their managers. Such people tend to be risk-averse. They feel uncomfortable with the idea of performance evaluation unconnected to how well they execute specified tasks. They want control over the variables that affect their rewards, and being responsible for executing well-defined activities gives them more control. They want their compensation to be based on their ability to carry out these tasks skillfully—an attitude Frederick Taylor thought all "high price" workers should have.

Business will continue to need people with this attitude, but not in roles requiring adaptiveness. Good performance in these roles depends on a capability to create new ways of responding to unprecedented requests. The adaptive taxi driver can deliver such outcomes, while reliable bus drivers are held accountable for taking the actions prescribed by management.

People are unaccustomed to thinking about their roles in terms of commitments and accountability. Long after Frederick Taylor left the scene, many of us remain quite comfortable with being evaluated on how well we do what we are supposed to do, rather than on the consequences of doing it. The 1993 job description below, for example, outlined the role of offering owner at

IBM's Advanced Business Institute. As the job title suggests, the offering owner has overall responsibility for a particular course offering. Like many job descriptions, this one is couched as a list of activities.

- Market the course in the internal IBM electronic news network.
- Write course brochure.
- Write fact sheet.
- Communicate with the IBM sponsor of the offering.
- Assemble the teach-team.
- Facilitate the definition of teach-team responsibilities.
- Ensure vitality of the course content.
- Conduct formal post-class debriefs.
- Conduct an annual analysis of course quality and substance.
- React quickly and appropriately to changing audience requirements.
- Deliver message that enhances revenue opportunities for IBM.
- Run pilot offerings.
- Develop effective marketing strategy to attract target audience.
- Execute the current class-management process.
- Verify that new content development is consistent with ABI curriculum strategy.
- Communicate rapidly with ABI leadership.

No doubt this list would be useful to someone coming into the role. But, at the very least, such a role definition puts the cart before the horse. It emphasizes activities but ignores the outcomes that those activities exist to accomplish. Most of us have run into maddening individuals who refuse to do something because it is "not in my job description." They mean that the request does not match any item in the list of activities they are authorized to perform. By sticking to the letter of the law, however, these people may fail to achieve the purposes for which their jobs exist. They may not meet the needs of their customers or earn revenue for their companies. The fault is largely theirs, of course, but defining jobs in terms of activities rather than outcomes is a contributor.

Furthermore, describing a role as a list of activities sheds little light on why the position exists at all. Although one might infer the expected outcome or name the implied customer of some of the offering owner's activities, interpretations will vary. Guessing—even intelligent, informed guessing—about what the role owes to whom inevitably leads to ambiguity about its purpose and its relationship to other roles in the organization. A group of experienced Advanced Business Institute faculty needed five full days of meetings to agree on a redefinition of the offering owner's role recast in terms of accountability for outcomes to customers. The amount of effort required and the range of interpretations put forward—early discussions yielded more than ten possible key outcomes—show how much ambiguity existed about this one apparently straightforward organizational role. The specificity of the activities list did not make the role's *purpose* unambiguous. Eventually, the group defined the role's essential contribution to the Palisades reason for being with three outcomes for three customers. The revised role description appears in Table 8.1.

As Table 8.1 indicates, customers may be internal or external. Conditions of satisfaction provide local context for specific outcomes in the form of constraints that will be made specific through negotiations between customer and supplier every time the outcome is produced. The conditions of satisfaction can take various forms. They may specify *deliverables* other than the primary outcome, for example, a guarantee of minimum performance. They may set *acceptable boundaries for a measurement*, such as minimum return on investment or a specified level of customer satisfaction. They may dictate *mandatory behaviors*. And they will always include a *deadline*. Deadline and adherence to the organization's governing principles are the only mandatory condi-

TABLE 8.1

ROLE DEFINITION FOR ABI OFFERING OWNER

ROLE TITLE: ABI OFFERING OWNER

OUTCOME	CUSTOMER	CONDITIONS OF SATISFACTION
Educational Experience	IBM Customer Executive Attendees	Attendee evaluation of overall educational experience; attendee evaluation of content, importance, and delivery of topics
Marketing Opportunity	IBM Client Representative	Marketing Revenue Index*
Educational Events	ABI Leadership	Appropriate level of executives attending (decision-makers); overall customer satisfaction measurement

*A statistical measure of the degree to which a given event influenced customer buying decisions favorable to IBM within the four-month period following their attendance.

tions of satisfaction. Deadlines are not normally specified when the role is defined, but are negotiated when people assigned to the roles take action.

Readers may find it a useful exercise to define one of their roles in terms of accountabilities to customers. Complete this statement:

> In my role as [role name], I am accountable to [customer] for [outcome]. The conditions of satisfaction are [deadline, measurements, etc.].

How difficult or easy was it to identify a customer role? How difficult or easy to describe an outcome in terms of a deliverable (that is, using a noun) rather than as an activity (using a verb)? Would your customer specify the same outcome? Would you and your customer agree that the conditions of satisfaction you listed were the critical ones? Most of the ambiguity about what you owe to whom probably resides in the items you found hardest to complete. The conflict and frustrations of working in highly-matrixed organizations, discussed in chapter 7, follow largely from the failure to define roles in terms of outcomes, customers, and conditions of satisfaction. Application of this discipline often uncovers serious conflicts in particular roles or, more typically, between roles assigned to a given individual. Good business design, whether high level or lower level, avoids making a given role accountable for incompatible outcomes. Good personnel management avoids subjecting individuals to role conflict. This does not mean designing trade-off free roles, but it does mean avoiding conflicts of interest.

Benefits of Codifying Commitments and Accountabilities

Defining roles in terms of commitments and accountabilities goes a long way toward helping individuals and groups understand their relationships to one another and their personal contribution to the organization's reason for being. Moreover, specifying the relationships between roles exclusively in terms of customer-supplier commitments makes possible a powerful simplification of the complicated task of coordination in very large enterprises. Defining and tracking commitments rigorously creates universal, standardized connections among capabilities and modularizes the organization in the process. The quality of this modularization, of course, depends on the skill of business designers who specify the capabilities and the customer-supplier relationships among them.

Coordinating the many thousands of commitments needed to achieve organizational purpose demands a standard language of commitment. If everyone were left free to describe and create commitments in their own way, commitments could not serve as system-wide capability connectors. What is needed, in other words, is a common, universal protocol for describing how commitments between parties originate and how they should be carried out. *Protocol* has long meant a set of common terms and ground rules that allow two different parties to negotiate an agreement or work together. In the computer world, it refers to the shared interface rules and formats that allow two computers to communicate. Both definitions are relevant to our discussion.

THE COMMITMENT MANAGEMENT PROTOCOL

The needed commitment management protocol already exists. Developed in the 1980s but still not widely known today, it serves our purpose admirably.[1] As a general and universal description of the communications needed to define and produce a particular outcome, it can represent accountabilities ranging from "provide for the common defense" to "set up a lunch date with Bob." It applies equally well to stable, repeated processes and to ad hoc responses to unanticipated requests. Its rigor imposes clarity on processes that may otherwise be rife with ambiguity and misunderstanding. (How many commitment/accountability relationships have gone awry because of disagreements about precisely what was committed to and precisely how and when that commitment would be honored?) That same rigor makes possible the use of technology to register and track commitments and to coordinate the dynamic interactions among the components of adaptive systems.

The principle of defining roles in terms of outcomes rather than tasks allows us to apply the commitment management protocol to help govern sense-and-respond organizations. Commitments involve outcomes. If a supplier who agrees to deliver a particular product of a certain quality by a certain date succeeds in fulfilling that commitment, why would the customer care how work was organized to achieve the result?

The commitment management protocol consists of four task phases—define, negotiate, perform, and assess—and seven communications of a special kind—offer, request, agree, report, accept, reject, and withdraw. The activity that goes on in the task phases may be specified in part, entirely, *or not at all*. The communications between customer and supplier are sufficient to define and track the status of the interaction between them. The protocol, shown in Figure 8.1, completely describes the life cycle of any commitment.

FIGURE 8.1

THE COMMITMENT MANAGEMENT PROTOCOL

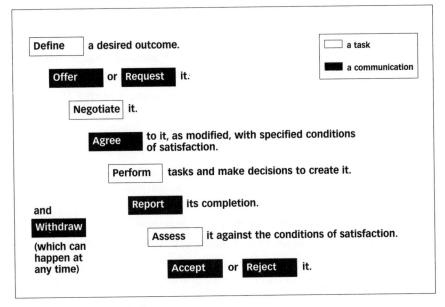

Sources: Alan Scherr, Fernando Flores.

The task phases (shown in the white boxes in the figure) consist of activities. Ad hoc decisions about what to do must reflect the priorities established by the organization's reason for being, and be limited by its governing principles. Technology can ensure that this is the case by automatically adding the firm's governing principles to the conditions of satisfaction associated with every commitment. This ensures that all outcomes called for in the business design, and all activities producing them, will be assessed for compliance with organizational context before they are accepted. With an assist from technology, the integrity of commitments and the interdependencies among parts of large organizations can once again be effectively managed. Only now leadership governs by context and coordination, not command and control.

The communications acts (shown in the figure's black boxes) are performed by saying them. Linguists call them *commissive verbs* or *speech acts*. Saying, for example, "I agree," constitutes a speech act, an act carried out by saying it. Saying "I am running," in contrast, describes an action and is not a speech act. The seven verbs shown with dark backgrounds in Figure 8.1, including the speech act *withdraw,* which causes a breakdown and prematurely terminates the execution of the protocol, can be used to represent any commitment both rigorously and exhaustively. Again, the procedures in each task phase may be left unspecified, or they may be spelled out in as much detail as the interacting parties find useful. For completely ad hoc processes, of course, only a general statement—for example, "Perform whatever tasks are necessary to meet the agreed-on commitment"—can be made in advance. The amount of detail added, if any, about those tasks does not affect the protocol's ability to track the creation and execution of any commitment.

This protocol makes possible the governance system required by the sense-and-respond model. Appendix C illustrates its application in more detail, showing how the protocol can improve a business process by explicitly incorporating human accountability and commitment.

Rigor is necessary but not sufficient for successful implementation of a commitment-based governance system. The commitments made and registered must also be authentic. By *authentic,* I mean two things. First, both parties must mean what they say and say what they mean—they must be *sincere.* Second, each party must know and understand what they mean—they must be *competent.*[2]

Any social system—no matter how rigorous—can be subverted by inauthentic behavior. Sincerity alone cannot prevent this. Customers must communicate what they know about what they need, and suppliers what they know about their ability to deliver. Agreeing to a commitment that one doubts can be or knows *cannot* be met, or knowingly requesting more than one needs, will defeat any systematic effort at commitment management. People in an organization may believe that expressing their uncertainties will be unpleasant, dangerous, or unproductive. They may then, for example, remain silent about problems that may delay an outcome or risks that should be considered. Or they may try to gain an advantage by manipulating rather than participating in the system. In either case, the governance system described here will suffer badly.

Unfortunately, inauthentic behavior in organizations is extremely common. Harvard's Chris Argyris, who has studied organizational behavior and learning for more than forty years, finds it to be the norm rather than the exception. He expresses the authenticity issue as a gap between "espoused theory and theory in practice." The causes are many, various, and systemic. They range from corporate cultures and compensation systems that punish people for telling it like it is to the nearly universal human tendency to avoid unpleasantness, embarrassment, conflict, and danger. Over the years, Argyris has compiled voluminous evidence of the mixed messages and tacit censorship that defeat the kind of communications and learning that would help employees work together more effectively.[3]

At a minimum, rigor itself can support authenticity in communications about commitments. Weaving into the fabric of the organization an unambiguous purpose, unbreachable principles, and clarity about who owes what to whom can only help legitimize and reinforce authentic communication. Employees who clearly understand their roles in the system and who have the authority and knowledge necessary to carry them out will be less likely to work against the system and more likely to align their own purposes with that of the organization. People have a natural desire to be part of a larger social structure. Systems with unambiguous purpose and structure fulfill this desire.[4] Argyris believes many people will want to use the commitment management protocol to communicate authentically with each other if they can be confident that such behavior will be rewarded or at least not penalized. He adds a caveat, however: Few people excel at authentic communication, and so the desire to communicate authentically will not necessarily ensure it. Like any other change of long-standing habit, this one will require practice and reinforcement.

A lengthy discussion about fostering authenticity lies beyond the scope of this book, but leadership will have to deal with this issue. Current and future work on the social structures of organizations will have more to say on this subject. For our present purposes, it is enough to emphasize that authenticity and trust are essential elements of a well-functioning adaptive organization. Chapter 10 features a case study of an organization in the process of implementing the context and coordination governance system that will make the importance of these "soft" issues abundantly clear.

CHALLENGES OF APPLYING THE PROTOCOL

Our earlier discussion touched on the difficulty of thinking about roles in terms of outcomes and commitments. The protocol does not just use a new vocabulary to describe the same old work. It reflects a shift from being held accountable for one's actions to being held accountable for the consequences of one's actions.

Authentic commitment to some outcomes is not possible. Uncertainties will sometimes be so great that negotiations must center on how the customer and the supplier will share the risk rather than on the desirability and specification of the outcome itself. Conditions of satisfaction, in any case, should include the terms under which renegotiation will take place as some uncertainties are resolved and others arise. Consider the patient-doctor negotiating process. No physician can authentically promise to keep us healthy, much as both supplier and customer may desire that outcome. Often, doctors cannot even commit to specific surgical outcomes. The process of negotiation relies on the principle of informed consent rather than on guaranteed results. The physician proposes alternatives, offers an assessment of benefits and risks, and perhaps suggests what she or he would do in the patient's place. The patient accepts a particular level of risk. The physician undertakes the risk of demonstrating competence in applying accepted medical practice. The outcomes to which the parties authentically commit may be no more than these: professional assessments, recommendations, demonstrations of due diligence, and performance that meets or exceeds specific standards of practice. Forcing anything more, as happens when the culture values aggressiveness over authenticity, changes the nature of the real commitment from an outcome into a best effort.

Some people, particularly in the early stages of unlearning inauthenticity, react adversely to the process of authentic negotiation. Many feel impatient with so-called nonproductive time spent in negotiation rather than action. But it is in the negotiation phase that the outcome, its specifications, and the risks are explored and made explicit. Ambiguities left festering because both parties want "to get on with it" usually come home to roost in execution, where the delays and costs associated with their resolution will be much greater. Ambiguity, particularly if "undiscussable," is a pernicious, ineffective way to deal with uncertainty. Better is a sequence of commitments that permit mid-course adjustments.[5]

Some individuals don't have the debating and salesmanship skills they assume necessary to successful negotiation. Notice the implicit assumption here that the best possible result of negotiation is a win-win agreement that represents the highest common denominator of two separate agendas. But the whole idea of a shared context is a *win* agenda that gets everyone in the organization on the *same* agenda—the agenda of achieving the reason for being. Once this is accomplished, debates about how best to support organizational purpose will not involve asking for more than one needs or offering less than one can provide.

Hovering near the surface here is the issue of *trust* and its role in negotiations. Trust means many things to many people, but it is clearly role dependent. Your children may trust you to feed and clothe them, but they probably won't trust you to pick out their music. You trust pilots to fly you safely to your destination, but you might hesitate to have them do your taxes or remove your appendix. For our purposes, *trust* means the certitude of a person in a specified role about another's competence and intent to deliver what they have agreed to in a negotiated commitment. Competence might be assessed objectively by asking for certain kinds of information during negotiation. But how does one assess intent? The impact of context on organizational culture becomes very important here. I trust your intent to the extent that I have confidence that you and I share the values and priorities set forth in the reason for being and governing principles. The length and detail of the conditions of satisfaction list is a good indicator of the amount of trust between two individuals in a customer-supplier relationship. This list will certainly be shorter for the merchants of Prato or for bond traders who consummate million-dollar transactions on the basis of a short phone call than for two people who don't know each other or who have had difficult dealings in the past. Trust has obvious commercial value. It has sustained the merchants of Prato for centuries.

Confusion and conflict can arise because individuals play multiple roles. We are not accustomed to consciously switching our frameworks from role to role. Yet we must do so if we want to authentically negotiate commitments in each of them. In a given negotiation, we may find ourselves unwittingly arguing points of view specific to another of our roles. Neither we nor those with whom we are negotiating may see clearly what role motivates a particular position at any given moment. Good systems designs minimize intra-person role conflict. For individuals assigned to different roles with different and incompatible trade-offs, such as revenue growth in the role of sales manager and sales expense reduction as administration manager, authentic negotiation in either role becomes extraordinarily difficult. Two solutions are possible. The conflicting roles can be integrated into a single, larger role, for example, general manager, so that the trade-offs can be made consistently in favor of a common outcome (that is, profit with a growth constraint or vice versa). Or, alternatively, these roles can be assigned to different individuals.

OTHER TRANSITION ISSUES

In empowered companies, most of the commitments that count are made horizontally, between people with accountabilities acting to produce business outcomes. But the commitments that are *counted* still tend to be those made vertically, between individuals and their managers. Some appraisal and counseling practices, well-established from our command-and-control heritage, interfere with effective governance by context and coordination. A few of the more serious follow.

- Outcomes and the measurements of those outcomes are not distinguished. As mentioned earlier, a measurement that has only a loose correlation with an outcome frequently replaces it as the objective, often leading to severe misalignment between individual effort and organizational purpose.

- The individuals to whom horizontal commitments are made go unspecified and may not be involved in assessing the outcome. Immediate managers, who typically play the role of evaluation administrator, frequently evaluate outcomes for which they are not the customers.

- Employees are either assigned or asked to commit to results at the beginning of the year without authentic negotiation. But these are not commitments. They are statements about the desirable year-end status of certain measurements. Occasionally, the statements are updated by management during the year, based on the changing needs of the business, but conditions of satisfaction are not systematically specified or renegotiated.

- Some commitments are inherited as line-of-sight pass-throughs of enterprise-level revenue, cost, and profit objectives. These involve no negotiation, and the link between year-end measurement status and individual contribution can be quite remote. If the outcome is a system-level effect, furthermore, no one except leadership can authentically commit to it.

- Better-than-committed outcomes are rewarded with bonuses for over-achievement. This fosters two-agenda negotiations and erodes authenticity by motivating providers to make low-ball offers and customers to ask for more than they think they need.

- No linkages between individuals' commitments are made. Therefore, no coherent design emerges from the collection of commitments and assignments registered.

Introducing the practice of negotiating rather than assigning accountabilities can be tantamount to initiating a cultural revolution. Our concept of order and authority has been shaped for decades or even centuries by the command-and-control model.

Some of us learned it in extreme forms in basic training or boot camp. Many learned when told by a boss with whom we were trying to negotiate, "If you can't do it, I'll find someone who can." Such an experience makes it clear that this request— and probably all future ones from the same source—are undiscussable.

Imagine imposing on such a culture the requirement that all requesters, most especially leaders, not only tolerate but *insist* on negotiating their requests with the people they want to carry them out. Adopting the commitment management protocol requires this shift. The goal is not a sociological or humanistic one. Negotiation is intended to create clear, meaningful, and authentic commitments with the people who are or will become dependent on them. Before a commitment can be authentic, the performer must be confident either that the conditions of satisfaction can be met or that they can be renegotiated as required by unfolding events. To deal meaningfully with uncertainty, mutually acceptable ranges of risk or performance should be negotiated and registered. Requesters and performers must be sufficiently confident that the specified outcomes meet their requirements. If the two parties agree that they cannot commit to a mutually acceptable outcome because of other commitments, one or both must consider renegotiating those commitments. Expecting and accepting *frequent* renegotiation is important. The sooner the parties become aware of changing conditions that invalidate an existing commitment, the more effectively they can deal with the situation, with the least cost to the organization.[6] Precisely because things change unpredictably, decommitments are frequent and normal in sense-and-respond organizations. But like commitments, decommitments must be *bilateral.* Only unilateral decommitments should be associated with negative consequences for the responsible individual.

The commitment management protocol solves the problems involved in dynamically linking empowered people to achieve organizational-level outcomes. Its successful introduction, however, depends on creating a culture whose foundation is a shared dedication to a compelling, unambiguous organizational purpose and whose local reward systems facilitate the creation and renegotiation of commitments. Creating such a culture is a formidable assignment for the leaders who must conceptualize, design, and realize the adaptive organizations of the future. The protocol does not make the task easy, but does make it practicable.

ENABLING MODULARITY WITH THE PROTOCOL

Like the standard interfaces that allow any Web browser to connect to any Internet server, the commitment management protocol serves as the common interface among any two or more of the modular capabilities in a sense-and-respond organization. These capabilities can snap together in virtually any configuration because they share a common understanding of how to connect. The protocol spells it out. This is a much easier and faster way to achieve modularity than is redesigning each capability to fit all others. It works the way telephone dialing protocols do to enable telephones around the world to work together. The alternative, Lego-block approach, would require that each block be designed and manufactured with male and female connectors in precisely the right places.

Any capability (that is, any role with skills and resources at its disposal) can initiate a commitment with a *request* or *offer*. A commitment ends with an *accept, reject* or *withdraw* speech act. Obviously an organization could not be effectively adaptive or genuinely modular if its elements had to build a shared interface each time they needed to work together [to meet an uprecedented request]. Yet this lack of commonality accurately describes the situation in many large companies now trying to be responsive and flexible. They have neither clearly defined their commitments and accountabilities nor developed a standard way of creating, tracking, and coordinating them.

Businesses that achieve modularity have a different attitude toward change. Just as investments in sensing more information about changing customer needs pay off with earlier and deeper knowledge about new opportunities to create value, so investing in modularization allows companies to rapidly commercialize these opportunities. When rapid response becomes possible, as Westpac found, firms can and do seek out opportunities to exploit that capability—often leaving discontinuous change for competiors.[7] Change becomes an ally, rather than a series of problems to be dealt with.

GOVERNING MODULAR ORGANIZATIONS WITH THE COMMITMENT PROTOCOL

What happens when an unanticipated request for an unprecedented response arrives? As illustrated by the high-level business design at Old Mutual's Employee Benefits unit, a role in the organization, such as the integrator, fields it. The people in this role are responsible for negotiating an agreement with the customer and dispatching the required capabilities to respond with a customer-unique value chain. Figure 8.2 presents a schematic diagram of how those in dispatching roles can use the protocol to manage the relationship with the customer and to secure commitments from both internal and external capabilities.

FIGURE 8.2

CREATING A CUSTOMER-SPECIFIC VALUE CHAIN

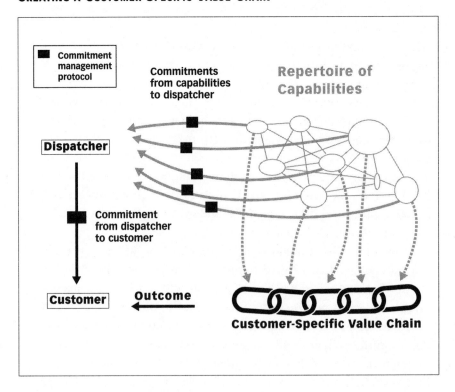

Through negotiations, the dispatcher and customer seek the closest match between needs and capabilities. But this is only part of the story. As suggested above, the internal relationships that really count, the dynamic horizontal commitments, must be negotiated and executed to integrate capabilities into systems-level responses. This is where the technology-assisted protocol makes an enormous difference in coordinating complex responses. (See Figure 8.3.)

Once a commitment has been registered in the system, software can track its status by recording the latest speech act communicated by either of the parties involved. Software can also remind individuals of pending requests and commitments for which they are either supplier or customer.[8]

FIGURE 8.3

ESTABLISHING "WHO OWES WHAT TO WHOM"

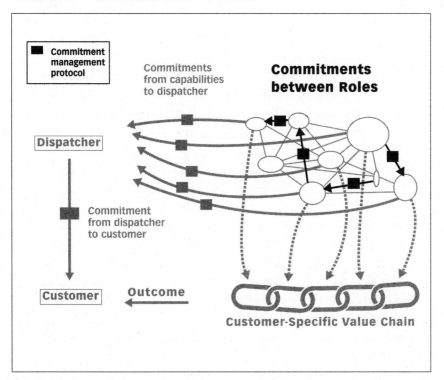

Remember from our discussion of hybrid organizations that most business designs will incorporate both make-and-sell and sense-and-respond capabilities. As long as each capability is dispatched in a standard way using the protocol, context and coordination can be used to replace command and control in any organization, even in a classic make-and-sell company. (Roles in a static functional hierarchy can easily be expressed as vertical accountabilities of subordinate providers to manager customers. Then technology can follow up on the commitments made at plan time, effectively replacing the central staff.)

The commitment management protocol was developed by computer scientists to improve the design and automated execution of business processes, even when some of the procedures required to automate the processes were lacking or unknown. I have coopted the protocol for the sense-and-respond governance system because it can represent all possible outcomes of a process without specifying any procedure. This feature makes it possible for leadership to create a high-level business design strictly in terms of outcomes, and to ensure that the business then operates in accordance with the design. Moreover, this design-execution correspondence can be maintained in the absence of any prior knowledge of the activities that will create the outcomes.

The protocol has the very important traits of rigor, universality, and generality. These attributes solve the problem of coordinating large numbers of modular capabilities constantly making, executing, and renegotiating commitments, thus allowing technology to replace the command-and-control staff. Technology tracks the dynamics of "who owes what to whom," indefatigably propagating governing principles—commitment by commitment—throughout the organization. The protocol's rigor also makes it possible for the technology to test for compliance, an absolute necessity for maintaining coherence. Technology thus can make it feasible, once again, for large organizations to seriously consider synergy, a systems-level effect, as a strategic option. The protocol makes it practicable to design and govern a large business as a synergy-producing system rather than as a collection of autonomous units and procedures.[9]

Technology plays another important role in sense-and-respond organizations. It enables the behaviors required for adaptation to occur *in time*. For this to happen technology must support key roles as they cycle through the adaptive loop described in chapter 5.

Imagine a corporate cockpit where corporate pilots view, in real time, the status of commitment networks displayed as in Figure 8.3. A commitment symbol turns yellow or red, signifying that it is being renegotiated or terminated due to an unforeseen event. Each of the linked commitments lights up as the respective roles determine whether they need to renegotiate their own commitments in response to the breakdown. A negotiated work-around alters the pattern of relationships on the screen. Additional information and other models help the pilots make decisions regarding the resources available to the capabilities that must frequently renegotiate their commitments. An enterprise model simulates the effect of possible changes in the high-level design.

Anyone in a role accountable for outcomes requiring such dynamic linking of capabilities would benefit from a heads-up display like the one just described. Decades ago the United States Air Force implemented a technology program to augment people's ability to cycle through their adaptive loops faster and better. The application of this concept to business is the subject of the next chapter, because, in more and more companies, technology-assisted adaptive cycles are fast becoming a requirement for keeping up with the unexpected.

Time and the world are ever in flight.

—WILLIAM BUTLER YEATS

MANAGING BY WIRE

ADVANCES IN JET ENGINE TECHNOLOGY DURING THE 1950S confronted aviators with a serious problem. Practically overnight, jet propulsion dramatically increased the speed of fighter planes—so much so that pilots could no longer fly them. They could no longer sense and interpret their changing environments rapidly enough to decide on and implement an action before the critical moment passed. The U.S. Air Force uses the term *OODA loop* to describe how pilots process information when they fly. Another name for the adaptive loop described in chapter 5, OODA stands for *observation* (sensing environmental signals), *orientation* (interpreting those signals), *decision* (selecting from a repertoire of possible responses), and *action* (executing the selected response).[1] Fighter pilots with faster OODA loops consistently win dogfights; those with slower loops get more parachuting practice.

High-speed jet fighters rendered every pilot's reaction time too slow: Imagine trying to drive a car down the highway at three thousand miles per hour. As we saw in chapter 5, "Successfully adapting systems have the property of translating apparent noise into meaning at a faster rate than the arrival rate of apparent noise."[2] In the 1950s, for the adaptive system consisting of jet-plane and pilot, the arrival rate of apparent noise outstripped pilots' ability to turn it into meaning.

Technology caused the problem and technology helped solve it. Aircraft designers today use computers to help pilots move rapidly through the OODA loop, vastly reducing the time it takes them to assimilate and react to information. Heads-up displays—computer-generated pictures projected onto helmet visors—show selected abstractions of a few vital environmental signals, helping pilots to see and understand "what's going on out there." In other words, the computer takes over much of the work needed to reduce a continuous flood of information into a few meaningful patterns. Other instrumentation and communication technologies help evaluate possible responses. When the pilot makes a decision—say to take evasive action by banking sharply left—software interprets the pilot's consequent actions, translating them into the myriad detailed, nuanced orders that orchestrate the plane's behavior in real time. When pilots manipulate cockpit controls, they no longer directly affect the plane's hydraulic systems. Instead, they provide input to the computers controlling these systems. The aviation world calls this *flying by wire*. Pilots need not understand all the details of what happens when they act, because the procedural specifics of "how we do things around here" have been codified and automated.

Flying by wire means much more than using autopilot. Autopilot automates flying. It carries out standard pilot behavior in situations that the plane's designers could anticipate. Fly-by-wire capabilities *augment* a pilot's functions. Pilots decide on and take ad hoc action. Software interprets the actions and modifies the plane's behavior. Pilot and software are parts of a single system, capable of responding to both anticipated and unforeseen events. The current generation of commercial fly-by-wire aircraft can taxi, take off, fly, and land without pilot intervention. But pilots remain at the controls of the Boeing 777 and the Aerobus 340, because they and only they can deal with unanticipated and un-precedented events not foreseen or planned for by the plane's de-signers. It takes people, not procedures, to deal with the unex-pected.

When a United Airlines 747 lost an engine and all three hy-draulic systems in 1992, for example, nothing in any flight manual told the pilot how to bring the plane down safely. Certainly, no au-topilot or computer system on board could handle the problem. In fact, no mechanisms or procedures existed anywhere for dealing with this unprecedented situation. Boeing's engineers had never seriously considered the minuscule possibility that *both* back-up hydraulic systems might fail simultaneously. The pilot, of course, had a clearly defined responsibility: Land the plane safely. He did so in this case by inventing an ad hoc procedure that used the dif-ferential thrust created by the loss of an engine to turn the plane around and steer it back to the nearest airport. Confronted by a new situation, the pilot made sense of it by thinking *outside* the system. He sought insights from other experiences to help him deal with the crisis—perhaps remembering a concept from his high school physics lab or the time a flat tire made his car pull to one side. We humans excel at thinking outside the box, using analogies and metaphors from other contexts to devise new alter-natives. We are the one part of any system that can step outside that system and modify it on the fly.

Two essential characteristics of flying by wire make it an im-portant foundation for discussing managing by wire. First, fighter pilots today do not fly airplanes; they fly informational representa-tions of airplanes. We can use technology to fly airplanes only after translating into symbols the highly dynamic business of flying. And we must use technology because only it can keep up with develop-ments taking place at speeds of Mach 1 and higher. Second, human beings remain essential for dealing with unexpected events. Flying by wire augments the pilot's role; it does not automate it.

MANAGING BY WIRE

Many of us working in today's information-intensive busi-nesses confront problems similar to those faced by aircraft designers and pilots in the 1950s. Events and the vast, complex flood of information move so fast that we cannot take in, interpret, and respond to signals from our environments quickly enough to act effectively. To survive, we, like jet pilots, need electronic augmentation of our ability to sense "what's going on out there" and an electronic representation of our knowledge about "how we do things around here." We cannot *automate* our most important activities, because rapid change and discontinuity make it impossible to predict what we will face and how we should respond. Like pilots dealing with emergencies, our capacity to move quickly through adaptive loops can be electronically enhanced. But the unique human ability to respond creatively to new situations must be an integral part of the adaptive system.

Managing by wire means running a business by running its informational representation. This is not simulation, any more than flying by wire is simulated flight. Flight simulators help pilots learn to fly by mimicking the experience of flying without leaving the ground. Similarly, business simulations use electronic models to help managers play out "what if" scenarios that enhance their ability to predict and understand the consequences of real-world decisions. Managing by wire is different. It incorporates an electronic representation of the business into the actual fabric of the business. The system carries out real actions, just as the Boeing 777 carries out the pilot's real actions.

Imagine an enterprise design describing the behavior of an entire business. This model, built into the corporate information infrastructure, could then use technology to connect users throughout the firm to one another and to relevant sources of information. Now imagine a crew piloting the organization, using controls in the firm's information cockpit. They respond to readouts of salient data about changes taking place inside and outside the business by appropriately modifying the flight plan. They monitor the performance of delegated responsibilities (accountabilities and commitments) and send coordinating decisions to subsidiary functions.

Such a system would indeed be complex. The current generation of fly-by-wire systems, for example, requires more than twenty million lines of computer code to represent the dynamic complexity of a modern jet airplane in flight. The success of those systems clearly suggests that technology and human imagination can meet the challenge of adequately representing the very dynamic behaviors of a large business. The challenge may seem daunting, but the survival of more than a few Information Age firms will depend on their ability to manage by wire. If they can't, they simply will not be able to keep up with the amount of change they face. They will fail to translate enough apparent noise into meaning.

Westpac's CS90 system provides an early and impressive example of such a system. Although Westpac is not now managed as a sense-and-respond organization, the bank's Product Development Application system demonstrates that systems supporting manage-by-wire operations can be built. It was possible to do so, in fact, even with the now outmoded technology of the 1980s. Westpac's system builders successfully accomplished the following significant results.

- They created a robust symbolic representation of the business and of the changing environment in which it operates.

- They demonstrated the feasibility of using information technology to execute a business strategy directly from a symbolic representation of it, changing what the business does by changing the symbols representing what it does.

- They used technology to propagate management policies that set boundaries for, but did not dictate, the actions of empowered employees. The technology both communicates and enforces these policies, ensuring that responses to customer requests falling outside the boundaries are not executed.

Westpac's PDA, combined with its data warehouse and its people accountable for making profitable loans and developing new products, created a human-electronic system capable of running its complex commercial and retail banking businesses. Even as part of a make-and-sell speed-to-market system, PDA dramatically reduced product development time, increased efficiency, and put Westpac in a position to lead in the introduction of new financial products.

Westpac's system established the operational and technical feasibility of managing by wire. A more recent initiative at Aetna provides an example of the intentional use of the management by wire concept to solve operational problems in the firm's investment sector.

THE AETNA PORTFOLIO MANAGEMENT GROUP

In the early 1990s, when Glen Salow became CIO of the Aetna business unit responsible for managing a portfolio of more than $50 billion in securities, the group faced business challenges familiar to the leaders of any money management firm. Salow has described these challenges in terms of several information management issues.

- **In search of last week's position.** Information about the Portfolio Management Group's "current" investment position came in the form of a two-and-a-half-foot-high computer printout that was out of date by the time it hit executives' desks. Buried in multiple places in the report was week-old information about the distribution of securities in Aetna's portfolio. Aetna "pilots" were flying at three times the speed of sound, with only a blurry video of last week's battles to guide them.

- **Deluged by dirty data.** "Thirsting for knowledge and drowning in data" describes the investment managers' plight. The ocean of data overwhelming them was not only vast, it was polluted with errors and important omissions. No one owned the data, so no one was accountable for its quality.

- **Two different worlds.** External and internal data were managed as separate resources. As a result, signals from the environment were often inaccessible and could seldom be related to actions taken by portfolio managers.

- **The "paperful" office.** Much of the current information that investment managers actually used took the form of notes scribbled on slips of paper. On average, a trader's desk was littered with more than one hundred such slips.

Not surprisingly, Aetna's IT department had a very poor reputation among the investment managers, whose work depended on—in fact, consisted of—obtaining and manipulating information.

In September 1993, Salow attended a Harvard Business School Executive Program at which Richard Nolan and I talked about managing by wire.[3] He found the metaphors of jet pilots, OODA loops, and heads-up displays relevant to the information support needs of Aetna's investment managers. Back at Aetna, he developed an information strategy using the adaptive loop and managing-by-wire concepts.

Working with the traders to customize their own heads-up displays, Salow's staff replaced the scribbled notes with two monitors on each desk. One, a Bloomberg terminal, provides a constant stream of signals about current business events in general and security markets in particular. The second monitor displays an interpretation of those signals. It links to databases containing abstractions of carefully chosen elements of the Aetna Group's business. It represents companies, for example, by name, type, value to Aetna, and current credit rating. It represents security assets by attributes, such as type, the amount of Aetna's investment in them, face value, estimated maturity, and estimated prepayment risk. Clients are abstracted into symbols describing the size of their portfolios and their individual risk and portfolio mix constraints. The market is defined by symbols representing prices, interest rates, and so on. Unlike earlier information sources, the contents of these databases have been carefully scrubbed to ensure accuracy and consistency.

The system also includes models embodying some of the essential knowledge of experienced investment managers. One relates changes in credit rating to changes in security values. Another sorts many thousand investment opportunities into a dozen or so clusters with similar properties. A third simulates the impact of potential investment decisions on portfolio value. Figure 9.1 shows the kinds of information incorporated by the system, and its relation to the steps of the adaptive loop.

FIGURE 9.1

MANAGING BY WIRE AT AETNA

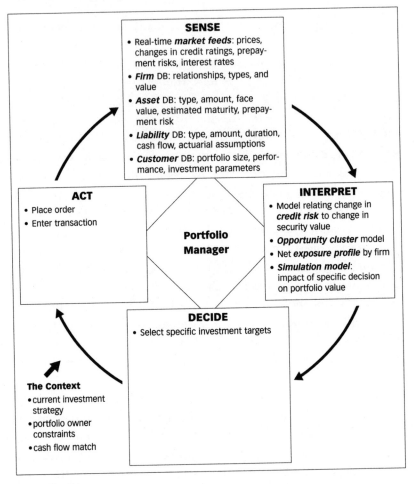

SENSE
- Real-time *market feeds*: prices, changes in credit ratings, prepayment risks, interest rates
- *Firm* DB: relationships, types, and value
- *Asset* DB: type, amount, face value, estimated maturity, prepayment risk
- *Liability* DB: type, amount, duration, cash flow, actuarial assumptions
- *Customer* DB: portfolio size, performance, investment parameters

ACT
- Place order
- Enter transaction

Portfolio Manager

INTERPRET
- Model relating change in *credit risk* to change in security value
- *Opportunity cluster* model
- Net *exposure profile* by firm
- *Simulation model*: impact of specific decision on portfolio value

DECIDE
- Select specific investment targets

The Context
- current investment strategy
- portfolio owner constraints
- cash flow match

Source: Glen Salow.

Investment managers, accountable for maximizing the return on the portfolios they oversee, are subject to three constraints: Aetna's current investment policy, which defines limits on the amount of types of securities in the company's portfolio; similar constraints imposed by the individual owners of the portfolios; and an Aetna cash flow management policy requiring that every investment be matched with insurance policy premiums. Decisions by investment managers are executed by making a call to a broker. The manager then enters symbols representing the transaction into the system. Software updates the books, keeping status information current. Except for the phone call to the broker, the entire interaction between trader and market takes place within the system, in the world of electronic abstractions.

Because it involved such a significant change in work patterns, Salow and his staff made use of the new manage-by-wire system optional. They also took care to tailor simulation models to the idiosyncrasies of individual traders. In the first full year of operation, two-thirds of the traders began using the system, and Aetna achieved an eight-basis-point increase in portfolio performance. Not surprisingly, the IT department's reputation among portfolio managers soared. According to many of the traders, however, the most significant change was that, for the first time, they felt personally accountable for the performance of the portfolios they managed. They now had quality information and an adaptive loop cycle short enough to illuminate the cause-and-effect relationship between their decisions and changes in portfolio value. By "flying" in a representation of the market, they could keep up with a rapidly changing environment making decisions much more closely attuned to the real market. Using heads-up displays instead of rearview mirrors made their work both more productive and more satisfying.[4]

SCALING UP MANAGEMENT BY WIRE

At Aetna, managing by wire was applied to the trading function of the Portfolio Management Group, one part of a much larger organization. At Westpac, a much more extensive effort produced a more nearly comprehensive management-by-wire system, one used by many people developing and selling a wide range of financial products. Even Westpac's CS90 system, however, did not incorporate commitment management or propagate policies unrelated to products. Westpac does not, therefore, constitute a complete example of enterprise-level management-by-wire.

Enterprise-level systems are becoming increasingly necessary, however. Fortunately, they will also be increasingly practicable as understanding of sense-and-respond principles improves and as technology continues to advance. David Ing, of IBM's

Advanced Business Institute, and Ian Simmonds, of IBM's Research Division, have completed a sense-and-respond support system specification independent of any particular technology platform. The system, as specified, enables a manage-by-wire implementation of sense-and-respond. It has the following key features.

- A complete representation of a firm's current version of its organizational context.

- Support of role-specific adaptive loops and management-by-wire.

- Support of the collaborative decision process (described in appendix B).

- Status tracking of commitments made using the commitment management protocol (described in chapter 8).

Assuming validation and successful operational testing, this specification will become a major contributor to the implementation of sense-and-respond in large enterprises. Techniques, methodologies, and technologies to support sense-and-respond organizations are now emerging as by-products of applying the principles and contexts to early adopter businesses. In the next chapter, we will look at the progress made, and understanding gained, by an organization that for three years has been moving toward sense-and-respond.

Nothing is more practical than a good theory.

— K U R T   L E W I N

The facts will eventually test all our theories.

— J E A N   L O U I S   R O D O L P H E   A G A S S I Z

Managing the

Transformation

A Case Study

WE HAVE EXPLORED THE INFORMATION AGE REALITIES THAT call for adaptive enterprises, and considered how such organizations can be created and led. Although their sense-and-respond efforts are all works-in-progress, the experiences of early adopters of the concept reveal much about the problems and benefits— expected and unexpected—of the ongoing transformation process.

The sense-and-respond model is so new and differs so greatly from the Industrial Age make-and-sell model that, as yet, no complete examples exist of large companies fully transforming themselves into companies using context and coordination to ensure adaptive, coherent behavior. Parts of large firms, however, are making the transition. Their experience shows that the change is necessary, possible, and that it can be productive. Appropriately enough, IBM's Palisades Executive Conference Center, where many of these ideas were developed, itself provides an example. Given its moderate size, the center cannot exemplify all the issues that large corporations will face. The Palisades experience does, however, offer insights into the process of developing buy-in and commitment to sense-and-respond. In its case, the road from command and control to context and coordination passed through an interim experiment with ungoverned empowerment.

IDENTIFYING THE NEED FOR SENSE-AND-RESPOND

The Palisades Executive Conference Center is dedicated to educating executives from IBM's customers, consultants, and business partners on subjects ranging from business strategy to computer concepts to electronic commerce. Three groups within the center serve these three constituencies. The Advanced Business Institute (ABI) educates customer executives on management issues relating to technology. The Executive Consulting Institute provides certification training for IBM consultants. The Business Partner Executive Institute offers executive education to the senior management of IBM's business partners. More than eight thousand executives attend courses, seminars, briefings, and conferences at the facility each year. The center is a legacy of IBM's founder, who believed education to be one of the most effective forms of marketing. To this day, accordingly, attendees at ABI courses pay no tuition.

The Palisades facility was built in 1989 to consolidate many smaller education centers spread around the country. Within a few years, it had achieved a noteworthy record of success. Palisades became the first IBM service organization to win a Silver Quality award in the company's internal Baldrige competition. Its overall Customer Satisfaction Index has been greater than 99 percent every year since 1992, and more than 60 percent of attendees describe their experience there as the best or one of the best of its kind they have ever had. Results like these would lead many managers to say, "It ain't broke, so don't fix it." But they would be wrong. Jack Hammond, director of executive education in 1992, explains why.[1]

> I was lulled into complacency by the quality results, and by the fact that empowered employees from seven different corporations were working harmoniously together to produce them. Based on cus-

tomer feedback, we were getting better and better at doing what we did. Why would I want to tinker with a well-oiled machine that generated customer satisfaction ratings of 99.5 percent year after year? I didn't, until the IBM executive responsible for client-server marketing suddenly took his customer-education business to another company. He didn't think the ABI was teaching what his customers needed. This was totally unanticipated and a major problem. It made me realize that getting better and better at doing the wrong thing is not a good survival strategy.

Although Hammond had thought that the sense-and-respond concepts being taught at the center had little application for him, the major shock of losing a good customer made him wonder. "The ABI's antenna was not picking up signals about a very important sea change in the industry," he says, "and we needed a much better way of sensing what we should be sensing. The sense-and-respond concept suddenly seemed highly relevant." He understood, too, that performance measures could only measure what you were doing. They offer little insight into what you *should* be doing that you weren't. As was true of Old Mutual's Employee Benefits unit, developing sense-and-respond capabilities meant creating new outcomes with new roles, not just reengineering old ones. Hammond saw this, as well.

> Having learned the lesson that customers can change their minds without warning, and in ways that current measurements don't reflect, we created a role whose primary responsibility is to scan for changes about what is important to both customer execs and to our IBM sponsors—and to keep an eye peeled for potential new constituencies.

Hammond's sense of urgency increased due to the turmoil prevailing at IBM in 1992. He could not be certain that the Palisades center would survive the downsizing then affecting virtually every sector of the company. This threat provided a further incentive to get better at both understanding and doing whatever the *right* thing was, even if that was far from clear at the time.

Hammond rejected the idea of concocting a strategic plan, telling the managers reporting to him that he wanted to focus on "what we are going to be" rather than "what we are going to do."

Judging that the success of the organization grew from process excellence and that the people who executed the processes understood them best, he eliminated most management positions, replacing them with process leaders empowered to figure out what to do and then do it. This worked well for the clearly-defined, stable processes used to manage the physical facility. But the ad hoc processes for developing and delivering education at the Advanced Business Institute could not as readily be pinned down. New ideas, new material, and the unique character of each class meant processes changed continually. Hammond had confidence that the seasoned professionals in the ABI would be able to figure out what to do by focusing on processes, so he eliminated all but one of the ABI managerial positions. Even that position was not involved in operations, but fulfilled IBM's requirements for salary administration, performance, appraisal, and career counseling.

For a year, ABI faculty and process leaders met interminably but came away with little other than a growing sense of frustration. They had been told they were empowered, but had no idea how resources were to be allocated, priorities set, or conflicts resolved. Faculty kept doing what they had been doing in the classroom, and performance indicators remained high, but morale was low. Many felt the institute was drifting, a rudderless ship. Empowerment creates such problems when no context exists to support consistent decision-making.

Seeing this, Hammond decided to create the context needed by testing some of the ideas being taught at the ABI about governing empowered, sense-and-respond organizations. He resolved to determine a reason for being and develop governing principles and a high-level business design. These would declare the kind of unambiguous goals, boundaries, and accountabilities needed to foster coherent, yet unplanned, behavior. The context would apply equally to the more predictable facility management organization and to the very ad hoc ABI and ECI. (The BPEI did not yet exist.)

THE PALISADES REASON FOR BEING

Hammond first solicited possible reasons for being from the staff. Most submissions received boiled down to this: "The Palisades exists to educate customer executives in a world-class environment." The statement seemed self-evident. After all, it described what the Palisades *did*. Hammond was dissatisfied, however. He asked himself whether the center's customers or IBM would miss its services if the Palisades disappeared. Customers had other educational options, and IBM account reps could offer their clients other types of IBM education. After considerable thought, Hammond decided that the center's primary constituent was and should be IBM. The value it provided IBM should be a positive influence on revenue. Lost revenue would most certainly be missed by the company, but the impact of education on revenue could not be measured directly. IT decision cycles can take years, and knowledge is never the only decision factor. But Hammond believed he could get statistically valid estimates of the extent to which customer decisions were influenced by their Palisades experience. He presented his thoughts to the staff, listened to their comments, and then declared the Palisades' reason for being: "The Palisades exists to influence customer buying decisions by educating customer executives in a world-class environment."

The primary outcome was now clearly stated: influenced customer buying decisions. IBM was established as the primary constituency. Providing customer executive education and a world-class environment are non-negotiable boundaries constraining the way buying decisions can be influenced. Hammond summarized his reasoning in this way.

> The more I thought about it, the more I became convinced that IBM's marketing and service organizations were our *primary* constituency. The reason for being reflects that clarification: From IBM's standpoint, we may educate to exist; but we exist to influence customer buying decisions. Although many in the faculty would have preferred it to be the other way around, at least the ambiguity had been resolved.

Hammond made a commitment to the general manager to whom he reported that, in exchange for its annual budget, the Palisades would positively influence customer buying decisions to the tune of more than $1 billion per year. Achievement of that figure would be determined by a survey technique independently veri-fied by experts at Columbia University.

GOVERNING PRINCIPLES

Hammond spent several weeks developing governing princi-ples. He chose to phrase them all as positive statements, avoiding the "we will never" formula sometimes used to express these boundaries. Very much a governance minimalist, Hammond strove to devise the smallest number of principles that would en-sure integrity and coherence of action while leaving the greatest possible latitude for discretionary decision-making. He settled on these five.

- The overall Palisades experience will always be maintained at a world-class level, as assessed by our customers.

This boundary makes it clear that only customers can decide whether the facility meets world-class standards. Benchmarking against other world-class conference facilities could be used for continuous improvement but not to determine compliance with the reason for being constraint of offering a world-class environ-ment.

- We will continually find ways to spend less.

Since IBM cut the budget at least once a year, the Palisades had to adhere to this principle to survive.

- We will continuously improve based on feedback from our customers.

Hammond saw continuous process improvement as an orga-nizational core competence and believed that customer feedback could best test such progress.

- We will develop those skills that enable us to provide world-class services.

This puts the onus on Palisades leadership to provide opportunities and resources for skill improvement and on individual employees to exploit the opportunities.

- Everyone will operate in compliance with their respective organizational audit standards.

The Palisades Conference Center operates as a system whose components include several independent subcontractors, with IBM employees making up less than 20 percent of the total population. Positions normally accountable for ensuring audit compliance had disappeared when most managerial jobs were eliminated. This principle makes every IBMer who contracts with a vendor, visiting scholar, or lecturer, responsible for ensuring that the relationship meets IBM procurement standards. Employees of Marriott, Johnson & Johnson, and other subcontracting firms must also comply with the audit standards of their own organizations.

The reason for being and governing principles were prominently posted at the employee entrance to the building, along with evidence that current performance was within the boundaries established by the principles. The next step was to complete the context by creating a high-level business design.

THE HIGH-LEVEL BUSINESS DESIGN

It had taken months to come up with a reason for being for the Palisades, but Hammond, true to his minimalist instincts, created a high-level design in a week. He reasoned that a system designed to "influence customer buying decisions by educating customer executives in a world-class environment" needed only two subsystems. One, the Advanced Business Institute, was responsible for producing influenced customers through education. The other, Palisades Operations, was responsible for producing a world-class environment.

Hammond spent most of that week deciding whether he would be comfortable delegating so much responsibility to the subfunction leaders. The role of establishing a context for deci-

sion-making differs from the traditional managerial role of deciding what people should do or supervising their actions. As director,
he understood, however, that the people in the two subfunctions
knew far more than he did about doing their work. In addition,
with their compensation directly tied to how well they delivered
the outcomes specified in the business design, they should have
responsibility for designing their own subsystems. For each subsystem Hammond developed appropriate specific financial performance and minimum levels of measured "customer satisfaction."
Leaders, however, were left free to determine how to achieve the
required outcomes. Undirected empowerment did not work, but
Hammond also knew that old-style hierarchical management was
inappropriate to the center.

> When unbridled empowerment failed in the ABI, I didn't want to
> bring back the management hierarchy because I had seen from the
> success of our quality effort how much creativity and magic empow-
> ered people can contribute. I opted for context and coordination be-
> cause it offered the prospect of *bounded* empowerment. The deci-
> sion to commit the organization to sense-and-respond was less a
> stroke of insight than an act of measured desperation.

Hammond's commitment to sense-and-respond and context
and coordination grew out of his understanding that the center's
environment was changing. The old way of doing things—even at a
very high level of quality—would not work any more. He also recognized that some of his own long-held assumptions were no
longer valid.

> [H]eads-up sensing led to a new ABI institute for business partners
> in 1998. Prior to my retirement, I had turned down proposals for
> this based, again, on what I thought was solid evidence about a mis-
> match between our skills and business partner needs. The real mis-
> match turned out to be between my conviction and a changed mar-
> ketplace reality. Because we hadn't considered business partners to
> be one of our constituencies, we hadn't been tracking the changes
> in their needs. What you don't know *can* hurt you.

Understanding how to operate in this context came easily to the procedure-intensive facility management function. For the Advanced Business Institute, however, it was a major issue. Hammond built the center's context with clarity and thoughtfulness, but it still failed to provide a basis for coherent behavior in the ABI. The ABI leadership, a confederation of former managers, shared a collective title but had no common understanding of their role and its relationship to other roles. They did not understand how the system was meant to work. Hammond's minimalist high-level business design did not incorporate important logistical interactions between the ABI and facility management, nor did it provide ABI leaders with the guidance they needed to design their own subsystem.

When Hammond retired in 1997, his successor Carol Schoenfeld decided to lead the ABI leadership through the process of system design. She adopted the Palisades reason for being and governing principles she had inherited from Hammond, but saw that more work needed to be done. The ABI leadership would have to learn to think and act differently. Schoenfeld believed that the essential first step in bringing about change in an organization that already exceeded its objectives was for individuals to "personally become totally convinced and committed." Although earlier work in other parts of IBM had shown her the importance of sense-and-respond concepts, she had to educate herself in the specifics.

> A previous assignment in leading a global speed-to-market development project made it easy for me to buy into the need for rapid adaptiveness, rigorous commitment management, and unambiguous context. It took a while to appreciate the distinction between the sense-and-respond meaning of these terms and the general ideas of "flexibility," "committed to doing the best you can," and "giving direction." For example, the difference between "having an approved plan" and being accountable to a customer for an outcome is subtle but very important.

Like Hammond, Schoenfeld found abandoning traditional top-down management for context and coordination necessary but difficult. As director, she was still responsible for system results.

The temptation remained strong to "take the reins" in a traditional sense to ensure their achievement.

> Adopting context and coordination means giving up a lot of tradi-
> tional management "friends": organization charts, buck slips, and
> distributing your own objectives all the way down the organization.
> I was, and still am, nervous about not having some one person re-
> sponsible for volumes. It's not easy to count on "the system"—
> which is what you do when you say an outcome is a "system-level
> effect." The buck stops here for those results, because if you lead an
> organization, you are the one accountable for the quality of the
> high-level business design.

The meetings during which Schoenfeld and the ABI leadership constructed the design stretched over four months. The goal
quickly changed from creating an ABI design to creating a Palisades design, as the number and importance of interactions between facility management and the ABI became apparent. The
manager of Palisades operations and the CIO joined the leadership
design team. The team struggled to understand and internalize the
implications of looking at the Palisades as a system of outcomes.
This very different perspective required participants to change
their thinking. This takes time. Schoenfeld used a series of workshops and exercises to engage the leadership team in the process
and to encourage them to work in new ways. She described the
process this way:

> Small doses break down an organization's immunity to change. Be-
> tween workshops, the leadership began asking people to identify
> outcomes, rather than activities, when talking about what needed to
> get done. We began to negotiate, rather than assign results. This is
> not nearly as easy as it may sound. Some of the greatest resistance
> comes from certain individuals who feel much more comfortable
> when they are told what to do.

What was true for the Palisades will be true in other organizations that make similar changes. The *process* of creating the design provides benefits every bit as essential to the new system as
the design itself. Faculty members asked several basic questions.

How do I get approval and resources for a new class? Who is responsible for volumes—class owners or the marketing process leader? How can someone not directly involved in the system that produces "influenced customer buying decisions" evaluate those who are? Several commented that they thought leadership had for the first time finally demonstrated a real understanding of their frustrations. Also for the first time, faculty members understood and described their roles in terms of accountability, of what they owed to whom. Most importantly, this work and the diagram derived from it revealed the relationships of the parts to the whole. Most people found themselves in the design multiple times. They could now see in full how their roles related to others' and to the system as a whole. Schoenfeld commented on this benefit.

> The difference between an organization chart and a high-level accountability design as a communication device is important. In an organization chart, everyone can find themselves once. In an accountability design, you find yourself in multiple places—one for each role. For most people, it's the first time they can relate what they do to what others do, and see how they influence organizational results.

In the work place, we generally do not think precisely about our role in a given situation. More likely, we maintain a general sense of our "job," which, in reality, is comprised of multiple roles. As a result, we may try to negotiate a commitment without adopting the viewpoint appropriate for the specific role in question. This role ambiguity fosters inauthenticity, defeating coherency and efficient system functioning. Schoenfeld found a creative way to confront this confusion during the development of the Palisades high-level business design.

> It is very hard for people to keep their multiple roles sorted out when they talk about who owes what to whom. So we make everyone literally change hats (which have the role names printed on them) when we catch one another switching roles in mid-argument. Although often frustrating and exasperating, the "who-owes-what-to-whom" discipline really pays off. We learned where and why communication breakdowns were occurring; why certain balls were

consistently dropped, and where work could be eliminated. It was an eye-opener to find out how frequently we either could not identify a customer or that a customer wanted a different outcome than the supplier was offering.

The design that emerged from these meetings was a hybrid of make-and-sell and sense-and-respond capabilities. The center made and sold formal classes with relatively fixed content and course descriptions, room schedules, and promotional brochures completed months in advance. These courses, designed for busy executives, had to be booked long in advance. Sense-and-respond elements were more flexible. Some were customized to individual clients. Others were four-day "college" events during which students built individual curricula from several standard modules to accommodate the number of days they had available. The design for these events requires both make-and-sell scheduling and sense-and-respond dispatching of capabilities. Both parts of the hybrid depend on the same clear context and commitments. Make-and-sell can be a special case of sense-and-respond, useful when customer needs remain relatively stable over time and can be met with the same "snapped together" response over and over again.

Schoenfeld came to appreciate the value of the high-level business design *process* itself in clarifying roles and accountabilities and in fostering communication among the people in the system. She sees, too, that the process never ends.

> Developing a high-level business design is an iterative process—one that will never be finished as long as things stay unpredictable. I consider continuous improvement of that design to be my primary responsibility.

A NEW DEFINITION OF LEADERSHIP

Schoenfeld understands that transforming the Advanced Business Institute into a sense-and-respond organization will transform her own role. Like most executives, she has been accustomed to spending the bulk of her time dealing with daily crises, making operational decisions, and translating current challenges into priorities for the people in her organization. In a sense-and-respond Palisades, she will do none of these—at least not in her leadership role.

Like the leaders of all organizations, she will continue to bear ultimate responsibility for delivering the outcomes promised to the Palisades' external constituencies, but internally she is responsible, as leader, "only" for the three outcomes identified in chapter 6.

- Creation and continuous adaptation of a viable organizational context.

- Establishment of a commitment management system to coordinate the behavior of people in accountable roles.

- Population of roles with the right people.

If Schoenfeld does these competently, the system will produce the required external outcomes; the organization will realize its reason for being.

On several occasions in the process of moving Palisades toward sense-and-respond, Schoenfeld has found it necessary to step out of her leadership roles and intervene in operations. She knows that every instance of this signals either that the context needs work or that staffing adjustments must be made to put the right people in important roles.

TOWARD TRANSFORMATION

Like employees of any organization, the staff of the ABI brought common human tendencies and the legacy of long-standing habits to the process of learning how to work effectively in a sense-and-respond context. During the months after the creation of the high-level business design, many still found it hard to turn down requests from colleagues, even if those requests were inconsistent with their roles. Staff members were not in the habit of having authentic discussions about which commitments would best support the organization's reason for being. Even some who fully understood the importance of authenticity remained skeptical about whether they would really be rewarded for renegotiating or withdrawing from existing commitments to take on new ones that would more effectively contribute to organizational purpose. As in other organizations, people continued to find themselves overcommitted and frustrated that others were not delivering on their commitments. Schoenfeld found herself intervening in conflicts and telling people how the reason for being should be used to determine their local priorities.

She discovered that everyone, herself included, tended to revert to command-and-control habits under pressure. The phrase *authentic commitments* still had little real-world substance at the Palisades. A few people, she felt, simply would not perform well in the empowered, accountable roles they occupied. Some personnel changes followed. The high-level business design was altered to substitute multiple individual roles for one dysfunctional team role. Many employees needed to learn and experience the meaning of membership in a sense-and-respond organization. Recognizing this, Schoenfeld has taken several actions specifically to bring practice in line with theory.

Keeping Track of Commitments

Deciding that the discipline of commitment management should be extended to lower-level commitments rather than limited to those captured on the high-level business design, Schoenfeld commissioned the creation of a Lotus Notes database to keep track of every important commitment at the institute. The commitment records that make up the database contain the following items:

- The name of the customer role

- The name of the supplier role

- The deliverable outcome

- The conditions of satisfaction (other deliverables, boundaries, and measurements)

- The most recent speech act (offer/request, agree, report, accept/reject, or withdraw)

- Upstream commitments (to customers for each of this role's outcomes)

- Downstream dependencies (on suppliers of outcomes to this role)

Following every update, the database is replicated for all users, keeping everyone current on the latest status of all commitments. Because interrelationships among commitments are made explicit, all roles affected by the renegotiation or failure of a particular commitment become immediately aware of the breakdown. Every commitment called for by the high-level business design is in the database. The individuals involved decide whether to register other, lower level, commitments. Registration carries a consequence. Both parties will be evaluated on the outcome: either successful completion of the protocol (with or without renegotiation), unsuccessful completion (rejection by the customer), or unilateral withdrawal by either customer or supplier. Periodic assessments of how well people manage their commitments has become an important part of their performance appraisals. Together, the commitment-defining business design, the commitment management protocol, and the database make it possible to govern the center's changing, interlocking commitments—a function that once belonged to and eventually overwhelmed the central staffs of large corporations. Currently, Palisades commitment database updates are entered manually by the customer and the supplier of a given outcome. When ultimately linked to a workflow manager, database updates will occur automatically. The organization will have moved a step closer to management-by-wire.

Creating this database signaled organizational intent to govern by commitment management. It gave employees the opportunity to see their work and the work of others in terms of commitments and accountabilities. But the database alone does not resolve the cultural issues that can inhibit the negotiation of authentic commitments.

Sense-and-Respond Workshops

The series of workshops launched by Schoenfeld provided opportunities for the holders of key roles to negotiate real commitments before their colleagues. These exercises have proved extremely valuable. They have precipitated lively, productive discussions of the relative importance of requests or offers measured against the reason for being. They have also increased awareness of the "upstream and downstream" repercussions, the system effects, that renegotiations carry for other commitments. The Lotus Notes database allows Palisades to track these effects and factor them into trade-off decisions. The workshops have also made clear the astounding amount of unconscious bouncing back and forth between roles that people do while negotiating.

In the process of communicating these important pieces of learning, the workshops function as behavioral laboratories. Anthropologist Karen Stephenson observes these sessions, taking field notes. She has been asked to identify the behaviors that promote or inhibit authenticity. When Stephenson has reached her conclusions, Chris Argyris will be invited to review the results and suggest ways to reduce the gap between what people say they will do and what they actually do. Institute leaders have called in these experts because even the best organizational design will fail if human and social issues receive insufficient attention.

EARLY RESULTS

Schoenfeld made certain that all of the outcomes specified in the high-level business design were incorporated into IBM's Personal Business Commitment system. IBM employees worldwide annually register their key commitments using this performance assessment tool. Their pay is partly based on their managers' assessments of the extent to which those commitments have been met. The company as a whole does not use this system to manage the dynamics of sense-and-respond commitments, but the Palisades has adapted it to support that purpose. Every commitment entered in the PBC system must specify an outcome and its conditions of satisfaction and must associate that outcome with a customer who verifies its satisfactory delivery. Palisades commitments are made between supplier and customer, not employee to manager. Supplementing IBM's Personal Business Commitment system with the commitment management protocol has led to significantly increased clarity about who owes what to whom. In fact, Schoenfeld now uses the formalisms of the protocol in her dealings with other parts of IBM, thus helping to sharpen negotiations and reduce confusion about what was being agreed to and under what conditions.

Some of the progress at the Palisades has been subtle but significant. First, as people became conscious of the distinctions between outcomes and the activities that produced them, their language changed. Several individuals began questioning how their activities fit into the high-level business design. Some simply stopped performing tasks for which they could identify no customer. Unsurprisingly, abandoning activities with no clear connection to essential outcomes had no noticeable effect on system performance.

Taking the lessons of commitments and accountabilities to heart, Marie Malley, who was responsible for administering the scheduling process for the entire Palisades facility, made an offer to leadership. She would accept sole accountability for meeting annual facility utilization objectives on the condition that her decisions no longer be reviewed by leadership. This time-consuming process was, in her view, not very productive. She enumerated the specific decisions she wanted excluded from any review and successfully negotiated this condition of satisfaction with the leadership. As a result, her job was transformed from administering a process to taking accountability for an important outcome: producing more than $15 million in recovered costs for the Palisades. Malley received the authority she needed by *negotiating* for it, not because it came with the job. She was well aware of the additional risk she was taking in terms of her performance evaluation, but this did not concern her. Malley is a natural taxi driver. In the first nine months of her newly negotiated commitment, Palisades utilization was 14 percent higher than in the previous year.

The workshops, intended to educate participants, evolved into a forum in which those in key roles identify and resolve conflicts. Schoenfeld uses them as a rich source of signals to help her decide if, when, and how to modify organizational context. The lessons they teach are beginning to translate into the kinds of organizational and behavioral change described above, and into other changes as well. Without a management "we" and employee "them" in the workshop exchanges, people in roles discuss issues and negotiate commitments directly in ways that can leverage everyone's knowledge. The value thus gained has begun to change the make-up of all decision-making and informational meetings at the Palisades center.

Because, for example, the high-level business design made it very clear (for the first time) that *offering owner* is the pivotal operational dispatching role, people in this role began to be included in leadership meetings. This eventually led to the demise of meetings with that title, a conceptual legacy of the "we know/you do" management concept. Now the roles directly affected by the issue at hand determine the make-up of all meetings, whether informational or decision-making.

The Palisades continues to move toward sense-and-respond, governing itself by context and coordination. Even after it arrives at that goal, however, it will not be able to rest on its laurels. An adaptive organization can never reach and lock in a final, perfect structure. As Schoenfeld says, the iterative process of developing and adapting a high-level business design "will never be finished." To remain viable—literally, capable of living—in an uncertain world, the organization must continue to adapt. Organizational context must adapt with it, both reflecting and shaping new organizational behavior.

CHAPTER 11

All that is not a true change will disappear.

— GEORGE SAND

CHANGING THE CORPORATE
DNA

I HAVE CHARACTERIZED THE CHANGE FROM MAKE-AND-SELL TO sense-and-respond as a business transformation, a phrase often too casually used. Russell Ackoff, a leading thinker on how to apply systems theory to business, likes to remind executives that most of their talk about business transformation is really talk about business reformation: doing pretty much the same thing, but doing it better. Reengineering, Total Quality Management, team-based structures, continuous improvement, and a host of other prescriptions may produce valuable operational improvement, but they achieve reformation, not transformation.

Ackoff maintains that transforming a business means changing both its function and its structure. A shift from make-and-sell to sense-and-respond is therefore a true transformation because it involves changing a firm's basic function from making offers to responding to requests, and also changing its structure from that of an efficient machine to that of an adaptive social system. After the transformation to sense-and-respond, the enterprise will be doing something fundamentally different in a fundamentally different way.

This distinction is important, because sense-and-respond can all too easily sink to the level of a mere slogan. The phrase immediately appeals to many people—and why not? Who would argue in favor of sense-and-ignore or guess-and-respond? For that matter, who would argue against getting closer to the customer, investing in better information, and reducing response time? But we have seen that becoming a sense-and-respond organization requires a dramatic transformation. Many executives who might gladly embrace sense-and-respond as a motivational theme will find the reality difficult and demanding. The early sense-and-respond adopters described in this book did not use the phrase as a communications device to remind people in their organizations how important it is to listen to customers, cut through bureaucracy, and get to market faster. They understood and presented sense-and-respond as a specific way of thinking about organizational purpose, structure, and governance. As one experienced executive put it, "There are some terrible truths lurking beneath these easy-to-love phrases."[1]

Transformation is hard. Reg Munro of Old Mutual's Employee Benefits unit attests to the difficulties of "trying to introduce a radically different idea in a time of major industry and environmental change." He goes on to say, "Of course, that's the very reason it has become necessary. Despite the very real problems experienced to date, I am convinced that the sense-and-respond transformation is a non-negotiable requirement for managing business in the future."

Significant reformation of a large organization can be difficult enough. Transformation, because it involves reconceptualization, will always be much more so. Even IBM's Palisades Executive Conference Center, a relatively homogeneous organization offering essentially one product, continues to find the process challenging. Larger, more complex organizations will find the challenge even greater. But given our premise of pervasive unpredictability, the survival of information-intensive organizations will depend on meeting that challenge. This final chapter further explores the question of how to get there from here. The following story may help make more vivid the demands and scope of the undertaking.

A SENSE-AND-RESPOND PARABLE

Dinosaurs ruled Earth for roughly 160 million years—not a bad record of market dominance. At a strategic planning conference approximately 140 million years into this reign, a futurist guru predicted that the furry, smelly, ugly little varmints running around the dinosaurs' feet would one day take over the world. "What are they called?" asked the dinosaurs. "We call them mammals; they call themselves niche players," answered the guru. Not surprisingly, given the available evidence, the dinosaurs ridiculed the mammals and beheaded the guru.

Ten million years later, the mammals had become real pests, polluting the savannas, swiping dinosaur eggs, and picking low-hanging fruit. Policy-makers convened an emergency session to deal with the problem. After two days of team-building exercises and motivational speeches, they adopted a strategy of all-out war against the mammals.

When another five million years had passed, it became clear that the mammals were winning the war. It seemed the futurist guru had been right after all. So the dinosaurs called in consulting gurus. "Not to worry," counseled these sages. "You too can become mammals. All you need are tusk implants, body wigs, and intensive immersion in our lactation seminars."

The dinosaurs followed this advice, and some actually became quite good at passing themselves off as mammals much of the time. To little avail, however. When the midday sun beat down, they still succumbed to an irresistible urge to lie down on flat rocks and go to sleep. They had modified their appearance and some of their behaviors—they had reformed themselves—but they hadn't altered their reptilian DNA.

THE PRAGMATICS OF TRANSFORMATION

The parable's moral is that transformation of a system entails changes in that system's fundamental nature that cannot be achieved with behavior changes and capability implants alone. A dinosaur in a fur coat is not a mammal; nor does adopting sense-and-respond techniques in itself create a sense-and-respond organization. Transformation, by its very nature, is not incremental change. But the process that achieves it can be gradual. There is nothing incremental, for example, about the change from water to ice. Yet it is possible to cause this transformation by gradually lowering the temperature of water.

Small units of large companies, as we have seen, can make themselves into islands of sense-and-respond in an ocean of make-and-sell. Entire companies have developed certain sense-and-respond capabilities, but not others. These incomplete examples reflect the newness of sense-and-respond as a requirement for large enterprises. They also demonstrate that, up to now, sense-and-respond concepts have not been fully integrated into a coherent model. To the extent that the model presented here satisfies that need, more complete sense-and-respond organizations will emerge in the coming years, after having passed through a transition period. No company—certainly no large company—can be make-and-sell one day and sense-and-respond the next. Such an instant makeover lies beyond the abilities of even the most determined leaders and most willing employees. The larger the organization, the more powerful its momentum is likely to be. And transformation can be very distracting. Managers focused on executing aggressive plans usually have little time for reflective thought and are more likely to devote what time they do have to solving problems, not to absorbing new concepts.

Fortunately, systems can be redesigned and then modified step-by-step. In general, leaders should focus first on the particular business areas experiencing the most unpredictable change. These will benefit most from sense-and-respond capabilities. A step-by-step approach may at first seem to contradict the requirement that the enterprise be managed as a system because it is true that piecemeal improvements conceived and carried out in isolation cannot improve overall system performance. But partial and local sense-and-respond initiatives can work if they interact—by design—with other parts. Sense-and-respond strategists must keep in mind how their local efforts affect and are affected by other elements of the business. Jack Hammond and Carol Schoenfeld of IBM Palisades and Reg Munro of Old Mutual Employee Benefits, for example, consciously developed their sense-and-respond designs in the context of the aims, capabilities, and boundary constraints of the larger organizations of which their units were part. Furthermore, they took care to think through the impact on other enterprise units of the changes they were contemplating. Most organizations will be hybrids, as noted several times in earlier chapters. Make-and-sell organizations will have some sense-and-respond capabilities or sense-and-respond organizations will need some make-and-sell capabilities. Treating an organization systematically does not mean that the structures of its parts must be homogeneous.

As the examples throughout this book show, every firm will approach the challenge in its own way, taking its own particular structure, environment, and organizational personality into account. Certainly, however, understanding the *need* for sense-and-respond must rank near the top of any priority list. These basic questions can help guide that assessment.

- Of the known factors important to our success, which are predictable (within acceptable limits) and which are not?

- Do new developments become important to our business before we begin taking them into account? How frequently does this happen? Is the frequency increasing or not?

- How information-intensive is our business? Is it becoming more so?

- How consistent is our current strategy with Glazer's list of implications for information-intensive businesses?

- How widely shared and unambiguous is the understanding of our purpose, boundaries, and essential structure?

- What roles in our organization require the most adaptiveness?

- What is our current contribution to the total bundle of customer values? Could we profitably provide or manage more of it?

- How do we achieve coherence in our business operation, ensuring behaviors are consistent with our strategic intent? Do we still use command and control? If not, what has replaced it?

- Do we manage our business as a system or as a collection of individually managed parts?

THE HYBRID CORPORATION: MOVING TOWARD SENSE-AND-RESPOND

Very few enterprises that conclude, like Westpac did, that unpredictability is *the* issue, should strive to become homogeneously pure sense-and-respond firms. Heavy investment in adaptive capabilities cannot be justified in situations where the changes sensed occur only gradually and where customers, whether external or internal, find little value in customized responses. The hybrid model is a viable option because the transition from make-and-sell to sense-and-respond can be gradual as long as it is systematic.

Vince Barabba, the general manager responsible for developing and implementing the strategy development process at General Motors, believes that GM will always be a hybrid and that it should move from make-and-sell *toward,* not *to,* sense-and-respond. Starting with the development of a new reason for being and governing principles did not seem fruitful to Barabba. Instead, he looked for places where the company could benefit from specific elements of the sense-and-respond model in both the short and long term. He also developed a multi-stage strategic framework to guide a GM transition from mainly make-and-sell to a mainly sense-and-respond hybrid. Without a clear path for getting from here to there, Barabba believes, sense-and-respond could not take root at GM. Barabba's framework serves as a tool, he explains, "to help each of GM's operating and functional organizations . . . move from independent unit business plans to an interdependent enterprise-based strategy that . . . takes advantage of our existing strengths, while developing . . . business designs that assist us in adapting to changing customer, market and business conditions." Here are Barabba's four stages.

- **Stage 1**

  Yesterday's Business Design: GM as a manufacturing company.
  Make-and-sell with emphasis on make. Highly leveraged and fixed economies of manufacturing scale. Assumed pre-

dictable customer requirements and economic growth and foreseeable competitive reactions.

- **Stage 2**
  Today's Business Design: GM as a market-based manufacturing company seeking global synergies based on our ability to predict future conditions.
  Market-based make-and-sell with emphasis on designing vehicles to match customer needs. Vehicles targeted at specific customer or market segments. Customer requirements addressed through flexible, lean production of different vehicle designs.

- **Stage 3**
  A "Next Step" Business Design: GM as a primarily market-based product company with increased involvement in distribution and services.
  Predominantly market-based make-and-sell incorporating supplemental sense-and-respond service elements into the value proposition.

- **Stage 4**
  Next Generation Business Design: GM as a highly adaptive enterprise.
  Predominantly sense-and-respond with some make-and-sell attributes.

For Barabba, the specifics of GM's hybrid will emerge from the changing mix of offers and responses in its value proposition. This will drive decisions about the sequence and cadence of the sense-and-respond transformations inside GM. The strategic framework helps the leadership think through, systematically, the necessary internal transformations.

Organizational capabilities can be mapped against these stages, as illustrated by the sample capabilities in Table 11.1. Barabba makes each capability accountable for developing its own transition to the next stage. GM strategists and those responsible for particular capabilities must cultivate an awareness of how their capabilities relate to the system as a whole. But not all capabilities need to reach a new stage simultaneously for the company to realize benefits from the move toward sense-and-respond. A Stage 3

TABLE 11.1

Hypothetical General Motors Business Evolution

	Portfolio Capability	Marketing and Communication Capability	Market Understanding Capability	Information Management Capability
Stage 1	Marketing division product portfolio constrained by economies of scale	Mass marketing	Division-specific	Host-centric mainframe, automation
Stage 2	GM product portfolio, constrained by bill of materials process design	Brand management and target marketing to segments	Sector-specific, broadly focused to address portfolio-level issues	Mainframe and client-server, common processes and systems, global infrastructure
Stage 3	Product portfolio of "Hit-the-dot" vehicles enhanced by services that provide revenues over the vehicle life cycle	Brand management with increasing precision. Marketing to highly specific segments	Improved understanding of consumer attitudes and social influences	Mainframe and client-server, common systems functionally integrated into process models
Stage 4	Portfolio of transportation capabilities increasingly customizable by individual customer	Emphasis on 1-to-1 customer relationship building	Understanding of individual consumer attitudes and preferences	Network-centric computing, shared access to anyone, anyplace, anytime

Source: Vince Barabba.

GM strategy, in other words, does not necessarily require that every capability reach its own third stage. GM uses tables like the one shown above to achieve a systems overview that helps the company synchronize the evolution of its component capabilities.

PREPARING THE GROUND: THE
IMPORTANCE OF EDUCATION

DSC Logistics, the largest privately owned third-party logistics company in the United States, provides integrated logistics and supply-chain solutions to Fortune 500 companies. Among their customers are Unilever, Nabisco, and Bristol-Meyers Squibb. As recently as the mid-1980s, the time required to adapt to new, significantly different changes in the needs of DSC's individual customers averaged three years. DSC prided itself on its willingness to respond to occasional special requests from customers to do something they had never done before.

But by the time Ann Drake took over the reins of DSC Logistics in 1992, the three-year cycle time had shrunk drastically. New customers called with one-off requests requiring a complete response in as little as eleven *days*. Driving this, of course, was the declining predictability of the requests received by DSC's customers from their own customers. The unprecedented was rapidly becoming routine. More and more, to provide value, DSC had to help its customers cope with discontinuous change. This proved very disruptive, and by 1994 internal operations at DSC had become very ad hoc and less and less profitable. The same request made to different parts of the organization now elicited different ad hoc responses to accomplish the same thing.

Drake concluded that DSC's future success depended on its transformation into a sense-and-respond organization. She made her first priority the establishment of common processes, a prelude to modularization. At the same time she launched a campaign to instill a sense-and-respond mindset throughout the company. She published her vision as a strategic imperative, telling both customers and employees that DSC Logistics would "become the premier adaptive sense-and-respond logistics company," and reinforced this message with an education program for operational and policy executives.

Drake believes that coming in as she did as an outsider was an advantage. She did not have to tear down her own preconceptions about how a logistics company *should* be run. Her mind was open to the need for transformation and to new ways of thinking. Most of the people she worked with had been part of the "old"

DSC, and, like Carol Schoenfeld at the Palisades, Drake saw an important part of her job to be fostering new ways of thinking and acting.

Drake understood that people not only needed to learn sense-and-respond, they needed to unlearn many of their ingrained ideas and habits. Unlearning can sometimes be the hardest part of changing. Drake says, "Unlearning 'plan your work and work your plan' took more time than I wanted it to." One of DSC's operations vice presidents remarked, "It's the opposite of everything you've been taught to think about a business and its customers."

Reg Munro of Employee Benefits makes the same point:

> I totally underestimated the work and time involved in teaching pragmatic managers a conceptually new approach to strategic management. Sense-and-respond is not an easy theory to put into practice, because it is so different from traditional management practices. In an early phase, one of my colleagues questioned the usefulness and value of governing principles: "I'm not sure our governing principles are that helpful, because they don't help me decide on [a current issue he faced]." Although he had been educated in sense-and-respond, in a tough spot he forgot that the purpose of governing principles is not to relieve managers of their decision-making responsibility, but to define how far they can go without seeking approval.

Such radical learning and unlearning cannot be accomplished passively, by sitting through a few courses. Drake makes this clear:

> It's very difficult to communicate a big new concept. People must be given an experience. Even though we conducted a wide variety of internal courses, the ones who became most zealous are the ones who went to the Palisades for a "retreat." Focused immersion in a new concept is not unlike being "born again."

Learning an entirely new way of working cannot occur on an abstract level. It comes from applying the concepts in human terms, from directly experiencing authentic negotiation and the rewards that follow from consistently making trade-offs in the firm's interest. Not everyone wants or has the aptitude to work this way. Drake saw that attracting people with the necessary skills and predispositions would be exceptionally important if DSC was to succeed in creating a sense-and-respond environment.

> We spent one entire year coming up with the human characteristics, capabilities, and traits that we thought we would need to operate as a sense-and-respond company. Because this forced us "inside the skin" of the people who would have to make the vision happen, it propelled us along the path to sense-and-respond much faster than would have otherwise been the case.

GM's Vince Barabba similarly understands that learning how to put a new idea to work is not a passive exercise; people need to absorb, adapt, and own the idea. In Barabba's view, they have to reinvent a new idea to accept it. "You know a concept has taken root when people believe they created it," he says. He points to the example of a GM divisional executive who responded to an invitation to attend the Advanced Business Institute's sense-and-respond course by saying, "Why should I go there to learn about it? Sense-and-respond is a GM idea." Barabba views this kind of feedback as a strong signal that sense-and-respond has taken root at GM; it is no longer someone else's idea.

Understanding that she was dealing with systemic, ongoing transformation, not just a new management style, Drake made sure that the learning process involved everyone in the company. Learning meant conversation, not a one-way transmission of management ideas.

> We have asked every employee to support sense-and-respond. When senior management visits a facility, they talk about it at the transactional level. Employees share what it means to them and to their work with customers. We learn a lot from their way of translating it.

Learning and doing are entwined. Although Drake has, necessarily, put a lot of emphasis on education in leading the transformation at DSC Logistics, no clear demarcation exists between education and implementation. The learning process leads to understanding that can be immediately put into practice. This unity affects how people think about carrying out their particular responsibilities and results in larger-scale changes. Drake describes the process this way:

> We have come to think of sense-and-respond at four levels: transactional, process, organizational, and strategic. This has not only helped us think about our own business, but structures our approach to helping our customers lower their total systems costs. We changed our sales training to emphasize facilitation of response definition, instead of selling predefined services.

DSC's transformation is far from complete. Drake sees the integration of technology into the sense-and-respond system as one area lagging behind others. She knows IT expertise must play a key role in representing and running the business.

> We still have a long way to go in using technology-based sensing mechanisms. We have now made the chief technology officer a part of the senior team, but it was not easy finding someone who could be conceptual in helping us with our business design and also good at managing the nuts and bolts of information systems.

Nevertheless, progress has been made on several other fronts. The entire organization is now in the mode of continuously improving common processes, and DSC was poised to begin modularizing these processes in the first months of 1999. The executive team has used scenario planning to assist in the creation and evolution of DSC's context and has identified the key capabilities necessary to realize the firm's purpose of responding profitably to customer requests for integrated logistical systems and supply-chain solutions. Policy-makers have codified what they have learned about sense-and-respond leadership imperatives in a set of "Leadership Practices and Characteristics," a document Drake uses in filling key executive positions. DSC has, in addition, developed a template for profiling customers that enables the firm to identify and invest in mutually profitable customer relationships based on information sharing. As a result, says Drake, "more and more of our customers and potential cus*^mers are asking us to take the logistics leadership role in their business. This is confirmation for us that we are moving in the right direction."

THE STORY DOESN'T END HERE

Let's briefly review the logic of this book. Starting with Westpac's premise of increasing unpredictability as the ultimate strategic issue, we identified the economic properties of information as the underlying engine of discontinuous change. Merrifield's curve supplied graphic evidence, and more than sixteen hundred executives polled at the ABI confirmed this as the reality at their companies. Brian Arthur's casino and Glazer's list tied the logic of an information economy to some important implications for business. We explored the inadequacy of a business model conceptualized as an efficient machine—the model that "got us here"—for dealing with discontinuous change. After looking at emergent strategy as a possible replacement for the integrated, analytic, and too rigid strategy-as-plan model, we concluded that complexity theory, while having much to offer, does not adequately deal with an issue too important to ignore: Large firms are social systems of humans with their own purposes, who can and do change the purpose and rules of the systems of which they are part. Introducing the sense-and-respond model as an alternative, I argued that it preserves the purposefulness of the classical model, while leveraging the information management principle that enables adaptive systems to adapt. Sense-and-respond, the model, was presented as a prescription for large enterprises to institutionalize and systematize sense-and-respond, the behavior. Throughout, I have emphasized that the logic of sense-and-respond flows from the logic of doing business in an information economy.

After comparing and contrasting the characteristics of sense-and-respond organizations to their make-and-sell counterparts, I described them as collections of modular capabilities orchestrated into systems whose purposes are defined by reasons for being, whose boundaries are established by governing principles, and whose structures are expressed in high-level business designs. Collectively, these elements comprise organizational context, within which empowered people in accountable roles make decisions about how to produce the outcomes required of them by the business design. (See Figure 11.1.) We looked at each of these elements in some detail, using the experience of some early adopters to suggest principles that could assist others who might follow in their footsteps.

I described the role of leadership in adaptive enterprises in terms of a specific competence. To deliver the outcomes that the business requires of them, leaders must successfully fulfill the following responsibilities. They must create and adapt a viable organizational context. They must establish an effective governance system for coordinating activities within that context. And, finally, they must populate organizational roles with capable people. After discussing the demise of command and control as an unintended consequence of dismantling large central staffs, I presented a replacement governance candidate: Coordination of the interactions between roles by tracking the commitments between them. I introduced a protocol sufficiently general and rigorous to accomplish this, and highlighted some very important issues associated with ensuring that people use that rigor authentically. Finally, I

FIGURE 11.1

LEADING AN ADAPTIVE ENTERPRISE

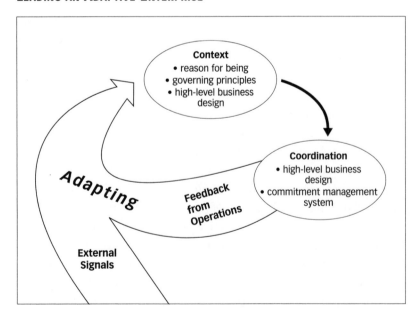

summarized what can be learned from the experience of pioneers in the transformation of their organizations to sense-and-respond.

How does a business know when it has completed the transformation? In one sense, of course, it never gets there, if by *there* it means finding another oasis of stability. The challenge of *becoming* a sense-and-respond organization gives way to the challenge of *being* a sense-and-respond organization. Further transformations are likely to become necessary—not to the sense-and-respond model, but within it. We have already seen that systematic adaptiveness requires that context be continually reviewed and adapted. Normally, the business design will adapt most rapidly, the principles more slowly, and the reason for being rarely. Since a new reason for being establishes a different purpose, which usually implies a different structure, changing the reason for being is likely to require yet another transformation. But because of their modularity and type of governance, transformations are much less traumatic for sense-and-respond organizations. Like other living systems, sense-and-respond organizations must continue to adapt—even if that means continuous transformation—or they will perish.

At a recent course, one thoughtful executive asked, "How will we know when we've become a sense-and-respond organization?" The question deserves consideration. Earlier I noted that the answer cannot be found by tabulating the number of a firm's sense-and-respond capabilities. Nor is it a question of how far leaders have progressed through a checklist of sense-and-respond. The following pro-forma checklist summarizes the prescriptions made in preceding chapters for creating very large sense-and-respond organizations. But more important than the checklist will be the *quality* of the decisions made while working through it. The competitiveness and viability of the context, and the way in which the people accountable for key roles execute the design—these determine how successful the adaptive enterprise will be.

- Create an unambiguous reason for being and governing principles.

- Create a high-level business design with a customer-back dispatching process.

- Codify the organizational context in technology.

- Define and support adaptive loops for the roles that must be highly adaptive.

- Implement a technology-assisted commitment management system.

- Place qualified people in key roles.

- Learn to communicate authentically about commitments.

In the final analysis, however, only experts can answer the question of whether a given firm has become a sense-and-respond organization. One group of such experts will be found in the organization's people. They will know whether customer requests truly drive the firm. The ultimate experts, of course, are the firm's customers. They are the final arbiters of value, and the only ones qualified to decide whether the firm has sensed their needs and is responsive to them.

These experts will tell you whether your firm is a dinosaur in a fur coat or if it has truly changed its corporate DNA. If it has transformed itself into a new species, it will no longer view change as a series of problems to be solved, but as an indispensable source of energy and growth.

APPENDIX A

CREATING THE MODULAR ORGANIZATION

Michael Shank

Sense-and-respond organizations are modular organizations. The design of these organizations, as Haeckel points out, expresses their adaptive strategies. Thus, strategy *becomes* structure as businesses seek to seize competitive advantage through modularity, using it to customize large numbers of profitable responses to individual customers. Advances in manufacturing technologies, marketing sophistication, services delivery, and interactive technology have already led to a much greater awareness of the potential of modular customization. Progress in e-business, knowledge management, organizational design, and capabilities for managing highly networked organizations have awakened interest in an even more fundamental issue implied by modular customization: modularizing the business itself.

In this appendix I will define and describe the modular organization and outline the choices executives must make when transforming their firms into successful modular organizations.

MODULAR FIRMS

Consider the varied approaches to modularization at four very different firms. A large insurance company studies its individual customers' needs and desires when facing a lifetime event, such as the birth of a child, retirement, or marriage. The company's customer service representative accesses a configurable knowledge base that matches the customers' wants and needs with the products and services offered by the company. Given the customers' state in life, the combination of life events they currently face or anticipate, and their expressed wants and needs, the representative can package a personalized set of products and services. These might include combining complementary annuities and insurance policies to manage risk and provide financial security. This visionary service has been a reality for years at USAA because of product modularity and a huge store of customer-specific information updated through constant dialog with individual clients.[1]

A large bicycle manufacturer faced cutthroat competition in a declining market with share moving offshore to companies offering commoditized products. Commoditization and increasing levels of obsolescent inventory threatened profitability for it and many other industry players. Japan's National Bicycle used that threat as an opportunity to capitalize on the inherent modularity of bicycles, 70 percent of the components of which are made by other firms. They modularized their order system to specifically capture and quickly respond to customer wants, needs, and dimensions. They now offer reasonably priced custom bikes to average consumers.[2]

Customers at distributors and retailers selling Andersen windows sit in front of a specialized personal computer system. The system provides both computer-aided design and a full electronic catalog with order-taking service. Dramatically reducing the time and error rate inherent in offering an ever increasing number of window design possibilities, the system allows customers to design their own windows using Andersen's multitude of modular window options. Customers get exactly what they want, while Andersen, its retailers, and distributors get a much more efficient and error-free ordering and production processes. Andersen now has a handle on the confusion formerly reigning because of its complex, varied offerings—through the logic of modular customization, the underlying logic of sense-and-respond structures.[3]

John Deere, to take a final example, uses a set of genetic algorithms that allow it to reconfigure its equipment manufacturing operations for large planters on a daily basis, if necessary. The algorithms ensure that each work station handles the optimal task in the right order to give customers the personalized planter they want, when they want it.[4] Real-time adjustments made in manufacturing operations and in the movement of work-in-progress through those operations match the changing mix of customer orders and delivery requirements.

As far as they have gone, however, none of these four firms pushes the envelope of product and process modularity quite as far as some systems integration and consulting firms do. General Electric's Steve Kerr points out that many firms today face the same conditions that consulting firms have faced for some years: unpredictable demand, both in degree and type; focus on a continuous stream of unique problems/opportunities; expansion and contraction in response to environmental opportunities; and the need to rapidly assemble and focus intellectual resources on evolving, ill-defined tasks.[5] Such organizations, he argues, require speed and flexibility more than efficiency and control, and more than most firms, they rely on fluid and temporary structures.

Systems integrators personify the respond-to-requests organization. Doing virtually only custom work, they yet must perform in a highly disciplined manner. Efficiency and effectiveness are crucial when bidding and executing large jobs and in maintaining high value-add as perceived by customers. Systems integrators often play single agenda games; that is, they have an equity interest in the customer outcome and, therefore, a higher motivation to be both efficient and flexible.

An effective systems integrator is essentially a dynamic pool of capabilities that must be configured (dispatched) both for bidding on contracts and for executing against contracts won. *Program* managers use this pool of capabilities to assemble the right team to judge the technical, business, schedule, project management, and industry-specific risk of a request-for-proposal opportunity. The configuration of these capabilities balances their cost against the potential risks and rewards of a given engagement to make a bid or no-bid decision. *Project* managers must then configure a different but complementary set of capabilities that builds upon the learning from the initial processes to dynamically configure the capabilities, skills, and resources needed to provide a customized modular solution that meets client needs.

Examining the operations of a systems integrator at a large consulting firm can shed light on important questions about modularity and provide some insights into the issues managers must consider if they are to transform their firms into sense-and-respond organizations. What capabilities are needed? How should they be organized? How are they configured or dispatched? How centralized or decentralized should the functions be? We will examine these questions below.

WHY MODULAR CUSTOMIZATION?

The capability to obtain, track, analyze, and compare increasing amounts of information about all customers allows firms to calculate the lifetime value of their customers (the expected profit over the time that customers continue to do business with the company). As firms get better at understanding the potential costs and benefits of individual customer relationships, they will become more interested in responding to the needs of high-value customers rather than following traditional make-and-sell strategies aimed at broad, if-we-build-it-they-will-come markets. As businesses develop or acquire both modular marketing and flexible production capabilities, others in the field will be forced to develop them as well to remain competitive. Another former trump card becomes an opening bet.

Furthermore, companies no longer see their options as either/or in the limited choice between a low-cost or a differentiation strategy. Manufacturing firms classified by Michael Porter as "stuck in the middle," that is, implementing both low-cost and differentiation strategies, either outperform or appear statistically inseparable from the performance of Porter's differentiators and cost leaders.[6] Advances in product and process innovation, especially modular customization, account for this result.

Brian Quinn found similar results in services. He points out that a number of firms have achieved "both lowest-cost outputs and maximum personalization and customization for customers."[7] Given the advances in manufacturing technologies, the growing importance of service to firms and customers, new levels of marketing sophistication, and rapidly developing interactive technologies, modular customization holds great potential for both physical and electronic commerce.

John Landry, IBM strategist and IBM/Lotus chief technology officer, recently assessed the potential impact of modular customization, broadly implemented, on the competitive landscape.

> I'm not talking about incremental change here. I'm talking about a set of technologies that will be as significant in impact as assembly-line technology was to mass production, and as mass-media technology was to mass-marketing. But this internetworking technology will replace many of the advantages of mass production and mass marketing by allowing for mass customization . . . creating, in some industries, custom goods better, faster, and cheaper than mass-produced goods and providing the framework for addressing individuals with custom marketing and individualized service.[8]

Some firms are beginning to realize these benefits today. The IBM Global Services Consulting Group studied mass customization in the United Kingdom manufacturing sector. The study's survey indicated that 72 percent of the respondents provided some form of product customization, as did 60 percent of their competitors. Over the next five years, 78 percent of the customizers intend to extend their customization. The study found that firms that had implemented mass customization averaged a 21 percent increase in market share, 24 percent less time to respond to customer orders, 14 percent greater profitability, and a 5 percent reduction in manufacturing costs.[9]

Implementing mass customization, of course, was not easy. The most significant barriers to mass customization reported by these firms included the following conditions.

- Inflexible factories

- Customization expense (unaffordable customized products)

- Rigid information systems

- Change management

- Management skills and attitudes

- Difficulties understanding customers' real needs

- Suppliers unable to match mass customization requirements

The report examined a number of ways to customize. Eighty percent of the respondents preferred "mass customization in the factory where products are customized on a mass basis using modular designs and fast, flexible, modular production processes enabling individual products to be delivered directly to the customer." Lean production, modular processes, successful integration of IT, fanatical customer focus, and flexible supplier partnerships were identified as the most important factors in achieving mass customization.

This study and others like it point to the importance of product and process modularity, driven by a customer-back approach that combines operational effectiveness and unique, strategically driven configurations of internal and external capabilities.

WHAT IS ORGANIZATIONAL MODULARITY?

Modular organizations respond in a dynamic way to the articulated and unarticulated wants and needs of customers through the reuse and reconfiguration of modular products or services and modular processes. Organizational modularization requires a standard way of linking capabilities and assets, which may be people, parts, process activities, or chunks of codified knowledge. An especially important capability is the "meta" process by which other modules are configured. While the outcome may be one of a kind, the way of getting there is not—not if the firm truly wants to reach the full benefits of modular customization. "Making this up as we go along" by using a new ad hoc process each time is "invention," not customization through a modular organization.[10] Firms that want to customize efficiently at large scale do so through modular organizations.

WHAT MODULARITY DECISIONS SHOULD A FIRM BE MAKING?

Executives may think they face a black-and-white choice: Customize or not. But neither highly integrated operations nor modularity are cure-alls. In fact, modularity can be very expensive if personalization doesn't create real value for customers. Executives should consider the following when thinking about where modularization may bring their firms the most benefit.

- **Products**

  Product modularity is driven by the reuse of modular components configured to gain economies of scope through the production of multiple responses to market requests.

- **Processes**

  Process modularity is driven by reuse to lower the cost of producing offerings with acceptable price-performance trade-offs.

- **Organization**

  At one level, organizational modularity is driven by the mix of product and process modularity for different parts of the organization and the markets they serve. At a higher level, managers may come to see the firm itself as a modular unit (or a configuration of modular units) existing within a value net or industry map. Deciding which capabilities to modularize and how to modularize them becomes a key question for executives and managers.

Companies undertake modularization strategies to enhance their adaptiveness for a variety of reasons, including the following:

- To increase the firm's inherent flexibility in process by allowing the firm to reconfigure subprocesses and activities in proven and well understood ways. The motivations for doing this are increased efficiency, faster change, and greater variety in process technology.

- To increase returns on product and process innovation by reusing components of that innovation in other processes, products, and services, thus accelerating experience effects and learning curves.

- To understand and optimally configure the trade-offs between product and service variety on the one hand, and production and marketing complexity on the other.

- To incorporate the customer into the needs specification and into the product/service design and configuration processes that provide marketing, manufacturing, and design input.

- To develop more robust designs that can more easily be modified for multiple markets, including markets of one customer.

- To compensate for the shorter life cycles of products and processes by extending the life cycles of their component parts.

- To move, with minimum disruption to the overall system, toward new business models, facilitating response to changed market conditions both through reconfiguration of product and process modules and through internal alteration of modular elements of products and processes.[11]

- To allow a firm to combine existing capabilities and open standards of process and technology in unique ways. Rather than having to continuously develop and defend proprietary methods and offerings, modularization facilitates the use of partnerships and alliances to improve the speed and quality of responses.

The use of modularity continues to evolve. Today, different firms approach its development and implementation in different ways. Two primary ways of organizing and coordinating a firm's modularity have emerged and are examined below: object-oriented modularity and protocol-oriented modularity.

OBJECT-ORIENTED MODULARITY

The object-oriented approach to modularization features Lego-like linkages that are conceived and implemented during the initial building phase of a system and further developed over time. Westpac Bank of Australia took this approach in the mid-1980s.

In his work on software-based innovation, James Brian Quinn noted that service activities can be divided into smaller critical units of service that can "be endlessly combined or manipulated to satisfy individual customer and operating needs." Quinn likened this to object-oriented software programming.[12]

In object-oriented programs, software objects represent real-world things and concepts. Objects carry both a method (instructions used by the object to carry out certain actions) and a variable (locations of data referring to other objects). Objects and variables in the same class carry references to partner objects. These partner object references have hooks that allow the objects to combine with one another using rules the objects are capable of interpreting. Thus, they create a *potential* for combining rather than a predetermined, hardwired set of combinations, the way procedural software does. Some firms attempt to approach modular organization in this way.

Here, the interface between modules is critical. The goal is a Lego-like ability to snap modules together. This approach works best when processes are well understood. When processes and procedures change dynamically in ways difficult to predict or imagine, this approach will be much more difficult and risky. Typically, too, it entails a very slow and burdensome process, subject to large budget and time overruns, as was the case at Westpac. A final drawback is that object-oriented systems may have difficulties linking to or incorporating external modules from suppliers that cannot build to the Lego-like interface used by the rest of the system.

Protocol-Oriented Modularity

A second way to modularize uses a shared protocol. Common protocols function like a telephone system dial tone. Using a dial tone and its associated standards, people from different geographies can place and receive calls from individuals in distant places using multiple telephone systems. Protocols act as general common connectors, joining diverse pieces (modules) across a broader range of differences than those possible with an object-oriented approach. Protocol-based systems function much the same way as TCP/IP and HTML do to bring together the diverse and dynamic parts of the World Wide Web.

Haeckel has described a commitment management system for keeping track within a business of who owes what to whom. The standard way that he proposes for communicating about commitments serves the protocol needs of a modular organization very well. This commitment management protocol is general, thus enabling a company to manage external capabilities as part of its own internal system design, using a single system to govern the interactions of all capabilities. The protocol also handles the ad hoc parts of modular processes both inside and outside the business more effectively than object-oriented modularity. For these reasons, new and changing alliances and partnerships, as well as changes within the firm, can be better handled using the protocol approach than using the object approach.

Furthermore, as the constant evolution of the World Wide Web suggests, the protocol approach fosters more experimentation and evolution than does the object approach. Firms do not have to anticipate the end state as completely when designing protocol versus object interfaces. More intelligence can be placed in the elements being configured using the protocol, in contrast to the object approach, thus allowing for increased decentralization closer to the dynamic marketplace and increased experimentation in sensing and responding. The dispatching or configuring function can better focus on bringing appropriate people, information, and components together to develop additional ways of capturing more value from the customer back to the organization.

MODULARITY IN ACTION

IBM's Global Services Consulting Group provides an excellent example of evolving modularity in action. In seven years, the Consulting Group has grown from a start-up unit to one of the world's largest consulting organizations, generating over $1 billion in annual revenues. While it has always delivered customer-unique solutions, the group has dramatically evolved the way in which it provides those solutions. Originally, consulting was a small craft-based group of IBM veterans and professional hires who relied on their personal and professional experience to meet customer needs. As the Consulting Group grew and its breadth and depth of experience and expertise increased, it developed multiple methodologies to guide its practice around the world. Competencies and competency segments were created with specific skill requirements and operational guidelines. Knowledge networks developed to supplement these competency segments with new knowledge, analytics, and tools.

Over time, the strict reliance on craft, even supplemented by methodology and knowledge networks, imposed limitations on the unit's growth and customer service. IBM needed to share its increasing expertise across individuals, industries, geographies, and competency segments and to configure more dynamically the diverse skills and talents it brought to an engagement. It also needed to work more closely with the enormous array of products and services available in other parts of IBM and from IBM's business partners.

The Consulting Group reorganized around the specific industries it served, reinforcing its customer-back approach. It developed an award-winning intellectual capital management system to codify its best internal and external expertise and experiences. It disaggregated its multiple methodologies, rewriting them as modular *work products*. These work products represent the outputs produced during the course of multiple engagements and include the context and rationale behind each.

The group developed an engagement advisor technology to configure, within the context of customer-specific issues, work products and their associated knowledge, analytics, and tools across IBM's Intellectual Capital Management system. This technology made it possible for principals and engagement managers to link customer issues with the configuration of people, processes, technology, and activities required to address those issues in a customized way that leveraged IBM's experience and expertise. It enables the production of highly effective and efficient customer solutions from capabilities assembled from across IBM and external business partners.

In developing this system, IBM applied the modularization approach it has used to help customers transform their businesses. From manufacturing to services, retail to government, across a wide range of industries, IBM can now more effectively ask and answer the critical questions that must be addressed if it is to help its clients transform themselves from make-and-sell into sense-and-respond organizations.

MODULARIZE WHAT, WHY, WHERE, WHEN, AND HOW?

The subsidiary serving small businesses at a mid-sized financial services firm found itself increasingly surrounded by a host of large, high-volume, low-cost financial services competitors, as well as smaller local competitors specializing in personalized service. In the midst of an engagement to reengineer a client's business processes, this subsidiary stopped to examine its objectives. The phrase *faster, cheaper, better* was not understood in the same way across the firm. An analysis revealed that 100 percent success in achieving the stated objectives of the reengineering project would not materially advance the firm's competitive position. At best, it might continue to fall behind, but at a slower pace.

The reengineering project stopped as IBM helped the firm to rethink its competitive strategy and modularize its operations to facilitate a new approach to the market. This process started with an analysis of the existing marketplace and the creation of scenarios about customers' and competitors' potential development. The firm decided to move toward sense-and-respond as a strategic alternative to its competitors' differentiation and low-cost strategies.

Existing processes and functions were analyzed to determine the optimal degree of modularization needed to provide flexibility while avoiding unnecessary complexity. Careful attention was paid to specific whats, whys, wheres, and whens to determine which processes and subprocesses should be modularized and which could continue with incremental improvement.

Branch managers were assigned the role of initial configurators. Working with enhanced training and skills and a newly created portfolio of product and service components, these individuals used new diagnostics along with their personal expertise and experience to trigger the development and delivery of personalized products and services to customers. Using the original analysis, a number of fast-path configurations were developed to lead the firm's new marketing efforts and rapidly regain market presence.

While this story plays out differently with different clients, some consistent themes surface. First it shows that, in large companies, modularization should always proceed from the customer-back. IBM's Customer Value Management methodology helps identify those unique value-creating elements that would be enhanced by customization done early on. This identification leads to a customer-centric, evolving envelope of wants and needs linked to firm capabilities. Care must be exercised, however, that an ability to customize doesn't create organizational hubris of the kind that tries to be too many things to too many people.

This is not to say that dramatic advances cannot be made in the art of the possible. By modularizing products and services around those things that really matter to customers, a firm can change the nature of competition—opening up new competitive spaces for itself and others. Custom Foot does not customize everything about the shoes that it sells. It only customizes the *fit*. A consumer can find far more variety in service, styles, and colors from other shoe retailers. But they will be hard pressed to find a more customized fit at a lower price from any other firm. Other retailers may choose to customize along those lines or to combine shoe customization with other aspects of their consumers' total shoe-buying and shoe-wearing experiences.

By modularizing and getting closer to the individual customer, firms have a much better opportunity to learn about an entire industry's tacit compromises in meeting customer needs.[13] Leading-edge customers and aggregated trends can help firms like National Bicycle spot emerging personalization preferences early, and incorporate appropriate responses into both its standard lines as well as its custom line. Firms like Levi Strauss, with its Personal Pair stores, can use the information they accumulate on the changing "shape" of the marketplace, gained from thousands of pairs of personalized jeans, to influence the cut and style of their off-the-shelf offerings.

The head of operations for Streamline, a Boston based firm delivering customized grocery and related services (cleaning, videos, take-out) to the homes of delighted suburbanites was asked when the service would come to New York City. His answer: "No time soon." This response reflects the realities of a mismatch between Streamline's current delivery capability—using optimized routing to replenish refrigerator/pantry/closet units in its customers' garages—and the requirements of operating in an urban environment with no garages. The need to schedule deliveries when customers are home rather than according to an optimized schedule undermines the advantages gained from differentiated service. Streamline has too many opportunities to serve its ideal, high-value customers to risk urban-required modifications to its current modular competencies.

Firms should redesign their production process or their product to match the need for responsiveness and customization. Product designs and production processes that only allow for customization early in the production process limit the firm's ability to adjust to changes during production or to compete in situations where the time needed to produce a product exceeds the market's opportunity window. Companies like John Deere used to address this situation by starting many work-in-process variations early in the order season and modifying them as orders came in. By changing their product and process designs, however, they were able to cut their work-in-process levels exponentially.

TRADE-OFFS TO CONSIDER

Modularity presents firms with a number of choices about the scope of customer values it will provide and the capabilities it will build and maintain. A too-granular modularization of processes increases cost and complexity. Too little limits flexibility. Product modularity may be too great, frustrating customers with unnecessary and unwanted choices, or too little, failing to customize product or service elements that really matter. The protocol or object system put in place may extend outside the firm or be limited to coordinating capabilities inside the company. If extended outside the firm and aligned with innovative alliance and partnership arrangements, the firm may be able to overcome an historical inability to make system-level trade-offs, thus avoiding the suboptimization that occurs both inside and outside many firms.

Few businesses realize or resolve all of these trade-offs in their initial moves into modularization. All firms can capitalize on the experience of others who have learned these lessons over time. Each can capture and leverage the customer, product, and process knowledge that dramatically accelerates in modularized firms. Some of that knowledge is summarized below.

THREE KEYS TO SUCCESS

Many discussions of modularity begin and end with the concept of pulling together a string of capabilities to form a customer-unique value chain. But there is more to it than that. IBM's Global Services Consulting Group has identified three core components required for sense-and-respond modular organizations. These components constitute integral parts of the functioning and value-add potential of modular customization.

- *A customer interface* that allows customers to easily state their known preferences and adds value by assisting customers in determining tacit preferences.

- *A configuration system,* consisting of a person, a group, software, or a manual procedure, that starts with the customer's order and snaps together the capability modules needed to respond to the request.

- *A capabilities management system* that identifies the firm's required capability modules, adjusting them as needed, and manages extended enterprise interfaces for capabilities obtained outside the firm or across multiple business units.

The customer interface serves as one of the key sensing elements of a sense-and-respond organization. An appropriately designed interface captures both articulated and unarticulated customer wants and needs. Significant value resides in developing modular capabilities for evoking requests from customers. A systems integrator, for example, must have skills in helping shape the bid, using its experience to help clients learn what to ask for, why, and how. Building systems that allow customers to shape their bids helps them to make better requests and to make requests that better match the firm's repertoire of capabilities. Done correctly, this interface starts the commitment management process at the point of initial contact with the customer and extends it throughout the customer's experience.

The configurator sits at the heart of modular organizations. It is the primary source of knowledge about how to reuse and reconfigure organization capabilities in an efficient, effective, *repeatable* way. Management in any organization must make important design choices about how to tie capabilities together and where to place the organization's intelligence to enhance the firm's adaptiveness to changing customer values. Motorola and John Deere use very sophisticated, IT-based configuration (dispatching) systems. A large furniture manufacturer, relying on people rather than software, set up a new logistics and expediting group to act as its dispatcher. Successful modular organizations support the dispatcher with information flows that permit adaptation and improve the firm's configuration capabilities over time.

Ultimately, success depends on the capabilities an enterprise has available to configure. The ability to know and help customers to know and express what they want is valuable, as are excellent configuration capabilities. But they will be of little use if the needed capabilities aren't there to dispatch. Resource-based competitiveness cannot be ignored in the push to become more customer-centric. Successful modular customization embodies the combined power of integrating customers *and* capabilities.

E-BUSINESS CHANGES EVERYTHING

One note of warning—or perhaps of encouragement—to firms hoping to change the nature of the game quickly. E-business changes everything in the modular customization space. A few speculations might be useful, based on the experiences of our clients thus far.

The shape and pace of developing modular organizations and the nature of customization and personalization will continue to change dramatically. The amount and type of information used to represent the physical world will continue to increase. Today, information about an airplane seat has more value than the seat itself. (Consider the relative size and profitability of American Airlines and The Sabre Group.) Increasingly, the locus of today's and tomorrow's competitive battlefields will be customization by modular organizations using that information space. Businesses will have to become more modular to deliver this degree of customization.

Internetworked firms using the modularizing protocols of intranets, internets, and extranets will become the key competitors. Personalization and customization at low incremental cost will become the rule rather than the exception for highly valuable customer segments. Some virtual companies will exploit this advantage, while others will seize much of the cost leadership space by making differentiation through modular customization an imperative for many incumbents. Consumer power will continue to increase as e-commerce shifts from today's focus on the seller to tomorrow's focus on an empowered buyer. Some interesting twists will occur in today's notions of interactivity as the shift toward the customer changes in nature. *One-to-one* may take on a new meaning as customers and customer groups exploit their newly found power and start customizing their relationships collectively and individually across sellers rather than waiting for sellers to customize their experience. The death of distance and the end of time and space limitations may be overstated, but we are rapidly running out of time and space for firms who fail to assess and adapt to the impact of these changes on their strategy and operations.

We have looked at some of the concepts, major benefits, and barriers associated with creating modular organizations. Distinguishing between product, process, and organizational modularity, I described two different approaches to organizing and coordinating modularity—object oriented versus protocol. I explored some of the trade-offs and keys to success, emphasizing the importance of customer interface roles, configurator/dispatchers capabilities, and capability management systems. Finally, I briefly noted the key role that e-business will play in determining the shape and pace of modular organization development and its implications for competitive advantage in the next millennium.

Large sense-and-respond organizations require modular organizations. They need an economic way to respond with different value propositions to individual customers. Transformation into a modular organization does not occur overnight. Many choices must be made, but the most important are driven by a deep understanding of the value that customers place on personalized responses for different parts of the value proposition. Firms have the opportunity to start now to learn about modularization and assess its relevance to their competitive situation. They must, if they want to transform their firms into organizations capable of sensing and rapidly, efficiently, and effectively responding to their customers.

APPENDIX B

COLLABORATIVE DECISION-MAKING IN ADAPTIVE ENTERPRISES

Michael Kusnic and Daniel Owen

Sense-and-respond organizations require strategic, collaborative, and customer-back decision-making processes. This appendix describes a powerful process that satisfies all of these criteria.

TRADITIONAL DECISION-MAKING

Most organizations use a familiar strategic decision-making process to resolve conflicts over resource allocation. It usually starts with some individual or group in the organization proposing a "straw man" course of action that makes sense from their point of view. (See Table B.1.) These proposals may arise from individual initiative or as responses to management requests. Proposal content consists primarily of evidence supporting the suggested course of action. Information damaging to the proposal is often filtered out either consciously or unconsciously. Typically, the proposal includes a business case with assumptions about the future used to calculate the profitability to be expected from adoption of the proposed course.

The centerpiece of this decision process is a "pitch." The pitch, as the term indicates, is designed to "sell" the proposed solution to the decision-maker(s). This advocacy process, in turn, tends to create an adversarial culture. The advocate or champion intends to sell the proposal, and the reviewers counter with the attitude "Buyer beware."

TABLE B.1

A Fundamentally Different Approach to Decision-Making

	TRADITIONAL DECISION PROCESS	ADAPTIVE DECISION PROCESS
Frame	• strawman solution • selective, known facts • assumptions about the future	• broad range of alternatives • identification of unknowns • ranges of uncertainty
Result	• "pitch" showing detailed evaluation of recommended course of action	• shared learning about the sources of value and risk in each alternative
Purpose	• justify the recommended course of action	• new "hybrid" course of action combining most valuable elements of each alternative
Culture	• adversarial • distrustful	• cooperative • open and inquisitive
Quality	• "inspected in" after the fact • reviews	• "built into" the process • dialogues

This approach fosters a culture high in distrust, especially regarding information sharing. Since everyone justifiably suspects that others bring forward only selective and self-serving information, no one trusts the information presented. To maintain parity in the debate, all stakeholders to the decision must independently develop their own sources of information. This underlying distrust severely hampers, and may preclude altogether, decision-makers' ability to learn from one another during the decision process.

By analogy to a manufacturing process, the output of which is a flow of products, the output of a decision-making process is a flow of decisions. And, to take the analogy further, both processes rely on inspectors to ensure quality control. The real purpose served by the management review process is quality control, after-the-fact inspections of decision recommendations. Depending on the importance of the decision being made (usually measured in terms of the magnitude of the resources involved), the champion for the recommendation may have to go through several levels of review and inspection. In these reviews, the advocate will face predictable questions. "Did you consider X?" "What about the implications of Y?" The quality of the responses to these will determine whether the recommendation is approved or sent back for rework.

DECISIONS AND DECISION-MAKING

Many decision-makers do not distinguish between the process of decision-making and the content of the decisions they make. They tend to think of decisions as conclusions (as in "I decided to do X") and to think of decision processes as decision *support* processes (for example, "My staff's financial analysis of our options provided valuable input for our decision"). We will use the term *decision* to mean an irrevocable allocation of resources. This is not the typical definition, which approaches more closely the use in the statement "Management decided to strive for world-class quality." Without a concomitant resource commitment, the strategic "decision" to strive for world-class quality becomes a wish or an empty statement of desire.[1] The simple discipline of defining strategic decisions in terms of resource commitments can be profoundly clarifying to both management and subordinates, because it forces identification of specific actions necessary for implementation.

Not all decisions are alike. Managers do not need a formal decision-making process for many operational decisions. Experience, discussion, and some traditional analyses will be sufficient. All parties know and understand the important issues. Evaluation can be reasonably performed without a careful treatment of risk or uncertainty. But these conditions rarely exist for the kind of strategic decisions that must be made when a new business environment arises from competitive or government actions or from the emergence of new markets or technologies. In such cases, decision-makers often suffer from one or more of the following deficits.

- Lack of clarity on how prior experience applies.

- Lack of consensus on the critical issues to consider and feasible actions to undertake.

- Lack of certainty about what numbers to use in the evaluation.

When clarity, consensus, and certainty are lacking, a systematic, disciplined process can markedly improve the quality of decision-making.

AN ALTERNATIVE APPROACH: THE
ADAPTIVE DECISION PROCESS

Organizations attempting to become adaptive enterprises can utilize a fundamentally better way to make decisions: the Adaptive Decision Process, or ADP.[2] ADP is a collaborative, systematic way of making choices in complex, uncertain environments and of gaining organizational commitment to implement the result. The process consists of four phases—*framing, alternatives, analysis,* and *connection*—each culminating in a *structured dialogue* between the decision-makers and a decision support team.[3] Specific tools, analytics, communication templates, and deliverables, designed to induce clarity, support each dialogue.

The framework of the Adaptive Decision Process differs from the traditional process in three important respects.

- Rather than starting with a "straw man" solution, ADP identifies several significantly different but practicable courses of action that capture the range of debate within the organization about what ought to be done.

- Rather than beginning with what is known about the world, ADP identifies what is not known that would be useful to know in evaluating the relative merits of the alternatives.

- Rather than making specific assumptions about the future to calculate business case profitability, ADP identifies the ranges of uncertainty about the key factors influencing the desired outcome to learn what information is and is not important to the decision.

In our experience, this process results in significant shared learning about the sources of value and risk in each of the initial alternatives. Collaborative learning leads to a better alternative upon completion of the process. We call this alternative the *hy-*

brid. When the process works well, this hybrid alternative integrates the highest value-creating elements of each of the initial alternatives into a course of action with significantly more value than any of the original proposals. Moreover, the hybrid will be an intuitively compelling course of action for all relevant stakeholders because its rationale unifies the different viewpoints advanced at the beginning of the process.

Because it channels conflict resulting from different perspectives into a win-win hybrid by introducing a shared approach to sense-making, repeated application of ADP can change an organization's culture. Businesses that fully integrate it into their operations experience a marked shift toward a more cooperative, open, and inquisitive culture.

Finally, strategic decision quality is designed into ADP; quality is not "inspected in" after the fact. The revolution that took place in manufacturing during the 1970s and 1980s taught us that getting quality in the output requires building quality into the process. An end-of-the-line inspection will not do. The heart of adaptive decision-making lies in collaborative dialogues, not hierarchical reviews. ADP uses dialogue to lure into the open all alternative views, issues, and value conflicts, and then deals with them in a shared learning context. It effectively and efficiently involves all stakeholders in the sequence of dialogues to obtain shared clarity both on the strategic issue to be addressed and on the highest value course of action. ADP produces consensus, commitment, and closure *prior* to implementation.

CUSTOMER-BACK VERSUS FIRM-FORWARD DECISION-MAKING

Sense-and-respond organizations are flexible, modular systems of operational capabilities designed to respond rapidly to implicit or explicit customer requests. This customer-back principle applies equally to the management of the enterprise's network of strategic decisions. Adopting the creation of customer value, as opposed to shareholder value, as the enterprise's fundamental purpose is essential to the shift from firm-forward to customer-back decision-making. The Adaptive Decision Process provides an explicit mechanism for aligning all enterprise actions and resource allocations around an enterprise-level creation of customer value.[4] At this level, ADP addresses the two fundamental questions of business.

- What do our customers, both present and potential, want?

- How can we best respond to their needs?

The answer to the first question should be the same no matter where in the system it is asked, because all parts of the enterprise, by virtue of being elements of the same system, serve the same customers. The second question, however, will elicit answers that vary subsystem by subsystem, because actions by different parts of the enterprise generally have different impacts on the value delivered. (In a profound sense, customers define the systems that serve them. To the extent that subsystems serve different customers, they should be viewed as parts of different systems.)

The multiple answers expected for the second question have important implications for organizational alignment and coherence, decentralization of decision-making, and organizational empowerment. Using the ADP framework fosters decentralized, yet coherent, subsystem-level decision-making because all decisions use the same metric for evaluation: impact on customer value. This helps ensure that local reward systems will be consistent with one another and with the purpose of the system—aligning the organization's "arrows" in the direction of customer value.[5]

As described in the next two sections, ADP operates simultaneously at two levels. Level I aligns actions to add value within the context of the organization's current understanding of the environment within which it operates, what might be termed its *momentum world*. This level includes sensing selected environmental signals to improve the value of the current course and speed of the business. Level II deals with the problem of adapting the context—identifying if and when the world is likely to change in a significant way. This level focuses on identifying and scanning for potentially important discontinuous changes in the environment that would trigger reinitiation of the Level I process. In this sense, Level II makes this collaborative decision-making process adaptive. As a higher-level process, it can change the context in which Level I decisions are made. It uses scenarios to identify the environmental uncertainties most likely to yield information about relevant emerging discontinuities.

LEVEL I: RESPONDING WITHIN OUR CURRENT UNDERSTANDING OF THE WORLD

The starting point for implementing a sense-and-respond framework at the strategic level is alignment of the organization's responses around the delivery of value from the customer's viewpoint. Each iteration on this process takes place through four structured dialogues.

Framing

Framing establishes agreement about what the enterprise must respond to and how it defines a response. It also identifies the critical uncertainties that make choosing a response difficult. It does so by asking and answering three key questions.

- Who are our customers?
- What is our purpose?
- How will we accomplish it?

Since a problem poorly defined will never be effectively addressed, the framing stage focuses on minimizing ambiguity within the decision-making team about the problem's three critical elements.

Because ADP works from the customer back, the first step requires defining who the customers are and what they want. These questions are clarified by identifying the implicit customer value attributes delivered by the firm's existing offerings and responses. The question "What do our customers want?" can thus be subdivided into two specific questions. First, "What attributes do customers perceive and value?" Second, "How much would each customer segment be willing to pay in the future for a one-unit improvement in each of these attributes?" Answering the second question, of course, requires a clear answer to the first. To make meaningful judgments about marginal value from a customer perspective, the attributes of value perceivable to the customer must be sharply defined and measurable.[6]

Framing also requires clarity about the enterprise purpose. This comes from the reason-for-being statement and its associated governing principles. These elements of organizational context clarify and establish constraints around who serves whom and how.

The last task in framing is to articulate the uncertainties (and their interrelationships) that stand between the actions we have the power to take and the conditions necessary for delivering value to the customer. A powerful tool called a sensing diagram helps provide new insights into how the system creates value and its potential for creating more.

Alternatives

The alternatives phase helps to identify and articulate the range of possible strategy responses to customer needs within the environment defined in framing. It asks and answers the question, "What is the range of alternative coherent responses, given the context defined during framing?" Using a tool called a response table, each alternative response strategy is spelled out in terms of the value attribute levels it would deliver to each customer segment. In addition, it specifies the actions that would make possible delivery of those value attribute levels.

The set of alternatives should represent the range of perspectives within the organization on how the enterprise should respond to the challenge or opportunity in question. In this sense, the alternatives phase is designed explicitly to bring to the surface conflicting views about what should be done. Our experience shows that the value of the process lies in examining the conflict. Embedded within the different points of view lie powerful insights into how the system can create value. Inducing clarity about the implications of these different viewpoints is necessary in combining participants' insights into a win-win hybrid course of action.

Analysis

Straightforward but powerful analytic tools are now brought to bear to identify the sources of the value and risk embedded in each initial alternative. Participants ask themselves and one another, "What have we learned about the sources of value and risk from a side-by-side examination of the initial alternatives?" The intent is not to pick the best alternative but to create a shared understanding of the value and risk associated with each. Because of this, the analysis phase is often referred to as the search for value. The analysis phase delivers a heads-up display for management to use in guiding the enterprise.

Connection

Haeckel has noted that decision-making is the process by which people transform knowledge into action. In the ADP, connecting decisions to implementable action happens in the connection phase.[7] Connection defines a new, hybrid response combining the sources of value in each of the initially identified alternatives. It describes the actions to be taken, establishes accountability for those actions, identifies where flexibility is required, and sheds light on what must be sensed.

Invariably, the connection dialogue is the most valuable. The key questions asked are "What are we going to do? And why?" All of the insight issuing from the systematic analysis of each alternative produces a synthesized response strategy that incorporates the best elements of each alternative. An important outcome of this phase is a compelling rationale for why the synthesis "makes sense." This involves a systematic way of exploiting the intuitive and nonlinear thinking capability of humans. The decision-makers must determine whether the hybrid is internally consistent and makes real sense, or if it is merely a mechanical stitching together of each alternative's highest value elements. The result is "connected" to implementation by using the commitment management protocol to establish formal accountability for carrying out the underlying actions.

Depending on the level of unpredictability that surfaced during the analysis phase about either the environment or the firm's capabilities, elements of the hybrid response strategy may not be completely determined. Uncertainties may dictate specific contingency planning. In such cases, the connection phase identifies the investments in information acquisition (for example, additional sensing probes) required to trigger the contingent response.

LEVEL II: ADAPTING TO NEW WORLDS AND DISCONTINUITIES

The sense-and-respond adaptation in Level I takes place within a given set of environmental assumptions. We call this collection of assumptions the *momentum world*. An essential requirement for an adaptive enterprise, however, is an ability to deal with increasingly frequent, discontinuous change. The Level II loop identifies and anticipates which potential discontinuities warrant a fundamental revisiting of the enterprise's context and, therefore, of its hybrid response strategy.

The Level II inquiry, based on the same underlying collaborative decision process as Level I, uses the same four phases. What differs, however, are the key questions asked in each phase.

Framing

Level II framing identifies events that might trigger the emergence of a "new world." Decision-makers explicitly ask and answer, "What events define relevant new worlds?" For adaptive decision-making, such world-defining events can trigger a new customer value attribute or a discontinuous change in the customers' willingness to pay for previously identified attributes.

Alternatives

A new world does not usually come to pass from a single event. Its emergence will typically be characterized by several interrelated events interacting with one another. The challenge for decision-makers is to relate these events and their effects in a coherent pattern. Using a tool called a scenario table, those participating in the alternatives phase identify alternative sets of events that could give rise to fundamentally new worlds. They ask and answer the question, "What is the range of possible alternative new worlds?"

Analysis

The framing and alternatives phases establish the context required to relate the potential emergence of new worlds to changes in the customers' value structures. In analysis a series of questions aids in evaluating the Level I hybrid against different customer value structures corresponding to the alternative possible worlds. "In which new worlds is our hybrid response robust? Which of the new worlds represents a threat? Which represents an opportunity?" The answers lead to the understanding of the robustness of a particular hybrid strategy in different environmental scenarios.

Connection

Once the worlds are identified that would lead us to revisit the hybrid strategy, we use connection to identify and deploy information probes designed to give advance warning of impending new worlds that matter.[8] Decision-makers must ask and answer the following questions: "What must we sense about the environment to anticipate the emergence of relevant new worlds? Who will be responsible for deploying and monitoring those sensors?" Using the scenario table in reverse allows us to identify which uncertain events to monitor. The identification made through this high-level process of a likely new world signals the need to examine the Level I response strategy and, if necessary, adapt it. (Recall that, for sense-and-respond organizations, this entails changing the high-level business design, which expresses the hybrid strategy.)

An ADP Application at IBM's Advanced Business Institute

The ABI's reason-for-being and associated governing principles make quite clear the organization's two most important constituencies: the IBM corporation and the participants in its education programs. In a series of decision-making dialogues, ABI leaders came to grips with the issues behind adapting customer executive education to meet the changing needs of IBM's customers. They first clearly articulated, from the viewpoints of its customers, the value attributes that should determine the ABI's response.

For IBM, the primary customer's value attribute appears in the ABI's reason for being: additional revenue attributable to the influence of the ABI. The value attributes for customer executives attending ABI events include new ideas that can be implemented in their companies, the opportunity to network with executives in other companies, and the motivation to learn stemming from the Palisades learning environment.

The response strategy would have to involve the coordination of three high-level actions: choosing a curriculum, implementing a marketing strategy, and maintaining an e-business learning environment. The decision-makers identified several critical uncertainties, including the following:

- How will various response strategies affect the number of executives who attend the ABI?

- What qualities of the e-business learning environment are most important to our customers?

- How will changes in the curriculum affect the number of implementable ideas it delivers?

- What drivers underlie the ABI's ability to achieve greater influence over revenue for IBM?

The ABI developed three alternative responses. Each was given a name that reflected its character. (See Table B.2.) *Current Course and Speed* (CC&S) includes some currently planned changes but recognizes that without a concerted commitment by its leadership, the ABI will undergo little change in direction. Having identified the customers and their value attributes, leadership unanimously agreed that CC&S could not deal with the changes they anticipated. The *e-business Institute* response was attractive because it aligned strongly with IBM's e-business strategy. The *Magnet Institute* response targets a broader group of executives by broadening the curriculum from a management/information technology (IT) interface to the management/IT/*information* interface,

TABLE B.2

THE ABI "BASE CASE" (CURRENT COURSE AND SPEED) COMPARED TO TWO ALTERNATIVE STRATEGIES

	MARKETING	CURRICULUM	ENVIRONMENT
Current Course and Speed	• mass mailings • current customers • broadcast communications • primary channel = "rep"	• broad samplings of IT and management thought • synthesis of leading-edge thought	• reflective • technology enabled
e-Business Institute	• e-mail and focused mail campaigns • direct to customers • 1:1 marketing programs • information-intensive industries	• interface between management and IT • focus on e-business synthesis of IBM research • leading-edge topics	• technology learning experience • more meeting time • more collaborative learning
Magnet Institute	• all customers • 1:1 marketing programs • information-intensive industries • use new channels (consultants, alumni)	• interfaces between management and information • more strategy and information focus • more original research	• technology learning experience • more class time

the former being of interest primarily to the CIO and the latter to functional and policy executives as well as the CIO.

The deliverable of the analysis phase is not a recommendation but rather understanding about and insight into the sources of value in each of the responses. The e-business response, for example, includes electronic, customized marketing and thus reaches a broader audience than does CC&S. It would, therefore, increase sales for IBM *and* expand the potential for networking among the customer executive attendees. Other important insights and understandings included the following:

- The e-business Institute response minimizes value because it appeals to single individuals with this responsibility.

- Focusing on the management/IT/information interface rather than the management/IT interface significantly increases value because it appeals to executive team participation.

- An improved marketing strategy with electronic, customized materials increases value for both categories of customer.

- The ABI does not know whether participants would prefer more or less class time each day.

- Agreement among the management team about these insights and understandings constitutes the foundation needed to create a hybrid response.

The hybrid response, labeled *e-Magnet Institute,* emerged from the combination of the most valuable components of each of the initial alternatives (see Table B.3). It combines the management/IT/information-focused curriculum (which interests more senior executives) with electronic marketing (which increases overall attendance). It also includes more time for meetings within, between, or among participating firms to facilitate networking.

As usual, the creation of this hybrid involved more than an analytical exercise. The decision team synthesized the e-Magnet Institute during a dialogue. The starting points of the dialogue

THE HYBRID STRATEGY (e-MAGNET INSTITUTE) INTEGRATES THE
MOST VALUABLE ELEMENTS

	MARKETING	CURRICULUM	ENVIRONMENT
Current Course and Speed	• mass mailings • current customers • broadcast communications • primary channel = "rep"	• broad samplings of IT and management thought • synthesis of leading-edge thought	• reflective • technology enabled
e-Business Institute	• e-mail and focused mail campaigns • direct to customers • 1:1 marketing programs • information-intensive industries	• interface between management and IT • focus on e-business synthesis of IBM research • leading-edge topics	• technology learning experience • more meeting time • more collaborative learning
Magnet Institute	• all customers • 1:1 marketing programs • information-intensive industries • use new channels (consultants, alumni)	• interfaces between management and information • more strategy and information focus • more original research	• technology learning experience • more class time
e-Magnet Institute	• e-mail and focused mail campaigns • direct to customers • 1:1 marketing programs • information-intensive industries	• interfaces between management and information • more strategy and information focus • more original research	• technology learning experience • more class time

were the analytical results. Several components of the e-Magnet Institute strategy had not been elements of the alternatives initially defined.

ORGANIZATIONS AS VALUE-CREATING SYSTEMS

The enhanced value of the hybrid is a system-level phenomenon. It stems directly from an increased understanding by decision-makers of how to coordinate multiple actions in a way that increases the total value created by the system. When managers make decisions within organizational silos, they usually have a good understanding of the actions they can take themselves and of the local consequences of taking them or not taking them. But these managers typically cannot assess the impact of their local actions on over-all system performance, much less the impact of simultaneous actions being taken in other silos that might enhance or cancel the impact of their own decisions. By synthesizing a broad spectrum of organizational perspectives, decision-makers better understand how the parts of the system interact. Through the dialogues, they learn how to manage suites of actions to improve overall organizational performance.

This process consistently leads to unexpected, often dramatic insights. A recent application of ADP involved an enterprise-level allocation of resources across operating units. These units were accountable for meeting their committed objectives, but they were also required to contribute to a number of corporate initiative projects that cut across many units. Out of the ADP came a counterintuitive insight: The allocation of additional resources to *any* individual business unit in isolation would not improve corporate profitability at all. In fact, adding resources to increase the performance of certain units *reduced* overall system profitability. But the same exercise demonstrated that several interunit strategic initiatives could generate significant corporate-level returns. This insight had been hidden because funds had previously been allocated to units on the basis of local returns on additional investments. Allocations on the basis of interunit contributions to system outcome produced radically different strategies than those resulting from the allocation of funding to individual units based on a unit-by-unit analysis of return on investment.

ADP AND THE VALUE OF INFORMATION

The Adaptive Decision Process provides a powerful way to think about the relevance and value of information-gathering activities. Its logical framework can best be described as *decision pull*, as distinguished from *information push*. Decision pull means that the decision context establishes the pull signal for information relevant to the decision at hand. Information push characterizes the data glut situation in which one tries to guess in advance what data will prove to be of value. But without a clearly defined decision context, no reliable means exists to determine that. In sharp contrast, the decision pull frame of ADP incorporates a method for placing a value on additional information, so that its value can be compared with the cost of its acquisition.[9]

ADP is a powerful learning process specifically designed to fulfill the purpose of business, that is, value creation.[10] Only in the context of a value measure and a choice among alternative courses of action can one meaningfully talk about the value of information. Since business consists of the creation of value through action, ADP's decision pull serves business much more powerfully than does information push.

An adaptive organization must sense what information can contribute to the development of value-creating strategies. The value of information can be calculated based on the relative value of alternative response strategies and the likelihood that acquiring the information would result in a change in response.[11] Only information that leads to a change in the response strategy has any value, and its value is a function of the difference in the values of the alternative strategies. Once the organization knows how to determine what information is valuable, its investments in information gathering become more focused and productive.

At the beginning of an ADP application, participants will typically identify between forty and sixty different issues or areas of uncertainty about the future. (An *issue* can be defined as a dimension of a decision problem to which some uncertainty attaches. Acquiring additional information about the issue will change the level of uncertainty about it.) By the end of the effort, it is rarely the case that more than three or four of these issues continue to be *decision-relevant*. A decision-focused filter for information acquisition leads to a 90 percent reduction in the number of issues worthy of continued investigation. More importantly, the value of acquiring additional information on the remaining 10 percent is typically an order of magnitude higher than anyone believed at the outset.

A successfully adapting enterprise must be able to rapidly convert apparent noise into meaning. Exploring the uncertainty around future possible states of "what is going on out there" is an effective way to improve a firm's ability to distinguish real from apparent noise. ADP provides a systematic guide to where and where not to look in this sea of potentially relevant signals. And it yields a decision-relevant context for interpreting and acting upon this information.

We have presented a collaborative, customer-back process for making and adapting resource allocation decisions. It enriches the dialogue between decision-makers and the decision team by seeking out, rather than subduing, the diversity of perspectives that exist within the enterprise. Out of this diversity come hybrid strategies that create more system value than could come from any single perspective.

The Adaptive Decision Process manages information to sense customer value attributes and support adaptive responses. By encouraging systems-level decisions and aligning subsystem trade-offs among subsystems, ADP provides leaders with a powerful implementation tool for sense-and-respond organizations.

APPENDIX C

PUTTING THE COMMITMENT MANAGEMENT PROTOCOL TO WORK

Every commitment involves a supplier and a customer. The terms identify the provider and recipient of any specified outcome and so can refer to two parties within an organization or to an internal supplier responding to an external customer. A visualization of the commitment management protocol described in chapter 8 looks like the diagram in Figure C.1.

The vertical arrows represent the speech acts separating the task stages of a commitment. Defining or recognizing a need leads to a request, which leads to negotiation. Agreement in turn leads to the performance of the tasks required to achieve the outcome. (These tasks may, of course, involve subsidiary commitment workflows.) Reporting completion of the work leads to assessment of the outcome (that is, of whether it meets the agreed-to conditions of satisfaction) and its acceptance or rejection.

This sequence is always the same, except that it may start with an offer rather than a request. The specific positioning of the speech acts allows a process designer to affect the amount of risk associated with a particular commitment. Making a commitment, for example, (*agreeing*) immediately after receiving a request, and without negotiating the subordinate commitments on which its fulfillment depends, invites some risk. (A discussion of the problems created for an appliance manufacturer by that kind of process design—or lack of design—appears below.) But if the request will always be a standard one carried out successfully many times before, the risk will be minimal, and designing for an immediate agreement is reasonable. If, on the other hand, the request is unprecedented,

FIGURE C.1

ANOTHER VIEW OF THE COMMITMENT MANAGEMENT PROTOCOL

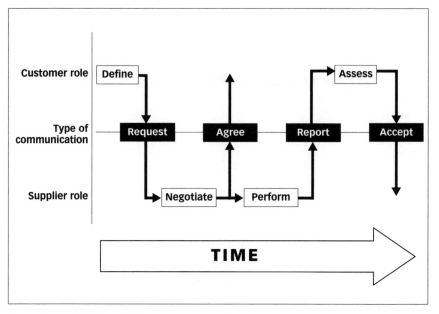

the supplier will want to minimize risk by positioning the agreement closer to the report of completion and adding subsidiary protocols in the negotiation phase to charter a feasibility study or develop a prototype. In especially high-risk circumstances, the supplier may even choose to carry out tasks normally not undertaken until the perform phase, such as conducting a feasibility study, before agreeing to the commitment.

Using the commitment management protocol to design adaptive processes involves these basic steps.

- Define the roles.

- Establish the customer-supplier relationships between roles, specifying outcomes and conditions of satisfaction.

- Sequence the speech acts within and between customer/ supplier pairs, making sure that necessary communications with subsidiary suppliers precede the communications that depend on them.

- Define the tasks to be accomplished in each of the four procedural, or task, phases in appropriate detail.

In addition to tracking commitments, the protocol can be used as a tool for diagnosing existing processes. Tom Morgan of Brooklyn Union Gas recognized this potential and used it to analyze failures in his company's business processes. He found that missing speech acts (especially *agree* and *accept* or *reject*), missing phases (especially negotiation and assessment), and, above all, missing customer roles correlated directly with process failure.[1] IBM consultant Kathleen Snyder used it to help a make-to-order appliance manufacturer understand some significant operational problems.

The company came to her because its customers complained that they were unable to get good information about the status of their orders. Worse, the products delivered frequently did not match the customers' specifications. Snyder used the protocol to map the relevant commitments that currently linked customer and supplier roles, and in so doing she identified the causes of this poor performance. (Remember that every commitment has a customer and a supplier, even when both roles are internal to the organization.) Figure C.2 shows the results of Snyder's analysis, with roles listed vertically on the left and speech acts indicated by arrows. The horizontal axis indicates time, from the placement of the initial order to product delivery and payment. (Tasks are not shown.)

The diagram clearly shows the communications failures largely responsible for the company's problems. For one thing, the sales function was out of touch with the rest of the organization. It committed product delivery to the customer without any consultation or agreement with planning and production about whether that commitment could be met. Its only communication with other parts of the company was to request an already promised product. The planning manager ordered supplies and requested production, but neither he nor anyone else assessed the results of production—one clear source of the mismatches between prod-

FIGURE C.2

APPLYING THE PROTOCOL TO DIAGNOSE A BUSINESS PROCESS

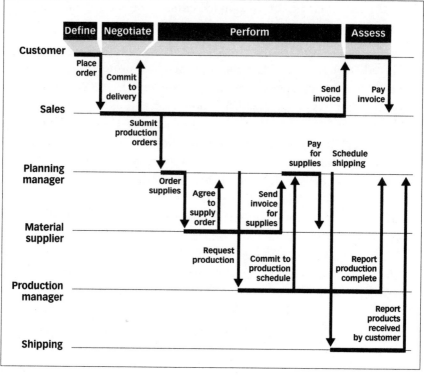

Source: Kathleen Snyder.

ucts specified and products delivered. The planning manager also scheduled shipping, but no further communication took place between planning and shipping until the customer received the product. Accurate information about order status could not be determined inside the company and could not, therefore, be made available to the customer.

Snyder's map of a redesigned appliance manufacturer process appears in Figure C.3. Missing speech acts have been added to complete every commitment protocol. Note, for instance, that the sales function now commits to delivery only after the planning manager has ordered supplies, requested production, and received confirming commitments from the material supplier and production manager. The design also provides for assessment of every

FIGURE C.3

REDESIGNED BUSINESS PROCESS WITH COMPLETE PROTOCOLS

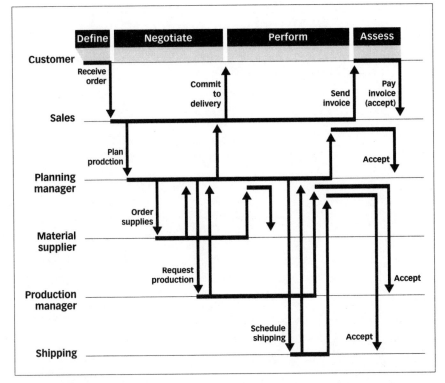

Source: Kathleen Snyder.

outcome requested by every role at the appropriate time so that problems can be caught and corrected before the product ships.

This exercise in process reengineering achieved significant improvement in organizational performance without the redesign of a single procedure. The only new procedures added were those to assess the results of each outcome. Everything else was a matter of adding and sequencing communications about outcomes between customers and suppliers—adding the dimension of accountability to this business process.[2]

NOTES

Chapter 1

1 D. Bell, *The Coming of Post-Industrial Society* (New York: Basic Books, 1973).

2 B. Arthur, "Positive Feedbacks in the Economy," *Scientific American,* February 1990.

3 P. Drucker, "Planning for Uncertainty," *The Wall Street Journal,* 22 July 1992.

4 From a 1985 interview with Hohne.

5 Seth Lloyd, "Learning How to Control Complex Systems," *Bulletin of the Santa Fe Institute,* Spring 1995.

6 S. H. Haeckel and R. L. Nolan, "Managing By Wire," *Harvard Business Review* 71, no. 5 (September–October 1993).

7 Russell A. Ackoff, *The Democratic Corporation* (New York: Oxford University Press, 1994).

Chapter 2

1 D. Bell, "The Social Framework of the Information Society," in *The Computer Age: The Next Twenty Years,* eds. M. Dertouzous and J. Moses (Cambridge, MA: MIT Press, 1979).

2 R. Glazer, "Marketing in an Information-Intensive Environment," *Journal of Marketing* 55 (October 1991). This article was based on research funded by the Marketing Science Institute, the results of which were first published by Glazer in a 1989 MSI research paper. In addition to the hypotheses, Glazer proposed a way to determine the value in use of a firm's transaction information and to use the result as a measure of the firm's degree of information intensity. Application of his methodology yields valid estimates of three sources of information value-in-use: increasing revenues from future transactions (for example, by using transaction data to cross-market, command higher prices, and so on); reducing the costs of future transactions (by reducing future distribution, repair, or promotional costs, for example); and by selling the information itself (for example, by selling scanner data). The sum of these three amounts, normalized as a percentage of total firm profits, forms an index of the firm's information intensity. Glazer's methodology has

been captured in software, permitting frequent sampling and trend analysis of the information intensity within a given firm—and the basis for correlating information intensity with firm performance data to test his hypotheses.

3 D. Bell, "The Social Framework of the Information Society," in *The Computer Age: A Twenty Year View,* eds. M. Dertouzos and J. Moses (Cambridge, MA: MIT Press, 1979).

4 B. Arthur, "Positive Feedbacks in the Economy," *Scientific American,* February 1990.

5 J. Kurtzman, "An Interview with Brian Arthur," *Strategy and Business,* Booz·Allen & Hamilton, Second Quarter (1998). Arthur summarizes three reasons for the increasing returns effect in Kurtzman's readable and interesting interview. They are *cost advantage,* resulting from the low cost of manufacturing and distributing information-intensive products once they are developed; *network effects,* attracting new users to products or information sources because they already have the largest user network (for an obvious example, the Windows 95 operating system); and *grooving in,* or the increasing reluctance of users to switch products or interfaces once they have become adept at using their current ones.

6 The first quote from Taylor appears in an unpublished paper by Bernard Avishai. John Whitney provided the other. This quote is also associated with "Meyer, 1914" in a handout for a course taught by Whitney at the ABI. Regrettably, neither he nor I have been able to find the original source. Both quotes, however, capture the now inconceivable certainty with which managers of a century ago assumed that they could know everything that needed knowing.

7 Alan Hohne, "Mass Customization: Avoiding the Need to Predict Change" (1996).

8 Rashi Glazer, "Marketing in an Information-Intensive Environment," *Journal of Marketing* 55 (October 1991).

9 From a presentation by Rashi Glazer at the Marketing Science Institute conference, Interactive Marketing, introductory remarks, September 1997.

10 Glazer's complete list includes other predictions, less directly connected with uncertainty, that are also proving true a decade after he proposed them. He noted, for example, that "businesses will focus more on profitability and less on market share." Shorter product life cycles will make it necessary to concentrate on the economics of product introduction and phase-out rather than on a sustained growth phase. At the same time, the distinction between long-term market share and short-term profitability will fade as the need to choose between high-volume/low cost and differentiation disappears.

11 The Economist Intelligence Unit and IBM Insurance Solutions, *Global Insurance to the Twenty-first Century,* Research Report (The Economist Intelligence Unit and IBM Insurance Solutions, 1996).

Recent research supports the argument that a focus on customers will be more likely to lead to success than a focus on competitors. W. C. Kim and R. Mauborgne (see "Value Innovation: The Strategic Logic of High Growth," *Harvard Business Review* 75, no. 1 [January–February 1997]) concluded that trying to beat competitors "is a waste [of] time and energy." In a five-year study of thirty companies around the world, they investigated the correlation between high growth and a variety of factors, including the age of managers, evidence of unconventional thinking, size, investment in new technology, amount of regulation, and the competitiveness of others in the same industry. None could be systematically connected with success. They did discover the following:

> The less successful companies were stuck in the trap of competing. Their strategic logic centered around building competitive advantages. They benchmarked the competition and focused on outperforming rivals. The result was a perpetual cycle of offering a little more for a little less than competitors. The competition, not the customer, set the parameters of their strategic thinking.

By contrast, high-growth companies paid little heed to matching or beating the competition. Instead, they sought to make the competition irrelevant by offering buyers a quantum leap in value.

Chapter 3

1 Paul O. Gaddis, "Strategy Under Attack," *Long-Range Planning* 30 (1997): 38.

2 *The Economist,* 1 March 1997.

3 In some individual cases, the strategic planning process does seem to work, even today. Emerson Electric provides a striking example. In a 1994 article about CEO Chuck Knight's success in maintaining what was at that date thirty-six consecutive years of increased earnings, *Forbes* reported, "Rigorous planning is the heart of Chuck Knight's Emerson, and it involves every aspect of the business. Emerson's exceptionally detailed planning is a classic of its kind, subject of countless admiring business school case studies. . . . [T]he most important part of the planning process is the forecasts." Emerson Electric is a rare exception, however.

4 From a conversation with Ackoff in November, 1997.

5 Arie de Geus, *The Living Company* (Boston: Harvard Business School Press, 1997).

6 From a 1996 conversation with Hendry.

7 Paul O. Gaddis, "Strategy Under Attack," *Long-Range Planning* 30 (1997): 43. Gaddis interprets the 216 B.C. battle of Cannae as one of the earliest historical clashes of the purposeful versus the emergent strategy philosophies. The Roman general Varro was an incrementalist with a super-organization. Varro's legions were better trained and better equipped. Varro "did not need any strategy. Hannibal, at the other end of the field, did have a preconceived game plan, which came to be called the military doctrine of the 'weak centre.' The result: devastating total defeat for the Romans." No suitable strategy emerged as the battle wore on.

Presumably Alfred Sloan, Theodore Vail, Henry Ford, Dwight Eisenhower, Walt Disney, Thomas Watson, Sr. and Jr., and Charles Knight (Emerson Electric) would be "purposeful" strategists. Margaret Wheatley, Dee Hock (VISA), Percy Barnevik (ABB), and John Walter (R. R. Donnelley & Sons) would be classified as emergent strategists.

8 This characterization of social systems derives from Russell Ackoff, who distinguishes four types of systems: *deterministic,* in which neither the parts nor the whole can display choice or purpose; *animate,* in which the whole can display choice and purpose but the parts cannot; *social,* in which

both the parts and the whole can display choice and purpose; and *ecological*, in which some parts can display choice and purpose but the whole cannot. See Russell A. Ackoff, *The Democratic Corporation* (New York: Oxford University Press, 1994).

[9] Kuldeep Kumar and H. G. van Dissell, "Sustainable Collaboration: Managing Conflict and Cooperation in Interorganizational Systems," *MIS Quarterly* 20, no. 3 (1996).

[10] C. Schelberg, "Parallel Scheduling of Random and of Chaotic Processes," in *Dynamic, Genetic, and Chaotic Programming,* ed. B. Soucek. (New York: John Wiley & Sons, 1992).

[11] See M. M. Waldrup, "Dee Hock on Organizations," *Fast Company* (October–November 1996), page 77. In a keynote address to the Pegasus Conference on October 3, 1996, Dee Hock offered his vision of the future organization as equitably owned by the participants, who will have common rights and obligations; organized with power and functions distributed "as far down as possible"; characterized by distributed governance; and malleable in form and function and durable in purpose and principles. (Notes on Hock's projections were provided by Richard Karash: rkarash@karash.com.)

[12] Banks, which are highly complex, multi-layered systems for carrying out their individual missions, appear as multiple instances of a very simple function in terms of the VISA mission.

Chapter 4

[1] See S. H. Haeckel, "Westpac Bank Corporation: A Sense-and-Respond Prototype," ABI Vignette, 1996.

[2] A. Hohne, "Mass Customization: Avoiding the Need to Predict Change" (1996). Alan Hohne, whom I met in 1985 as Westpac was in the throes of making their commitment to CS90, was and is my primary source on the Westpac story.

[3] Implementation of this on-the-spot tailoring capability entailed original work by Richard Taylor, the principal architect on the IBM development team, in an area called "dynamic parameter resolution." The idea is to partition the logic of the system such that programmers maintain the static parameters by which the system guides product development and business professionals maintain the dynamic parameters that change the bank's customer-specific value proposition. See R. E. Taylor, "Dynamic Parameter Resolution," IBM paper, October 1989.

[4] Alan Hohne, "Mass Customization: Avoiding the Need to Predict Change" (1996).

[5] The system was three years late and $20 million over budget—a drain, rather than an asset during a time when Westpac was losing money on bad loans. Some managers advocated abandoning the project, but the decision taken was to scale it back and extend its timeframe. A media release dated 5 November 1991 included this statement by CEO Frank Conroy: "The planned outputs of what has been called the CS90 project will continue to be provided to the Bank. However the timing of some of the component parts is likely to be changed and some of the priorities designated for the various elements are currently under review."

[6] Westpac home page, URL: http://www.westpac.com.au/, 24 November 1997.

[7] Robert White captured this insight about customer information in his articulation of a new vision for Westpac's future business: information interme-

diation. He understood this to be the information age culmination "of a business that (was) banking in the 1960s, became financial service in the 1970s, was becoming financial intermediation in the 1980s and would mature into information intermediation in the 1990s."

8 As of this writing, the Goodyear website asks only for the make and model of the prospective customer's car, from which it generates a best match. It does not solicit information about: preferences for safety, performance, or price range; driving habits; age or other demographics; or climate.

9 Some readers may find investment in the stock of Internet startups with infinitely high price-earnings ratios (because they will not earn a profit for several years) a closer-to-home manifestation of this logic.

10 Adrian J. Slywotzky and David J. Morrison, *The Profit Zone: How Strategic Business Designs Will Lead You to Tomorrow's Profits* (New York: Times Business Books, 1997).

11 Michael E. Porter, *Competitive Strategy* (New York: The Free Press, 1980).

12 See Michael Shank, "Porter's Generic Strategies: Becoming Unstuck in the Middle," Doctoral Dissertation, University of North Carolina at Chapel Hill, 1993; Andrew Boynton and Bart Victor, "Beyond Flexibility: Building and Managing the Dynamically Stable Organization," *California Management Review* (Fall 1991).

Chapter 5

1 Seth Lloyd, "Learning How to Control Complex Systems," *The Bulletin of the Santa Fe Institute* (Spring 1995). After asserting that the control of nonlinear systems requires intuition, which in turn requires learning, Lloyd goes on to say:

> The behavior of any system, whether a turbulent fluid, a robot, or the Dow Jones index, exhibits "regular" features that are predictable and deterministic according to some set of rules, and features that the rules fail to predict, and that are apparently random. . . . [T]he amount of information required to describe unpredictable, apparently random behavior can be identified with the Shannon information [that is, apparent, not true noise] of the ensemble of the residual random behaviors of the system after its predictable, rule-based behavior has been specified. These two types of information: algorithmic information to describe rule-based behavior, and Shannon information to describe apparently random behavior can be added together to give the total information required to describe both predictable and unpredictable behavior.

> Building on work done by M. Gell-Mann and J. B. Hartle ("Quantum Mechanics in the Light of Quantum Cosmology," in *Complexity, Entropy, and the Physics of Information, Santa Fe Proceedings VIII,* ed. W. H. Zurek [Reading, MA: Addison-Wesley, 1989]), which combines algorithmic and probabilistic information to "make sense" of the transition from quantum behavior to classical behavior, Lloyd concludes that adaptive control requires the use of Shannon information to change the algorithm used to model the system—thereby changing what is regarded as regular and what as irregular. This change in the model incorporates Shannon information and results in successful adaptation "as long as addition of extra rules to describe regularities of a system is more than compensated for by a decrease in the system's apparent randomness."

2 J. Kurtzman, "An Interview with Brian Arthur," *Strategy and Business,* Booz·Allen & Hamilton, Second Quarter (1998).

3 G. Zaltman, "Rethinking Market Research: Putting People Back In," *Journal of Marketing Research* (November 1997).

4 This example is based on a vignette in J. B. Quinn, *Intelligent Enterprise* (New York: The Free Press, 1992). I have taken significant liberty with the actual decision process used by GMR (which I don't know) in order to more vividly illustrate the concept of "thinking backwards, and acting forwards" around the adaptive cycle.

5 To simplify the illustration, the role of "GM" is assumed to encompass authority for making trades on the futures market and setting prices. In reality, these decisions might be distributed among multiple roles, each of which has its own accountability and adaptive loop.

6 In this book, *interpret* means *sensemaking,* as used by Karl E. Weick, in *Sensemaking in Organizations* (Thousand Oaks, CA: Sage Publications, 1995), and by others who have studied the ways humans make meaning out of what goes on in the world. Weick's book provides an excellent synthesis of research and reflection on this subject going back to William James in the last decades of the nineteenth century. The irreducible "units of meaning," according to Weick, are a *cue* (for example, some triggering signal, stimulus, or input), a *frame* (for example, an ideology, a set of decision premises, or a paradigm), and a *relationship* between them. The meaning of any one of these units "is determined by your momentary awareness of the other two" (A. Upton, *Design for Thinking* [Palo Alto, CA: Pacific, 1961]), and the sensemaker can start with any one of the three. Weick's treatment of many topics, including commitment and governance, will be of interest to readers of this book.

Although using a different vocabulary, Weick's exposition of sensemaking and its relationship to commitment and action are very compatible with, and reinforce, the ideas about adaptiveness incorporated in the sense-and-respond model. Particularly enlightening is his discussion of three forms of organizational control. First-order control, defined as direct supervision, and second-order control, defined as programs and routines (that is, procedures) are hallmarks of command-and-control and play diminished roles in sense-and-respond organizations. Third order controls are what Weick calls premise controls, because they "influence the premises people use when they diagnose situations and make decisions. . . . [T]hey are the deep assumptions that are the foundations of culture." Weick continues:

> [P]remise controls are one means by which ideology is translated into action, and . . . this translation occurs most often where the technology is non-routine and unanalyzable, and where the potential for incomprehension is high. . . . People at the top often inadvertently make their task more difficult by their efforts to make it easier. *When they impose first- and second-order controls on subordinates, they create interactively complex situations that enlarge in unexpected situations that enlarge in unexpected dimensions, with unintended consequences, in ways that defy comprehension.* (Emphasis added.)

Weick goes on to say that in the face of incomprehension, third order controls are the primary resource available to management to deal with the resulting "mess."

The function of the context in sense-and-respond organizations is precisely to articulate, ingrain, and enforce a universal set of deep assumptions about purpose, bounds and essential structure. Said differently, the *context* of context and coordination is the enterprise-level premise; the *coordination* by commitment management is the means by which the premise is controlled.

[7] Vincent Barabba and Gerald Zaltman, in *Hearing the Voice of the Market: Competitive Advantage through Creative Use of Market Information* (Boston: Harvard Business School Press, 1991), describe what they call "Haeckel's Hierarchy," a synthesis of the epistemological distinctions among *data, information, intelligence, knowledge,* and *wisdom.* Briefly, data is transformed into information by *context;* information is transformed into intelligence by *inference;* intelligence becomes knowledge when sufficient *certitude* is established; and wisdom arises from knowledge through *synthesis.* An elaboration is given in Stephan H. Haeckel and R. L. Nolan, "The Role of Technology in an Information Age: Transforming Symbols into Action," in *The Knowledge Economy: The Nature of Information in the Twenty-first Century,* Annual Review of the Institute for Information Studies (Northern Telecom Inc. and The Aspen Institute, November 1993).

[8] Intelligence agencies provide excellent examples of investments in an organizational capability to sense and interpret. It is not much of an overstatement to characterize their essential function as pattern recognition and interpretation. Some patterns are stable. Human faces, for example, possess six to eight unchangeable unique characteristics, such as the distance between pupils. The CIA leverages this predictable uniqueness by using on-line technology to scan passport photos at immigration centers, matching these characteristics with photos in its database to arrive at the probability that an individual is a specific person. The agency uses this capability to identify even those who change passports every time they leave their countries.

Other patterns, however, are unstable. Seemingly predictable "givens" can change abruptly. Not too long ago, for example, analysts identified two primary types of terrorists: disaffected upper-class terrorists, driven by guilt; and destitute people with nothing to lose. Without warning, a third class has now emerged: "entrepreneurial" terrorists who act as consultants to factions interested in creating disruptions. In many respects, this type is the most frightening, since they render ineffective all existing, motivationally based pattern recognition systems.

To be effective, the CIA or any organization must quickly learn to recognize data that signals the presence of new variables: Signals that had been "noise" now contain important meaning. A company that segments its customers in terms of specific categories of preferences must systematically search for signals about new categories. Their existing segmentation scheme will likely continue sending comforting signals of stability, even as the organization becomes engulfed by real market turbulence.

[9] S. Chandler, "Data is Power. Just Ask Fingerhut," *Business Week,* 3 June 1996, 69.

[10] I am indebted to Lorraine Scarpa for her interpretation of what Kraft learned from the use of data mining and for her permission to quote from a speech she gave in March 1994. Michael Rothman, who has since joined the IBM Consulting Group, now applies his skills in helping financial institutions. At least in his case, a talent for extracting patterns from data is robust across industries.

11　From Scarpa's March, 1994 speech cited above.

12　Vince Barabba, Michael Kusnic, and Dan Owen introduced collaborative decision-making at GM in the late 1980s. See V. Barabba, *Meeting of the Minds* (Boston: Harvard Business School Press, 1995).

13　Accountability for the identification and update—that is, learning—of these key uncertainties might be assigned to a staff role or to some or all of the members of the leadership team, in which case they would be acting in a different, nonleadership role, with its own adaptive cycle.

Chapter 6

1　Vittorio Cassoni made his comments to Esther Dyson, who recounted them in November 1997 when she was a panel member at a *Harvard Business Review* anniversary event in New York. I was privileged to work with Vittorio for four years in the 1970s, when he was a rapidly rising star in Systems Marketing at IBM Europe when I was its director. Cassoni and I reported to an individual who was an inexhaustible source of ambiguity, uncertainty, and inauthentic communication—a man whose priorities and decisions changed week by week. Vittorio was extraordinarily effective, even in this difficult environment. He shielded the people reporting to him from the maelstrom of uncertainty, giving them consistent messages about objectives and priorities. At the same time, he successfully navigated the chaotic waters stirred up by the senior manager by framing the results he got to fit the manager's context du jour.

2　All of Sloan's quotes are from Alfred Sloan, *My Years with General Motors* (New York: Doubleday, 1996).

3　One exception is Royal Dutch Shell's "helicopter" test. Candidates for positions at policy-making levels are screened both for their success in fighting operational brush fires and for their ability to conceptualize "big picture" frameworks. Peter Schwartz, formerly a scenario developer at Royal Dutch Shell, and founder of the Global Decisions Network, provided this information.

4　R. F. W. Nelson, "Four-Quadrant Leadership," *Planning Review* (January–February 1996).

5　Translated by Wing-Tsit Chan. I am grateful to John Deighton for supplying the complete text:

> If names are not rectified, then language will not be in accord with the truth. If language is not in accord with the truth, then things cannot be accomplished. If things cannot be accomplished, then ceremonies and music will not flourish. If ceremonies and music do not flourish, then punishment will not be just. If punishments are not just, then the people will not know how to move hand or foot. Therefore the superior man will give only names that can be described in speech and say only what can be carried out in practice. With regard to his speech, the superior man does not take it lightly.

6　George-Yves Kevern, in "Cindynics: The Science of Danger," *Risk Management* (March 1995), described five categories of ambiguity, which he calls "teleological, deontological, epistemological, axiological and statistical." Attributing them to Herbert Simon, he included them in a discussion of factors that increase the danger threatening a system. I interpret them as types of ambiguity that lead to incoherent system behavior.

7 The description of IBM and Apple's personal computer projects that follows is based on the report by G. S. Lynn, "Organizational Team Learning for Really New Product Development" MSI report 97-113 (Cambridge, MA: Marketing Science Institute, 1997).

8 Thomas Hout and John Carter, "Getting It Done: New Roles for Senior Executives," *Harvard Business Review* 73, no. 6 (November–December 1995).

9 From a sense-and-respond class discussion at IBM Palisades in 1996.

10 This is a particularly pernicious effect of the widely held belief, "If you can't measure it, you can't manage it." A strong argument can be made for the opposite belief: If you can't measure it, you *must* manage it.

11 The Philadelphia city department responsible for street maintenance is evaluated in part by the number of potholes it repairs annually. A graph in the city's annual report shows that this number has increased steadily over the years. If compensation is tied to this measure, one can easily imagine that a mild winter might trigger some extracurricular pothole creation by members of this department.

Chapter 7

1 From a 1995 letter from Munro to the author.

2 A. Campbell and M. Alexander, in "What's Wrong With Strategy?" *Harvard Business Review* 75, no. 6 (November–December 1997), also emphasize the importance of making this distinction.

3 Some strategists call this the "marketing concept." For an excellent discussion of the history of the marketing concept, business strategy, and the issues associated with implementing it, see the following three chapters, Stephen Greyser, "Janus and Marketing: The Past Present and Prospective Future of Marketing," Frederick Webster, Jr., "The Future Role of Marketing in Organizations," and George Day, "Aligning the Organization to the Market," in D. Lehmann and K. Jocz, eds., *Reflections on the Futures of Marketing* (Cambridge, MA: Marketing Science Institute, 1997).

4 Russell Ackoff, *The Democratic Corporation* (New York: Oxford University Press, 1994).

5 A relevant feature of the collaborative decision-making process described by Michael Kusnic and Daniel Owen in Appendix B is the insight it offers into how considering alternative possible *combinations* of resource allocations to different subsystems can enhance system value. The orchestration of interrelated moves, rather than isolated improvements, generates value at the systems level greater than the sum of the value created by the individual moves. The fallacy of trying to improve enterprise performance by doing every single thing better becomes very clear during this decision process. Implementing it has proven to be eye-opening for many firms.

6 It has been argued that Sloan *did* design GM as a system. If so, his was a design for an efficient mechanism, rather than for an adaptive social system.

7 The introduction to the speech Munro gave to managers and employees attending the fifteen group sessions on "Context Setting" reads in full, as follows:

> In an environment of unpredictable change, in which many underlying assumptions about our business are constantly placed in doubt, EB must be reconceived. It must become a *system*—a purposeful, adaptive,

empowered system. To create an empowered system that works, it is crucial that we have clarity and agreement about its purpose; its primary constituency; the constraints placed on empowered behavior by our values and obligations to all constituencies; the subsystem outcomes necessary; and the business design that links them to produce the outcomes defined by our purpose.

We will use a different vocabulary to describe this reconceived EB, and our roles in it. We will not talk about jobs and job descriptions, we will talk about roles and accountabilities. We will describe EB's purpose as its "reason for being," and the universal boundaries on all of our behaviors as "governing principles." Each of us will play several roles. In each role we will have well-defined but dynamic accountabilities to produce subsystem outcomes required by people in other roles. These accountabilities will be renegotiated as unpredicted change dictates, in a manner consistent with our business design.

As parts of an empowered system, each of us will have the license and responsibility for making decisions within the parameters of the governing principles and our negotiated commitments to produce what the system needs from us. Many of our most important commitments will be horizontal, rather than vertical. Our concept of a command-and-control management system operating within a functional hierarchy will change radically. We will be mutually interdependent, and rewarded on the basis of our contribution to achieving EB's purpose. We share a collective accountability for creating and executing the business design that ensures that result.

We will need to hone new skills and a culture of collaboration to make this reconceptualization of EB a reality. But our ground will be the shared values that define us as a unique organization. What follows is designed as a beginning of the dialog necessary to clarify the purpose, values and obligations that will bound our behavior.

Chapter 8

[1] The commitment management protocol is based on the "conversations for action" theory of Fernando Flores, and subsequent work by IBM Fellow Alan Scherr. Flores's integration of linguistics, computer science, and philosophy to represent actions in terms of producer/user dialogues about commitments has been formalized by Action Technologies as workflow software; it is available over the Internet, including a version that uses Lotus Notes, at http://www.actiontech.com.

Much of this chapter's discussion about accountability is based on conversations with Scherr about his insights that commitments are essential to accountability, and that human accountability is the "missing dimension" of business process design. In his words, Flores's schema was the first with sufficient rigor to "go to code with." Scherr developed a way of representing business process designs that could be directly executed by a computer that uses workflow software and that incorporates both ad hoc and procedural behavior. Scherr's representation of the schema has been patented. It reduces the number of "speech acts" required to exhaust all possible outcomes of a process from the twelve defined by Flores to seven, and facilitates the process design task by mapping both the tasks and the communications against a time line. Some former IBM employees have implemented Scherr's version of the protocol in software and use it in their business design consulting practice, Business Transformation Designs, Inc.

2 Karen Stephenson and Stephan H. Haeckel, "Making a Virtual Organization Work," *Zurich Insurance Management Review* (June 1997). A customer may not be able to specify a complete request with accuracy at the outset. In this case, customers should state both what they think they need and their degree of uncertainty. During the negotiation phase, the opportunity arises to estimate the amount of risk associated with the request, to agree on a series of preliminary checkpoints that will bring the risk within tolerable limits, to state the conditions of satisfaction, and so on. It occurs all too frequently that people request more than they need because they don't know what they need and they want to play it safe. This can turn a sincere request into an inauthentic one, because the supplier remains unaware of risk that the customer recognizes but neglects to communicate. By the same token, suppliers may agree to do something without adequately understanding their ability to do it. Other commitments may not allow the amount of time necessary, lack of experience may mean necessary skills will be lacking, and so on.

Inaccurate requests and premature agreements to produce them may be sincere or insincere, but they are *always* inauthentic.

3 Chris Argyris asks individuals to listen to tapes of their business conversations and then to write down, next to a transcription of their statements, their actual meaning. The exercise makes clear the often yawning chasm between spoken words and real meaning. See Chris Argyris, *On Organizational Learning* (Cambridge, MA: Blackwell Publishers, 1992).

4 Anecdotal evidence indicates that most of us want to associate ourselves with a group or purpose beyond ourselves, even when the reasons for which that larger entity exists are trivial or unclear. The social psychologist Henir Tajfel, for example, demonstrated that groups formed on the basis of an affinity no stronger than sharing the last digit of their social security numbers showed favoritism for members of that group within hours of its formation. See D. Berreby, "What the Heck Is a Company, Anyway?" *Strategy and Business,* Booz·Allen & Hamilton, Second Quarter (1997).

5 Chris Argyris, in *On Organizational Learning* (Cambridge, MA: Blackwell Publishers, 1992), 42, points to the mixed or contrary messages inherent in statements such as "I really like that idea, but have you thought about *X.*" Argyris's formula for systematically producing inauthentic communications sounds bizarre but describes a common pattern.

- Design a message that is inconsistent.

- Act as if the message is not inconsistent.

- Make the inconsistency in the message and the act that there is no inconsistency undiscussable.

- Make the undiscussability of the undiscussable also undiscussable.

6 This logic underlies Toyota's andon system, in which assembly-line workers are empowered to pull the andon cord that stops the transfer line if they see a problem. In spite of the enormous cost of shutting down and starting up a line, Toyota recognizes that the earlier they spot a problem, the greater the chance of coping with it and the lower the cost of doing so. People should not be punished for reporting that they cannot meet a commitment.

7 See R. A. D'Aveni, *Hypercompetition* (New York: The Free Press, 1994), for several examples of this phenomenon.

8 The importance of reducing designs to their "essentials" applies also to the registration of commitment workflows. Being nagged about nonessential commitments can and will alienate people. Seeing a list of five hundred "to-do's" on a computer terminal every day would keep most people away from work—or at least motivate them to work around the commitment management system.

9 General Electric and ABB are examples of very large conglomerates that have succeeded through *sharing*, not synergy. Sharing, like modularity, is a strategy for achieving economies of scope. In GE's case, these economies are achieved and sustained not by an enterprise design for synergy, but by Welch's relentless, vigorous, and personal follow-through on his policy edicts about sharing information, people, knowledge, and certain other assets. Managers are punished if they do not proactively disseminate their knowledge to other GE divisions or if they take action that impedes the free flow of money, people, or information between companies. One condition of staying in the GE portfolio is that each business conform to Welch's policies about developing, sharing, and leveraging GE's brand name, its deep pockets, its world-wide network, its best practices and customer knowledge, its AAA debt rating, and, as a direct report once said, "access to the best business consultant on the planet: Jack Welch."

Chapter 9

1 T. M. Hout and M. F. Blaxill, "Make Decisions Like a Fighter Pilot," *The New York Times,* 15 November 1987.

2 Seth Lloyd, "Learning How to Control Complex Systems," *The Bulletin of the Santa Fe Institute* (Spring 1995).

3 The session was based on the version of managing by wire that appeared in Stephan H. Haeckel and R. L. Nolan, "Managing by Wire," *Harvard Business Review* 71, no. 5 (September–October 1993a).

4 Glen Salow and his staff were very generous with their time in describing what they accomplished and how they did it. This brief summary cannot do justice to their efforts, which involved a large-scale redesign of the application at the heart of the business of the Aetna Portfolio Management Group.

Chapter 10

1 Unless otherwise noted, the citations from Hammond and other early adopters of the sense-and-respond model are extracted from descriptions of their experiences they provided to the author, and from conversations with them during the period of 1994–1998.

Chapter 11

1 Unless otherwise noted, the citations in this chapter are extracted from descriptions provided to the author of the experiences of early adopters of the sense-and-respond model and from conversations between them and the author during the period of 1994–1998.

Appendix A

1 J. Pine, B. Victor, and A. Boynton, "Making Mass Customization Work," *Harvard Business Review* 71, no. 5 (September–October 1993).

2 For additional detail on National Bicycle see: S. Kotha, "Mass Customization: Implementing the Emerging Paradigm for Competitive Advantage,"

Strategic Management Journal 16 (1995): 21–42; M. L. Fisher, "National Bicycle Industrial Co.," Case study (Philadelphia: Wharton School, University of Pennsylvania, 1993); R. Westbrook and P. Williamson, "Mass Customization: Japan's New Frontier," *European Management Journal,* March 1993.

3 Justin Martin, "Are You as Good as You Think You Are?" *Fortune,* 30 September 1996, 142–152.

4 W. Fulkerson and M. Shank, "The New Economy, Electronic Commerce, and the Rise of Mass Customization," in *The Electronic Commerce Handbook* (New York: Springer Verlag, 1999).

5 S. Kerr, *Consulting Practice Communique* (Briarcliff Manor, NY: Academy of Management, 1998).

6 Michael Shank, "Porter's Generic Strategies: Becoming Unstuck in the Middle" (Ph.D. diss., University of North Carolina-Chapel Hill, 1993).

7 See James Brian Quinn, *Intelligent Enterprise* (New York: The Free Press, 1992), 101.

8 D. Tapscott, *The Digital Economy* (New York: McGraw-Hill, 1995), 30.

9 The Foundation for Manufacturing and Industry, Department of Trade and Industry, and IBM Consulting Group, *Making It For You—Personally* (The Foundation for Manufacturing and Industry, Department of Trade and Industry, and IBM Consulting Group, 1997).

10 B. Victor and A. Boynton, *Invented Here* (Boston: Harvard Business School Press, 1998).

11 Note that if functional changes are made to any module they will have to be done in concert with changes in the design of the systems of which they are a part.

12 James Brian Quinn, J. J. Baruch, and K. A. Zein, *Innovation Explosion* (New York: The Free Press, 1997).

13 George Stalk, David K. Pecaut, and Benjamin Burnett, "Breaking Compromises, Breakaway Growth," *Harvard Business Review* 74, no. 5 (September–October 1996).

Appendix B

1 Haeckel calls this approach communicate and hope. The problem is that a real change in strategic direction requires a reallocation of resources.

2 The approach to decision-making described here has its intellectual roots in the academic field known as decision analysis. Developed during the 1960s and 1970s, decision analysis integrated two distinct disciplines, decision theory and systems analysis. Decision theory had as its primary focus the problem of a single decision-maker facing a choice among alternative courses of action in environments of significant uncertainty. The complexity associated with this class of problem stems from its probabilistic nature. Systems analysis, in contrast, focuses on the problem of controlling large-scale systems with many variables but within which uncertainty is not the critical feature. The complexity in this class of problems stems from the number of control variables, along with their numerous interactions. Decision analysis, therefore, was developed to deal with the problem of complex systems involving significant uncertainty.

Early experience with decision analysis was unsuccessful, due in large part to its heavily analytical, "black box" orientation. In this approach, very bright Ph.D.s would disappear into a back room with what they considered a good understanding of a decision problem facing management. They would emerge some time later with a recommended course of action backed up by a detailed, highly complex, probabilistic model. Managers, refusing to delegate understanding, were reluctant to underwrite decisions that they could not defend. Decision analysis faded away from the executive suites, along with many other operations research techniques.

During the late 1970s and early 1980s, the usefulness of decision analysis was significantly improved by embedding its tools and analytics in a collaborative process that engaged management in a series of dialogues around problem formulation, analysis, and the development of recommendations. In the late 1980s, General Motors began integrating decision analysis into their business decision processes. GM's process came to be known as the Dialogue Decision Process (DDP), an approach to redesigning strategic business processes centered on collaborative decision-making. DDP focused on improving the overall cohesion of the business as a system. Its goal was to reduce the frequency of coordination disconnects that fostered individual, isolated decisions.

Making decisions more effectively (as the DDP did) was a good thing; but reducing the need to make them independently was even more valuable. In thousands of applications over the last twenty years, DDP has been used to develop corporate strategy, clarify the risks and returns associated with alternative capital investment opportunities, and provide organizations with a common language and approach for making decisions in the face of uncertainty. Many major corporations, including Alcoa, Chevron, DuPont, EDS, Eli Lilly, General Motors, IBM, Kodak, and Westinghouse, have internal staff capable of applying DDP. They use it routinely for significant decisions and teach its principles in internal seminars.

[3] The parties to these dialogues consist of two groups of people: a *decision board,* comprised of individuals who command the resources to be allocated, and a *decision team,* made up of individuals who have studied the relevant issues in the required depth and who will be involved in implementation. During the four dialogues that occur at the end of each phase of ADP, the decision board provides the decision team with management's experience and a broad perspective on the issues, alternatives, analysis, and hybrid. The decision team brings to the decision board the insight and understanding that result from careful deliberation. In addition to dialogue between the two groups, considerable dialogue occurs within each group. The process provides a forum for discussing cross-functional and cross-organizational issues, thus allowing genuine understanding of the reasons underlying multiple viewpoints and organizational conflict. ADP is not a lockstep set of procedures but a systematic, disciplined approach for assuring quality in strategic decision-making.

[4] Considering the customer as external to the system (as defined by the enterprise) has some very beneficial properties. First, the existence of an external reference point is a necessary condition if a system's components are to consistently align their behaviors. Second, choosing the customer as the external reference point is intuitively compelling.

[5] The result is significant. Use of a common, external reference point for assessing the value of internal decisions reduces ambiguity about organizational purpose and facilitates managing the organization as a system. It simplifies complex decisions by eliminating internally inconsistent objectives. To allocate enterprise resources, management only needs from each organi-

zational unit the answer to this question: "How would more or fewer resources allocated to your unit affect your contribution to the delivery of each of the customer's value attributes?" The operational management task becomes how to get higher attribute "payoff" over time for each unit of resource.

6 The value customers place on an improvement in these attributes is not directly observable from the perspective of the provider of them. Since these attributes are not directly exchanged in the marketplace, an observable price is never associated with them. Hence, their value is implicit and, as such, can only be inferred.

7 We call this stage of ADP *connection* instead of *decision* because it involves connection among the conflicting viewpoints in the organization, as well as connection between the decision process and implementation. For a more in-depth discussion of these and related issues see Michael W. Kusnic and Daniel Owen, "The Unifying Vision Process: Value beyond Traditional Decision Analysis in Multiple Decision-Maker Environments," *Interfaces* 22, no. 6 (November–December 1992): 150–166.

8 At this higher level of ADP, connection involves bringing together the function that scans for new worlds and discontinuities with the function that decides what to do about them, that is, the Level I ADP. Note that this linkage is *the* explicit connection previously missing between scenario planning and strategic decision-making.

9 Our references here to the "value of information" pertain to the concept of value-in-use (when a piece of information may or may not be useful in the achievement of some other valuable end) as opposed to direct value (when acquisition of the information is directly valued, that is, when someone "just wanted to know").

10 The information-push paradigm is deeply rooted in the intellectual heritage of the scientific method. Science, with its theory-hypothesis-test-update methodology, is an information-push learning system designed to support the express objective of science: the value-free (that is, objective) accumulation of knowledge for its own sake. Value, a subjective phenomenon, has no place in science. The notion "value of information," therefore, is fundamentally alien to science.

11 See Ron Howard, "Information Value Theory," *IEEE Transactions on Systems Science and Cybernetics* SSC-2, no. 1 (August 1966).

Appendix C

1 For a more complete discussion of these concepts, see Fernando Flores, *Management and Communication in the Office of the Future* (Fernando Flores, 1982), T. Winograd and Fernando Flores, *Understanding Computers and Cognition* (Reading, MA: Addison-Wesley, 1991), and A. L. Scherr, "A New Approach to Business Processes," *IBM Systems Journal* 32, no. 1 (February 1993).

2 See Gabriel A. Pall, *Designed to Respond: The Process-centered Enterprise* (Atlanta, GA: St. Lucie's Press, 1999) for a discussion of ad hoc process design using the Flores schema modified by Scherr.

ACKNOWLEDGMENTS

Over breakfast one day in the summer of 1985, I heard Alan Hohne describe Westpac's strategic intent in these terms: "We aim to develop a system that will enable us to sense change earlier and respond to it more rapidly than other banks." The phrase struck me as a very different way of thinking about strategy. I am very indebted to Alan, who, with Peter Douglas, originated the strategy-as-adaptive-structure idea at Westpac. He has been exceptionally helpful to me in the preparation of this book, providing source documents and objective assessments of what went right and wrong in Westpac's implementation.

In speeches, presentations, and early publications on the concept in the late 1980s and early 1990s, "make-and-sell versus sense-and-respond" proved to be effective shorthand terminology for me in communicating what was essentially different about Westpac's approach. Richard Nolan and I subsequently used these terms in a 1993 *Harvard Business Review* article, and *sense-and-respond* became the name of a research project and course taught at the ABI. In a 1995 article in *Planning Review,* I presented sense-and-respond as a model for adaptive enterprise design. *Sense & Respond: Capturing Value in the Network Era,* edited by Stephen Bradley and Richard Nolan and published by Harvard Business School Press in 1998, offered a collection of essays written by individuals who participated in the 1995 Harvard Business School colloquium "Multimedia and the Boundaryless World." The collection provides many rich examples of how firms use technology to, in the words of the editors, "sense their environment in real time," and to respond rapidly with "dynamic resource allocation and execution."

Generalizing Westpac's way of thinking into a comprehensive model involved integrating it with some other big ideas introduced to me over the years by colleagues and authors. In 1972, Walter Trux made me understand the difference between integrated and modular systems. That year, he and I proposed to the vice president responsible for systems software development at IBM a way of reducing the "application" part of IBM's application software to its pure algorithmic content. We argued that this would allow each customer to "snap onto" this kernel the specific IBM systems software components that best matched their computing environment. We thought this would eliminate IBM's need to rewrite the systems components every time it developed a new application.

The vice president was a huge bear of a man with a marvelous sense of humor but very little admiration for stupid marketing theories about managing software development. Writing software, he told us, was an art form in dire need of becoming a science. The first step, which he was in the process of implementing, was to avoid hiring any programmer with more than a high school diploma. He wanted to make programmers replaceable parts and have them write predefined blocks of code according to standard procedures in a highly compartmentalized software-making factory. This would allow him to shift development missions around the world on short notice to maximize the utilization of low-skilled coders. After sharing with us several hilarious formulations of his opinion about our proposal's merits, he was kind enough to remind us that our job, as marketers, was to SELL WHAT IBM MADE. Both he and the shareholders would be much obliged if we would return to that task at our earliest convenience.

Which, of course, we did, having been properly chastised by someone who actually had to *produce* something. This executive had faithfully articulated the logic of make-and-sell, the received wisdom of more than a half century of business thinking and experience. Neither Trux nor I were about to challenge that towering intellectual edifice. (Nor were we aware that computer scientists at Xerox's Palo Alto Research Center had already begun to think rigorously about modularity, developing the concepts behind what would later become known as object-oriented systems.) Nevertheless, the distinction between modularity and integration stuck with me. So did the notion that the trade-off of flexibility for efficiency might be finessed, given sufficient reuse of modular components.

Seven years later, I took a position on IBM's corporate staff as resident futurist. In March 1980, sitting in a conference hall waiting my turn to speak, I heard Leon Martel of the Hudson Institute talk about Daniel Bell's 1972 conclusion that "codified information and knowledge are replacing capital and energy as the world's primary wealth-creating resources." After reading Bell's work and later meeting him, I became convinced that any long-term scenario was inherently implausible if it was inconsistent with the implications of increasingly information-intensive businesses operating in increasingly information-rich economies.

To understand as many of those implications as possible, I began paying less attention to what leading edge companies were doing with technology and more attention to what they were doing with information. In 1988, IBM, through the Marketing Science Institute, sponsored a research competition on the implications for marketing strategy of the information revolution. In the winning paper, Professor Rashi Glazer proposed a way of calculating a firm's information intensity, a way of estimating the economic value of its transaction information, and several hypotheses (called Glazer's list in this book) about the business implications of increasing information intensity. The intuitively appealing notion that market power would migrate toward the customer had now been tied logically to the economics of information.

In 1989, Fernando Flores introduced me to his schema for representing processes as a formal structure of communications between customers and suppliers. IBM Fellow Alan Scherr, building on Flores's work, had developed the notion of human accountability as the second, and missing, dimension of a process. I am embarrassed to say how long it took me to grasp the significance of Scherr's formalization of accountability, but it eventually became an indispensable mechanism for implementing the high-level design and governance of sense-and-respond organizations.

Modularity, information as the primary wealth-creating resource, the formal incorporation of accountability into business designs, and the principles of systems design are distinct ideas that I encountered at different times in different contexts. But over time, they came together as parts of my thinking about the business issues associated with unpredictability. They are now part of the warp and woof of sense-and-respond, along with the information requirements of complex adaptive systems.

Complexity theory provides rich metaphors for thinking about organizational adaptiveness. But as a robust model for business, it is suspect. (Murray Gell-Mann, Nobel laureate and cofounder of the Santa Fe Institute, responding to a question in November, 1995, told me that he was unaware of anyone doing research on complex adaptive systems whose elements act consciously to change the systems of which they are part.) But the conclusion of Gell-Mann and Seth Lloyd about the information processing requirement of successfully adapting systems is pivotal: Apparent noise must be continuously translated into meaning. Accordingly, in adaptive organizations, the generic adaptive loop becomes a template for the management of information and knowledge both within an existing context and of the context itself.

The individuals mentioned above provided some of the seminal ideas now synthesized as the sense-and-respond model. The intellectual fingerprints of Russ Ackoff, too, are readily discernible in the sections dealing with managing organizations as systems. Other thinkers and practitioners have contributed to the development of sense-and-respond implementation methods and tools. Michael Kusnic, Dan Owen, and Mike Shank are so important in this regard that the book would not be complete without their appendices.

I use examples from many firms to illustrate the nature and value of specific aspects of sense-and-respond as *behavior* even though what they did was not inspired by the model. The companies featured as early adopters are different, however, because they are implementing *from* the model. Their experiences represent the beginning of a learning curve about how to create and implement *good* adaptive designs. The Portfolio Management Group of Aetna, Old Mutual Insurance in South Africa, DSC Logistics, General Motors, and my own organization have all been early adopters of parts or all of the sense-and-respond model. The change agents in these organizations were, at Aetna, Glen Salow, chief information officer; at Old Mutual, Reg Munro, general manager; at DSC, Ann Drake, CEO; at GM, Vince Barabba, senior strategist and chief knowledge officer; and at IBM, Jack Hammond and Carol Schoenfeld, directors of customer executive education. These executives work daily to resolve implementation issues—including the difficult one of transforming existing businesses on the fly. I have learned more from them than they realize. The least I can do is acknowledge it here.

At GM, Steve Carlisle amazes me with his ability to rapidly absorb and apply the ideas of sense-and-respond. Arv Mueller and Ken Baker were early supporters. The sense-and-respond governance system is largely a response to one of Arv's dangerous questions. Jay Stark, Wendy Coles, and Nick Pudar have been creative and indispensable in orchestrating the introduction of sense-and-respond into the GM Knowledge Network and strategy development processes. IBM client executive Shay Dembicki played a major role from the beginning by orchestrating and participating in educational sessions with GM executives.

An important catalyst at Old Mutual was their 1997 Circle of Excellence Group. Reg Munro sent the group to the ABI sense-and-respond course, after which they pushed for a week-long exercise by top management to develop the Employee Benefits division's context. Wisely, Munro included them in the exercise. Led by Gary Palser, the members of this special team were Gordon Anthony, Howard Buck, Mitzie Ginsberg, Heather McLeod, and Mike Van Heerden.

I have been fortunate to have the support and encouragement of Bruce Harreld, senior vice president for strategy at IBM. Doug Sweeny, VP of strategic development, whom I've known and worked with for more than a decade, has followed the development of many of the strands woven into this book. I value his suggestions and insight almost as much as his humor.

My colleagues at the ABI have provided a rich source of ideas, criticism, and unstinting help. Jack Hammond, at first skeptically, and then with growing conviction, began implementing sense-and-respond ideas at the Palisades and supported my early research. Carol Schoenfeld has turned the place I work into a living laboratory of context and coordination governance. I am as impressed with her conceptual grasp and pragmatic application of sense-and-respond ideas as I am thankful for her enthusiastic support. Al Barnes, Marion Atwater, Dan Gassert, Donna Lee, and Bob Singley have been valiant guinea pigs, struggling with the people issues of implementing authentic commitment management. Al has made it possible for me to get comments and reactions from many leading thinkers in his seemingly infinite network of them. And a special debt of gratitude is owed to the faculty members who have taught sense-and-respond with me for four years: Pat Brown, Bob Goett, Steve Joern, Bob Keiser, Marianne Kosits, and Dirk Owens. David Ing joined the team in early 1998 and has made substantial contributions to our understanding of how to use technology to support sense-and-respond. Marleen DeSilva has somehow found time to help administrate the process of coordinating reviews and updating drafts. I am very grateful to her, Rich Russo, Ralph Capria, Ken Skorka, Zavier Berrios, Carol Quinn, and many other ABI staff members for their selfless willingness to help.

The ideas and perceptions of Lou Carbone and Karen Stephenson are now a part of the way I look at the world. Working with them on other projects has benefited me greatly—and has been a lot of fun. Alan Clifford and Malcolm Clark encouraged me with their interest, suggestions, and friendship over the years as the ideas in this book developed. I am certain that I have so completely integrated the thinking of many other associates over the last two decades that their ideas have become indistinguishable in my mind from my own. To them I can only offer a plenary apology for whatever they may find of theirs in these pages, cite unseen.

The suggestions of several thoughtful reviewers have made this book better. In particular, I would like to thank Chris Meyers, Tom Hout, Gordon Wyner, Chris Argyris, and Bill Ghormley for the time they invested and for the quality of their comments.

Larry Prusak, in addition to his encouragement and advice, did me a great favor by introducing me to Don Cohen. Don invested a great deal of time in understanding the sense-and-respond idea in depth. He has substantially improved the organization and flow of the book. The talented Ralph Wileman translated my primitive graphics into much more meaningful illustrations and helped me formulate new ways of expressing several concepts. At the Harvard Business School Press, Marjorie Williams shepherded me past many hurdles. She is very good at what she does and a pleasure to work with. If in spite of all this help any errors remain, the book, of course, stops here.

Writing a book can be an immense distraction, and there are times when it simply takes over. No one suffers the consequences more directly and inexcusably than a spouse. My wife, Ursula, has never complained and even sounds authentic when she asserts that she enjoyed having me around the house so much. My list of deferred obligations is, however, appallingly long.

And finally, my deep gratitude to Adrian Slywotzky for his foreword and for telling me it was time to write the book on sense-and-respond.

GLOSSARY

This glossary contains definitions, as clear and unambiguous as possible, of sense-and-respond terms *as used in this book.* It does not provide general or universal definitions.

Accountability

Personal acceptance of the consequences of making a commitment. Only people can have accountability. (Processes, machines, and systems cannot.) Accountability is codified by specifying who owes what to whom. It differs from the traditional mission statement in its requirement that the role to whom the outcome is owed be specified. No one, therefore, can be generically accountable for sales, manufacturing, logistics, quality, or the Acme account. Accountabilities arise exclusively from commitments.

Capabilities and Competencies

Capabilities are organizational subsystems with a potential for producing outcomes that contribute to the organization's purpose. *Competencies* are demonstrated by people in roles where they use capabilities to produce outcomes. *Core competencies* are those essential to the purpose—it cannot be fulfilled without them.

Collaboration

The interaction of two or more individuals to achieve an outcome that cannot be achieved by their independent actions. Successful collaboration requires reconciliation of purpose, values, and activities among the collaborators.

Commitment

An agreement between two roles to produce (and accept, if produced) a defined outcome in a way that satisfies a specified set of conditions. One role is accountable for producing the defined outcome; the other is accountable for accepting it if it meets the conditions specified.

Conditions of Satisfaction

The agreed-to criteria that will be used to assess a specific outcome.

Context

A declaration by policy-making executives of the organization's reason for being, governing principles, and high-level business design. When used in conjunction with a specific role, *context* refers to the outcome and conditions of satisfaction for which an individual is accountable.

Coordination

The linking of accountabilities to achieve a defined purpose. At the highest level, this purpose will be the organization's reason for being. The way key subordinate accountabilities are linked constitutes a high-level organizational design.

Decision

An allocation of resources (as opposed to the reaching of a conclusion).

Essential Structure

The necessary and sufficient (but not complete) specification of how elements of the organization interact with one another to produce the system-level outcomes required by the reason for being. The high-level business design is a representation of an organization's essential structure.

Governance

The systematic propagation and enforcement of organizational context.

Governing Principles

The boundaries of permissible behavior that constrain the way all people in the organization may act in carrying out the reason for being. Violations have serious repercussions on the ability of the organization to carry out its function. Exceptions, on a case-by-case basis, may be negotiated with the issuing authority.

High-Level Business Design

A systems design that depicts essential structure in terms of key accountabilities and the outcomes committed among them to carry out the organizational reason for being. The design is expressed as commitments between roles rather than as a flow of activities.

Leadership

The competence to create and adapt a viable organizational context, to establish an effective governance system for coordinating activities within that context, and to populate organizational roles with capable people. It is not a collection of techniques or a personality trait. At the highest organizational level, leadership is a core competence.

Organizational Integrity

Congruence of organizational behavior with organizational design. As a personal trait, integrity implies that people do what they say they will do. As an institutional trait, it indicates that business designs are executed as defined. It does not signify a good design, only that the organization behaves in accordance with it.

Procedure

An ordered sequence of the tasks and choices required to produce a specified output from specified input. A procedure describes "who or what does what with what to produce what." Note that process reengineers commonly use this definition for *process*. But *procedure* only captures one dimension of process—the predictable. If it is the *only* dimension, the process is bureaucratic. Accountability, which can apply even in unpredictable environments, is the missing dimension in most process descriptions. If accountability is the only dimension, the process is "ad hoc."

Process

An ordered sequence of, first, the procedures and, second, the communications between accountable roles about commitments required to specify and produce an outcome.

Reason for Being

The essential function of the organization, without which it loses its rationale for existing. An essential function is one that the organization exists to fulfill, as opposed to the functions it fulfills in order to exist. The reason for being should be unambiguous regarding both the organization's primary constituency and the outcome to be delivered to that constituency. Once declared, it is non-negotiable.

Role

A name assigned to a class of accountability holders (for example, instructors, sales representatives, process leaders, and so on). A role can be assumed by an individual or a group of individuals.

Sense-and-Respond Organization

A collection of modular capabilities, structured as a purposeful, open, complex adaptive system. Its design exploits information, technology, and the capacity of humans to think outside the system context to respond to discontinuous change and unpredicted requests. It is governed by an unambiguous, universally shared context that defines its purpose, the boundaries set on permissible behavior, and its essential structure, and by a commitment management protocol that propagates the context as capabilities link dynamically to create system-level responses.

Skills

The capabilities of the individuals in an organization.

Team

Two or more individuals with a collective accountability who interact to achieve an outcome that cannot be realized without their collaboration. This definition excludes groups of people with diverse purposes, individuals who do not require coordination, and individuals who relate to one another solely to exchange information.

Trust

The degree of certitude one individual has about another's intent to fulfill a commitment, the other's competence to do so, and the values that will constrain the other's behavior in carrying out the commitment. Trust is subjective and role-specific, because individual competence varies by role.

BIBLIOGRAPHY

Ackoff, Russell. *The Democratic Corporation.* New York: Oxford University Press, 1994.

A.C.T. *High Performance Internetworked Enterprise: Diagnostic Survey.* Alliance for Converging Technologies, 1996.

Argyris, Chris. "Empowerment: The Emperor's New Clothes." *Harvard Business Review* 76, no. 3 (May–June 1998).

———. *Knowledge for Action.* San Francisco: Jossey-Bass, 1993.

———. *On Organizational Learning.* Cambridge, MA: Blackwell Publishers, 1992.

Arthur, Brian. "Increasing Returns and the New World of Business." *Harvard Business Review* 74, no. 4 (July–August 1996).

———. "Positive Feedbacks in the Economy." *Scientific American* (February 1990).

Bak, Per. *How Nature Works: The Science of Self-Organized Criticality.* New York: Copernicus, Springer-Verlag, 1996.

Baldwin, C. Y., and K. B. Clark. "Managing in an Age of Modularity." *Harvard Business Review* 75, no. 5 (September–October 1997).

Barabba, V. P. *Meeting of the Minds.* Boston: Harvard Business School Press, 1995.

———. "Revisiting Plato's Cave: Business Design in an Age of Uncertainty." In *Blueprint for the Digital Economy,* edited by Don Tapscott. New York: McGraw-Hill, 1998.

Barabba, Vincent P., and Gerald Zaltman. *Hearing the Voice of the Market: Competitive Advantage through Creative Use of Market Information.* Boston: Harvard Business School Press, 1991.

Bell, Daniel. *The Coming of Post-Industrial Society.* New York: Basic Books, 1973.

———. "The Frameworks of the Future." In *Proceedings of the Marketing Science Institute Twentieth Anniversary Conference.* Cambridge, MA: Marketing Science Institute, 1981.

———. "The Social Framework of the Information Society." In *The Computer Age: A Twenty Year View,* edited by M. Dertouzos and J. Moses. Cambridge, MA: MIT Press, 1979.

Berreby, D. "What the Heck Is a Company, Anyway?" *Strategy & Business.* Booz·Allen & Hamilton (Second Quarter) (1997).

Bickerton, Derek. *Language and Species.* Chicago: University of Chicago Press, 1990.

Blattberg, R., R. Glazer, and J. Little, eds. *The Marketing Information Revolution.* Boston: Harvard Business School Press, 1994.

Bower, J. L., and C. L. Christensen. "Disruptive Technologies: Catching the Wave." *Harvard Business Review* 73, no. 1 (January–February 1995).

Boynton, Andrew C., and Bart Victor. "Beyond Flexibility: Building and Managing the Dynamically Stable Organization." *California Management Review* (Fall 1991).

Bradley, Stephen P., and Richard L. Nolan, eds. *Sense and Respond: Capturing Value in the Network Era.* Boston: Harvard Business School Press, 1998.

Braxton Associates. *Growth-Driven Companies Achieve Sharply Higher Performance.* Braxton Associates, Deloitte & Touche Consulting Group, 1996.

Campbell, A., and M. Alexander. "What's Wrong with Strategy?" *Harvard Business Review* 75, no. 6 (November–December 1997).

Carbone, Lewis P., and Haeckel, Stephan H. "Engineering Customer Experiences." *Marketing Management Magazine* 3, no. 3 (Winter 1994).

Chandler, Alfred D. *Scale and Scope: Dynamics of Industrial Capitalism.* Cambridge, MA: Belknap Press, Harvard University Press, 1990.

Collins, J. C., and J. I. Porras. *Built to Last.* New York: Harper Business, 1994.

D'Aveni, Richard A. *Hypercompetition.* New York: The Free Press, 1994.

Drucker, P. "How to Be Competitive Though Big." *The Wall Street Journal,* 7 February 1991.

———. "Planning for Uncertainty." *The Wall Street Journal,* 22 July 1992.

Dyson, Esther. *Intellectual Value.* Release 1.0, EDventure Holdings (December 1994).

Flores, Fernando. *Management and Communication in the Office of the Future.* Fernando Flores, 1982.

Flores, Fernando, M. Graves, B. Hartfield, and Terry Winograd. "Computer Systems and the Design of Organizational Interaction." *ACM Transactions on Office Information Systems* 6, no. 2 (April 1988).

Foster, T. R. V. *101 Great Mission Statements.* Kogan Page, 1993.

Gaddis, Paul O. "Strategy Under Attack." *Long-Range Planning* 30 (1997).

Gell-Mann, Murray, and J. B. Hartle. "Quantum Mechanics in the Light of Quantum Cosmology." In *Complexity, Entropy, and the Physics of Information, Santa Fe Proceedings VIII.* Edited by W. H. Zurek. Reading, MA: Addison-Wesley, 1989.

Gilmore, James H., and B. J. Pine II. "The Four Faces of Mass Customization." *Harvard Business Review* 75, no. 1 (January–February 1997).

Glazer, Rashi. "Marketing and the Changing Information Environment: Implications for Strategy, Structure, and the Marketing Mix." Working paper 89-108, Marketing Science Institute, Cambridge, MA, 1989.

———. "Marketing in an Information-Intensive Environment." *Journal of Marketing* 55 (October 1991).

Goss, T., R. Pascale, and A. Athos. "The Reinvention Roller Coaster." *Harvard Business Review* 71, no. 6 (November–December 1993).

Haeckel, Stephan H. "Adaptive Enterprise Design: The Sense-and-Respond Model." *Planning Review* (May–June 1995).

———. "Commitment Management." ABI white paper, 1996.

————. "From 'Make and Sell' to 'Sense and Respond.' " *Management Review* (October 1992).

————. "Westpac Bank Corporation: A Sense-and-Respond Prototype." ABI vignette, 1996.

————. "Why You Aren't Re-Engineering Your Business Processes." ABI white paper, 1995.

Haeckel, Stephan H., and Richard L. Nolan. "Managing By Wire." *Harvard Business Review* 71, no. 5 (September– October 1993).

————. "Managing By Wire: Using IT to Transform a Business from Make-and-Sell to Sense-and-Respond." In *Competing in the Information Age: Strategic Alignment in Practice,* edited by J. Luftman. New York: Oxford University Press, 1996.

————. "The Role of Technology in an Information Age: Transforming Symbols into Action." In *The Knowledge Economy: The Nature of Information in the Twenty-first Century,* Annual Review of the Institute for Information Studies, 1993–1994. Northern Telcom Inc. and The Aspen Institute, November 1993.

Hall, B. P. *Values Shift.* Rockport, MA: Twin Lights, 1994.

Hohne, Alan. "Mass Customization: Avoiding the Need to Predict Change." Unpublished paper.

Hout, Thomas M., and M. F. Blaxill. "Make Decisions Like A Fighter Pilot." *The New York Times,* 15 November 1987.

Hout, Thomas M., and J. C. Carter. "Getting It Done: New Roles for Senior Executives." *Harvard Business Review* 73, no. 6 (November–December 1995).

Jaques, Eliot, and S. D. Clement. *Executive Leadership: A Practical Guide to Managing Complexity.* Arlington, VA: Cason Hall & Co., Ltd., 1991.

Katzenbach, Jon R. "The Myth of the Top Management Team." *Harvard Business Review* 75, no. 6 (November–December 1997).

Keen, Peter. *Shaping the Future.* Boston: Harvard Business School Press, 1991.

Kevern, George-Yves. "Cindynics: The Science of Danger." *Risk Management* (March 1995).

Kim, W. C., and R. Mauborgne. "Manager's Journal." *The Wall Street Journal,* 21 April 1997.

————. "Value Innovation: The Strategic Logic of High Growth." *Harvard Business Review* 75, no. 1 (January–February 1997).

Knight, Charles F. "Emerson Electric: Consistent Profits, Consistently." *Harvard Business Review* 70, no. 1 (January—February 1992).

Kumar, K., and H. G. van Dissel. "Sustainable Collaboration: Managing Conflict and Cooperation in Interorganizational Systems." *MIS Quarterly* 20, no. 3 (1996).

Kumar, Kuldeep, H. G. van Dissel, and P. Bielli. "The Merchants of Prato Revisited." *MSI Quarterly,* forthcoming.

Kurtzman, J. "An Interview with Brian Arthur." *Strategy and Business.* Booz·Allen & Hamilton, Second Quarter (1998).

Lehmann, Donald, and Kathryn Jocz, eds. *Reflections on the Futures of Marketing.* Cambridge, MA, Marketing Science Institute, 1997.

Lloyd, Seth. "Learning How to Control Complex Systems." *The Bulletin of the Santa Fe Institute* (Spring 1995).

Lubove, S. "It Ain't Broke, But Fix It Anyway." *Forbes,* 1 August 1994.

Lynn, Gary S. "Organizational Team Learning for Really New Product Development." Report 97-113. Cambridge, MA, Marketing Science Institute, 1997.

Mintzberg, Henry. *Mintzberg on Management.* New York: The Free Press, 1989.

————. *The Rise and Fall of Strategic Planning.* New York: The Free Press and Prentice Hall International, 1994.

Nelson, R. F. W. "Four-Quadrant Leadership." *Planning Review* (January–February 1996).

Ong, Walter A. *Orality and Literacy: The Technologizing of the Word.* New York: Routledge, 1982.

O'Toole, James. *Leading Change.* San Francisco: Jossey-Bass, 1995.

Pall, Gabriel A. *Designed to Respond: The Process-centered Enterprise.* Atlanta, GA: St. Lucie's Press, 1999.

Pepper, Donald, and Martha Rogers. *Enterprise One To One.* New York: Doubleday, 1997.

Pine, B. J. II. *Mass Customization.* Boston: Harvard Business School Press, 1993.

Pine, B. J. II, B. Victor, and A. C. Boynton. "Making Mass Customization Work." *Harvard Business Review* 71, no. 5 (September–October, 1993).

Porter, Michael E. *Competitive Strategy.* New York: The Free Press, 1980.

Prigogine, I., and I. Stengers. *Order Out of Chaos.* New York: Bantam Books, 1984.

Quinn, J. B. *Intelligent Enterprise.* New York: The Free Press, 1992.

Quinn, J. B., and F. G. Hilmer. "Strategic Outsourcing." *Sloan Management Review* (Summer 1994).

Schelberg, C. "Parallel Scheduling of Random and of Chaotic Processes." In *Dynamic, Genetic and Chaotic Programming,* edited by B. Soucek. New York: John Wiley & Sons, 1992.

Scherr, Alan L. "A New Approach to Business Processes." *IBM Systems Journal* 32, no. 1 (February 1993).

Sloan, Alfred P. Jr. "The Most Important Thing I Ever Learned About Management." *SYSTEM, The Magazine of Business* 46, no. 2 (August 1924).

———. *My Years With General Motors.* New York: Doubleday, 1964.

Slywotzky, Adrian J. *Value Migration.* Boston: Harvard Business School Press, 1996.

Slywotzky, Adrian J., and D. J. Morrison. *The Profit Zone: How Strategic Business Designs Will Lead You to Tomorrow's Profits.* New York: Times Business Books, Random House, 1997.

Stephenson, Karen, and Stephan H. Haeckel. "Making a Virtual Organization Work." *Zurich Insurance Management Review* (June 1997).

Stewart, I., and J. Cohen. *Figments of Reality: The Evolution of the Curious Mind.* Cambridge, England: Cambridge University Press, 1997.

Upton, A. *Design for Thinking.* Palo Alto, CA: Pacific, 1961.

Vogt, E. E. "Learning Out of Context." In *Learning Organizations,* edited by Sarita Chawla and John Renesch. Portland, OR: Productivity Press, 1995.

Waldrup, Mitchel M. *Complexity: The Emerging Science at the Edge of Order and Chaos.* New York: Simon & Schuster, 1992.

————. "Dee Hock on Organizations." *Fast Company* (October–November 1996).

Walter, J. R. "How to Leap Before You Look: Lessons for a Digital World." *The New York Times,* 10 November 1996.

Webster, Frederick E. Jr. *Market-Driven Management.* New York: John Wiley & Sons, 1994.

Weick, Karl E. *Sensemaking in Organizations.* Newbury Park, CA: Sage Publications, 1995.

Wheatley, M. J. *Leadership and the New Science.* San Francisco: Berrett-Koehler, 1992.

Wheatley, M. J., and M. Kellner-Rogers. "The Irresistable Future of Organizing." *Strategy and Leadership* (July–August 1996).

Winograd, Terry, and Fernando Flores. *Understanding Computers and Cognition.* Reading, MA: Addison-Wesley, 1991.

Wolff, H. A. "The Great GM Mystery." *Harvard Business Review* 42, no. 5 (September–October 1964).

Zaltman, Gerald. "Rethinking Market Research: Putting People Back In." *Journal of Marketing Research* (November 1997).

INDEX

ABOUT THE AUTHOR

Stephan H. Haeckel is Director of Strategic Studies at IBM's Advanced Business Institute (ABI) and Chairman of the Marketing Science Institute. During his IBM career, he has held executive positions in Europe and on the corporate staff. As Director of Advanced Market Development, he led the project that formulated IBM's corporate strategy for entering the commercial systems integration business and coauthored IBM's services strategy. His interest in the strategic challenges of coping with unpredictable change stems from an assignment as IBM's Corporate Futurist in the 1980s.

At the ABI, Haeckel teaches and advises executives on the design, implementation, and leadership of adaptive organizations. He is currently working with colleagues on the specification of a comprehensive information technology support system for sense-and-respond. His other interests include business strategies for transforming firms' customer value propositions into total customer experiences. Haeckel has served on the Advisory Council of the Federal National Mortgage Association and on the panel of judges for the McKinsey Awards; he represents IBM on the Marketing Council of the American Management Association.

Publications by Haeckel have appeared in the *Harvard Business Review*, *Planning Review*, the *Annual Review of the Institute for Information Research*, *Journal of Interactive Marketing*, and *Marketing Management*.